Liberating the learner

Educational management series
Series editor: Cyril Poster

Liberating the learner

Lessons for professional development
in education

Edited by Guy Claxton, Terry Atkinson,
Marilyn Osborn and Mike Wallace

London and New York

First published 1996
by Routledge
11 New Fetter Lane, London EC4P 4EE

Simultaneously published in the USA and Canada
by Routledge
29 West 35th Street, New York, NY 10001

Typeset in Times by
Ponting–Green Publishing Services, Chesham, Bucks
Printed and bound in Great Britain by
Mackays of Chatham PLC, Chatham, Kent

British Library Cataloguing in Publication Data

A catalogue record for this book is available from the
British Library

Library of Congress Cataloguing in Publication Data

A catalogue record for this book has been requested

ISBN 0–415–13127–8

I have always thought it rather interesting to follow the involuntary movements of fear in clever people. Fools coarsely display their cowardice in all its nakedness, but the others are able to cover it with a veil so delicate, so daintily woven with small plausible lies, that there is some pleasure to be found in contemplating this ingenious work of the human intelligence.

De Tocqueville

Contents

Part III The facilitation of learning

Illustrations

List of contributors

(All at the University of Bristol School of Education unless otherwise stated)

Terry Atkinson, Lecturer in Education (Modern Languages)

Patricia Broadfoot, Professor of Education and Head of School

Laurinda Brown, Lecturer in Education (Mathematics)

Guy Claxton, Visiting Professor of Psychology and Education

Alan Dobson, Participant, MEd Programme

Valerie Hall, Senior Lecturer in Education; Programme Coordinator of the Taught Doctorate Programme

John Hayter, Senior Lecturer in Education (Mathematics)

Peter D. John, Lecturer in Education (History)

Elisabeth Lazarus, Lecturer in Education (Modern Languages)

Agnes McMahon, Senior Lecturer in Education (National Development Centre for Education Management and Policy)

Marilyn Osborn, Research Fellow in Education (Centre for Curriculum and Assessment Studies)

Mike Wallace, Professor of Educational Managment and Policy, University of Wales, Cardiff

Paul Weeden, Lecturer in Education (Geography)

Jan Winter, Lecturer in Education (Mathematics)

Introduction

Gone are the days when one 'learnt' how to teach, and then spent the rest of one's career 'practising' it. At all levels and phases of education, as for the other professions, continuing professional development is not now an option for the ambitious, but a necessity for all. The reforms – structural, financial, curricular and technological – of the last few years in Britain, and in many other countries, have affected the working lives of every member of the profession. Classroom teachers have to grasp new curricula, new technology and new working practices. Senior school staff are learning to be financial managers, appraisers and 'critical friends'. As universities and colleges seek new markets, so lecturers in higher education are confronted with 'students' whose life experience, professional seniority and sense of themselves as 'consumers' require a major shift in attitudes and teaching styles. Even if you, the teacher, should want to, it is becoming increasingly difficult to hunker down, defend your patch, and trot out your venerable old notes.

All kinds of courses, seminars and training are springing up to cater for this upsurge in adult professional learning (APL), in education as elsewhere. Some are beautifully packaged; some are popular; some are effective; and these three qualities by no means necessarily go together. Slick, well-received presentations sometimes bear disappointingly small fruit. Like the learning of younger people, APL turns out not to be predominantly a matter of content and cognition – of preparing a 'good lesson'. Other, subtler, factors play an equally important role in determining whether, when, how and for what purpose adults will engage with the learning opportunities that present themselves.

These factors may broadly be grouped under two other 'Cs' – culture and connotation. Like children, adults swim in a complex stream of micro-and macro-cultural messages and assumptions about learning: what it is (and is not); how to do it (and not do it); when and how to protect yourself rather than 'have a go'; who needs it, and for what. A cynical clique in a staffroom may see learning as 'naive', and training days only as a source of respite or a target of ridicule. A well-intentioned inspection team may see their visits as 'learning opportunities' for staff, and be completely oblivious to quite different eddies and currents that surround them. An eminent professor may be totally perplexed by the rejection of his or her didactic teaching mode by a roomful of managers. And individuals have their own idiosyncratic and partly unwitting connotations and associations to learning: barely audible echoes of their own schooling, studying or training that reach, perhaps inappropriately and anachronistically, into the present, bringing up old attitudes, assumptions and apprehensions that may channel or even block the course of APL.

It is with these subtler aspects of APL that this book is concerned. The central interest, which all the contributions share, is in the largely tacit assumptions, or 'implicit theories', about learning which reside in people's heads, or in the cultural milieu in which they work; the effects that these belief systems have on teachers' attitudes towards professional learning, and how they engage (or not) with it; and the ways in which an understanding of these implicit theories can help providers of APL in education make their offerings more effective. The overall purpose of the book is to investigate, both conceptually and empirically, how teachers' largely implicit views about learning influence their reactions to the challenges of professional learning, their work as educators and, consequently, the learning experiences of those they teach. Its aims are fourfold:

1 To develop a conceptual framework which embraces the role of implicit views about learning in the teaching and learning process.
2 To explore the value of this framework through a wide range of case studies in distinctive settings, where links and comparisons between cases can be made.
3 To use this empirical base to identify generic features of the part played by educators' implicit views of learning in the facilitation (or otherwise) of learning.
4 To highlight the practical lessons of this framework for the professional development of educators.

In order to pursue its aim of distilling out what is generic, both conceptually and practically, the book comes at the issue from a wide variety of perspectives. It arose from the desire of an unusually broad cross-section of staff at the University of Bristol School of Education to pool and explore their collective experience of working with adult learners in education. The group included those whose primary responsibilities were initial teacher education and the development of school-based training; in-service education of schoolteachers, both at home and overseas; masters' degrees, again for both home and overseas students; a taught doctorate programme, the EdD, focusing on management, and on psychology, in education; and training courses for senior school and college staff in management. This group, comprising some thirteen members of the School of Education academic and research staff, met over the course of a year to develop a framework for the enquiry, and to plan individual and collaborative investigations which would, it was hoped, add up to something greater than the sum of the parts. Drafts of chapters were circulated and discussed by the group, and authors received detailed feedback from a few 'peers' within the group as a whole. Final drafts were collated by the editors, who then worked to create links and draw together some of the issues, and the tentative lessons for 'good practice', which were seen to recur.

The chapters were deliberately designed to represent not only different contexts and clienteles, but also a variety of ways of tackling the core concern. Some of the contributions, such as the pieces by Guy Claxton, draw on a formal research literature, and attempt to develop a practitioner-friendly language for conceptualising and conversing about these personal and cultural aspects of the learning process. Some, such as Patricia Broadfoot's chapter, draw on ideas that have been developed primarily in the context of school education, and argue for their applicability to the sphere of APL – in Patricia's case, this relates to the ways in which assessment drives learning, through the medium of learners' implicit theories. In some, as in Mike Wallace's essay, the research literature resonates with professional experience in order to uncover the taken-for-granted assumptions that have informed many kinds of professional training.

Many of the chapters, in contrast, report original pieces of research, though here again these are of a wide variety of scopes and kinds. Marilyn Osborn reports data from a large-scale funded project that explored the reactions of teachers in different national cultures – England and France – to imposed change. Agnes McMahon's evaluation of the learning problems and challenges encountered by new headteachers, and the kind of mentoring support that is appropriate, again draws on 'formal', funded research. But some of the most interesting data derives from much smaller-scale action research projects undertaken by individual members of staff to inform their own practice.

In several of these 'unsophisticated' studies, the researchers are clearly themselves 'in the frame' as learners, just as much as the students or teachers whose experience is also being unpacked. Paul Weeden and John Hayter, for example, use their small study of a trip to The Gambia with a group of PGCE students as much to reflect on their *own* implicit assumptions about learning as to uncover those of the students. Likewise Jan Winter's account of her work as an advisory teacher models, as well as elucidates, reflective practice. Research that is only very lightly theorised can sometimes be as revealing as that which positions itself self-consciously within a technical discourse. (We are often reminded that the dictionary defines 'sophisticated' as 'deprived of simplicity or naturalness; falsified by fallacious reasoning; adulterated'.) It is unusual for senior professionals in education to write of their own process of learning as openly as one or two of the contributors to this volume do; in fact, as Agnes McMahon and Valerie Hall both suggest, it is this status-induced reticence that may be one of the major factors that inhibits genuine (as opposed to rhetorical) moves towards establishing a learning culture within education.

Another fruitful 'tension' within the book is the attempt to juggle inner and outer, psychological and sociological, perspectives. Some of the contributors naturally focus on the way learning assumptions become embedded within, and embodied by, educational structures, practices and forms of discourse. The current enchantment with 'experiential learning' would be one example. The tendency to see assessment as neutral or 'innocent' with respect to learning is another. Others, however, explore the ways in which implicit theories are installed in individual minds, and the effects that they have on learners' resilience or resourcefulness in the face of a learning challenge. Peter John, in one of his two chapters, shows clearly how the 'ghosts of education past' frequently continue to lurk in the back of people's minds, so as to skew their interpretations of current uncertainties. One of the strengths of the book, in the end, is to show these two perspectives, the personal and the cultural, to be complementary rather than alternative. When we are unpicking what is going on in a conversation between a student teacher and a mentor, for example, we are looking simultaneously at the transmission of a culture, and the modification of a mind. (With the increasing insistence on the irreducibility of 'mind in context', we are all Vygotskeans, or 'social constructionists', now, it seems.)

Contributors vary too in how overtly they make use of the language of 'implicit theories', 'learning blocks', 'cultural assumptions' and the 'disinhibition' of learning. Some, such as Valerie Hall in her study of the assumptions and anxieties of senior professionals when they re-enter formal education as participants on the EdD programme, make explicit use of the framework, and add to it as they do so. Others, such as Mike Wallace, tend to presuppose it without articulating it. Whichever, there is a clear appreciation amongst the contributors that learning is not adequately conceptualised as a relationship between content and cognition; it is embedded within the broader life-world, the wider dispositions and the deeper values of the learner, and within the culture, formal and informal, micro and macro, of the learning context. We know that learners' *engagement* with learning is, for adults as it is for children, of greater significance than their so-called 'ability', and that this engagement depends on a largely intuitive and sometimes highly labile summation of the pros, cons and conditions of learning. We know that people make these decisions in very different ways. Our joint endeavour is to explore what this means in the context of APL, and to uncover the practical wisdom which it may contain.

Though the book does culminate in some guidelines for 'good practice', it necessarily raises as many questions as it answers. We actually know rather little about the peculiar dynamics of adult professional learners, and this collection should be seen as raising issues and attempting to map out an agenda for further study, as much as settling things. There is here empirical support for aspects of the conceptual framework, and some of the practical implications; but it is also a food-for-thought book, designed to promote reflection and stimulate research, across the whole range of practitioners, researchers and policy-makers concerned with supporting the learning of professional educators, institutional managers, trainers and lecturers. We hope you will find it interesting.

Guy Claxton, Terry Atkinson, Marilyn Osborn and Mike Wallace
Bristol, April 1995

Part I

Theoretical perspectives

The first four chapters draw on the research literature to establish the conceptual foundations for the empirical chapters that follow in Parts II and III. They do so by highlighting certain 'myths' that underpin much of current practice, showing their inadequacies as theoretical positions, and suggesting alternative bases on which a sounder approach to adult professional learning (APL) can be built. The opening chapter by Guy Claxton critiques the dominant 'mythology of learning' and offers in its stead 'integrated learning theory', an approach which places the learners' priorities, beliefs, affective responses and learning strategies at the centre of the framework. Learners are seen as tacit decision-makers, choosing their stance of engagement (or disengagement) towards learning on the basis of their perceptions and interpretations. In Chapter 2, Mike Wallace homes in on the 'myth of portability', arguing that much so-called 'experiential learning' in APL is founded on the false assumption that learning is inherently transferable from the context of acquisition back to the context of professional activity. Patricia Broadfoot in Chapter 3 exposes another cornerstone of the current learning orthodoxy: the 'myth of measurability'. The assumption that assessment is neutral with respect to learning is debunked, and she argues for innovative forms of assessment, in both APL and school contexts, which advance the 'learning to learn' agenda rather than frustrating it; while in Chapter 4, Guy Claxton returns to examine a whole range of other implicit (and illicit) theories of learning that lead to a variety of misunderstandings and barriers to successful APL.

Chapter 1

Integrated learning theory and the learning teacher

Guy Claxton[1]

This initial chapter provides an overview of the theoretical framework that underpins the various contributions to the book. It argues that learning has to be seen as reflecting a tacit, or at least intuitive, decision-making process that includes social, emotional and material, as well as cognitive, considerations, the resultant of which is a *stance* towards the learning opportunity that determines whether, and if so when, how and with what intent, learning will proceed. The decision-making process represents a kind of cost-benefit analysis, in which subjective estimates of the available resources, the loss or gain of social status, the consequences of failure, and the weight of conflicting priorities (for example) are integrated, and a 'minimax' solution computed. These subjective estimates in their turn depend upon a whole variety of 'implicit theories' about what is to count as a threat or a need; the likelihood of success; what material, social and time resources are likely to be obtainable; and the nature of learning and knowing themselves. It is argued that lack of apparent 'ability' or 'motivation', amongst both students and teachers, should be interpreted in terms of this underlying, but rational, process. It is also suggested that the ability to *defend* oneself against unwanted or threatening learning invitations is a valuable capacity.

INTEGRATED LEARNING THEORY

It is the intention of this chapter to sketch the outlines of an approach to learning that offers a research-based handle on learning in real-life contexts. It aims to be both genuinely psychological, in offering a way of conceptualising the resilience, resourcefulness and reflectivity of a competent learner, and also of genuine utility in planning and appraising learning programmes. It is on this psychological skeleton that the varied case studies in this book will attempt to put some practical flesh. By looking at the ways in which teachers learn, in a variety of contexts, the book aims to illustrate, test and amplify this approach to learning, and to ground it in current practice.

In particular it will investigate the personal and motivational issues that teachers-as-learners experience, and explore practical ways in which these difficulties can be addressed.

My task here is to lay out a view of adult learning – integrated learning theory (ILT) – based on five central ideas. The first is that learning has to be seen as reflecting an on-going decision-making process about whether to engage with the challenge presented, and if so in what way. The second is that this decision-making process resembles a kind of intuitive cost–benefit analysis, which attempts to compute the most desirable course of action on the basis of the perceived opportunities, demands, costs, rewards and risks inherent in the situation and in the learners' view of themselves. The third is that learning is not a homogeneous activity, and there is not a single 'best way' of learning. Rather learners have to be seen as possessing a repertoire of learning strategies and processes that they deploy on the basis of an acquired understanding of what each is good for and when it is appropriate.

The fourth idea is that, as well as a set of ways of enhancing their competence, learners need a complementary repertoire of defensive strategies. 'Good learning' reflects not a complete absence of defensiveness and avoidance, but the ability to make choices about when and how to learn, or defend, that are appropriate to the actual contingencies present in the situation, and which serve to further the learner's own valued goals. The corollary of this is that learning may come to be impeded, blocked or abandoned in ways, and under conditions, in which the learner's best interests are not promoted, if learning choices are based on bad information. And the fifth suggests that the significant risks, rewards and so on, which weigh in the balance of a person's learning decisions, are themselves underpinned by a host of views-of-the-world that are the residues of past experiences and teachings. This concern with learners' 'implicit theories' of learning, and of themselves as learners, I shall examine in more detail in Chapter 4. This chapter sets the scene for this concern by spelling out the first four of the foundation stones. First, however, I need to sketch in the background.

THE SOCIAL CONTEXT

The world has changed for teachers, as it has changed, and is changing, for other professional groups, and indeed for the entire adult workforce. 'Continuing professional development' is no longer a matter of the odd in-service course, or an MA for those with more academic leanings. It is not an optional extra, to be undertaken as a matter of individual choice by the teacher with ambition and some energy to spare. The continuous development of a teacher's skills is rapidly becoming a matter of necessity. The National Curriculum, GNVQs, information technology, mentoring and school-based teacher training, the Local Management of Schools, teacher appraisal, 'league tables' and competition between neighbouring schools and colleges . . . the list of changes that demand new attitudes and competencies is lengthy and familiar. Whatever their particular roles and responsibilities, no student teacher or manager is exempt from the demand to be a learner.

These professional challenges – or pressures, depending on how they are viewed – must also be located within wider social and educational contexts. The shifting and multiple patterns of religion, relationship, ideology, vocation, lifestyle and geographical mobility that characterise our pluralistic society all place demands, arguably unprecedented, on individuals to exercise choice and engage with uncertainty: to invent and reinvent their own identities. Full employment and lifelong job security are options that no government, no corporation, no trade union or professional association can honestly offer any more. Middle-class occupations and lifestyles are more insecure than they have ever been. We live in the notorious 'enterprise culture', in which arguably the best that societies can do is provide support; to put in place a learning infrastructure that will 'empower' (dreadful word) individuals, and perhaps communities, to face these challenges with resourcefulness and confidence.

We are thus in the midst of an economic and social revolution in which the 'industrial society' is metamorphosing into the 'learning society' (Ball, 1993; Husen, 1986). Learning can no longer be seen as a task for people in the first quarter of life. And *what* it is that needs to be learnt, and the level of flexible understanding that is required, is also undergoing a profound change. What is required of an ever-expanding majority of the workforce, as the Information Age gathers momentum, is 'mind work' rather than 'body work' (Ross, 1994). In this individualistic world, those who can acquire the requisite competencies – and keep on expanding and updating their 'cognitive capital' – are those for whom it will be relatively easy to find employment. Those who are unable to do so may, in the future, have an increasingly hard, and marginal, time of it. Thus are the political and social arenas being redefined as we approach the next millennium.

These changes are placing demands on education at all levels that we are only just beginning to grapple with. The traditional distinctions between 'education' and 'training', liberal and vocational learning, are breaking down. The institutions that embodied these distinctions – universities, polytechnics, training colleges, human resource development provision in the workplace – are conversing, merging and changing their character in the search for more powerful and appropriate models of education. Various new forms of 'experiential learning', and ways of assessing and accrediting prior learning, are appearing in traditional institutions of formal education; while industry is concerned to develop not just specific skills, but the more generic qualities of ingenuity, autonomy and reflective practice. These uncharted areas of learning pose challenges that are as relevant to the professional development of teachers, as they are to any other vocational group. The current concern with understanding the nature of mentoring, and the best ways of fostering the development of the requisite skills and sensitivities, is but one example of a more pervasive trend.

But the challenges for schoolteachers are even deeper than they are for other groupings, because it is their business to prepare all young people – and not just the traditionally 'bright' or academically inclined – for this world. Teachers and managers must not only be willing to become career-long professional learners themselves; they must be actively engaged in the development of new – perhaps radically new – forms of education that equip students to function well under uncertainty. No longer can this be taken to mean the provision of particular vocational or discipline-based intellectual skills and knowledge. Something altogether deeper is needed. Whether one views the situation from a political/economic perspective, with its concern for competitiveness in global markets; or a sociological perspective, with a concern with equity and opportunity for different groups within society; or a psychological, or even spiritual, perspective, with focus on individual well-being and fulfilment; whichever vantage point one adopts, vital benefits will accrue to a society that develops a form of schooling that reliably produces young adults who can engage with learning, in whatever form it appears, with enthusiasm, resilience and resourcefulness.

THE PSYCHOLOGICAL CONTEXT

This book addresses, jointly and in a variety of ways, the socio-cultural and the psychological aspects of learning. Learning happens in social settings – classrooms, conference rooms, staffrooms, laboratories – that are saturated with cultural meanings and assumptions. But it also happens in people's heads. And understanding the internal dynamics of learning, as well as its contexts and occasions, can only lead to the design of more reliable, powerful and effective learning programmes and procedures. The problem is that no even half-way adequate psychology of real-life learning exists.

On the one hand the traditional theories that have emerged from academic psychology have been partial and simplistic. They have emphasised 'behaviour' or 'problem solving' or 'self-esteem' without putting all the facets back together into an integrated but recognisable picture of a real-life learner. And they have, until very recently, focused on types of learning that have no counterparts in the 'real world': they lack, in Ulric Neisser's phrase, 'ecological validity' (Neisser, 1984). Warmed-over Piaget-for-grown-ups is not going to do the trick. On the other hand conceptualisations that have been distilled from the genuine complexities of some area of everyday life tend to be descriptive, and what they often lack is insight into the subtleties of the learners' inner world. The recent explosion of interest in 'experiential learning', explored by Mike Wallace in Chapter 2, for example, has produced much enthusiastic experimentation with educational practice without generating anything very helpful or sophisticated in the way of theory. Kolb's famous 'learning cycle' (Kolb, 1984) still seems to be about as good as it gets (see Keeton, 1994).

THE DECISION TO LEARN

A comprehensive approach must throw some light on the *when*, the *where* and the *why* of learning, as well as the *how*. To be a 'good learner' one must be ready and willing to learn, as well as able, and this means being alive to the opportunities that present themselves for pursuing valued goals; and free of any internal blocks and barriers that inhibit one from learning when it is appropriate to do so. Before one attempts to depress the accelerator and drive off on a learning journey, the 'clutch' that links the cognitive motor to the learning wheels must be engaged, and the brake must be off. There is much attention being paid, at present, to the *facilitation* of learning. But unless we understand equally the dynamics of *engagement*, which enables learners to commit themselves and their learning resources whole-heartedly to the process of learning, and of *disinhibition*, which enables learners to avoid or overcome tendencies to defend or withdraw unnecessarily, then our attempts at facilitation are always liable to founder.

It is a matter of widespread concern in the area of professional development and learning in education, for example, that the uptake and outcomes of learning opportunities – often expensively and thoughtfully designed – are disappointing. Where courses are voluntary, attendance is sometimes thin, even when the topic is one that teachers know to be important; while where their presence is expected, or even enforced, as in many whole-school training days and conferences, there may be teachers whose active participation is minimal, and whose attitude can be fatalistic or even overtly cynical. While teachers' previous experience may make such an attitude seem reasonable, it is capable of becoming a self-fulfilling prophecy. If one enters a learning event firmly believing it to be a futile exercise, it is quite likely that that is precisely what it will be. And the problem seems to run deeper than making courses 'attractive' and 'relevant', or instituting carrots for attendance and sticks for avoidance.

The decision about when and how to engage – or disengage – with a specific learning opportunity is not a simple matter of conscious, rational appraisal of its potential value. Rather, I suggest, it is better seen as reflecting a complex, largely tacit 'cost–benefit analysis' that may be influenced by a whole host of considerations – personal and emotional as well as vocational – which extend beyond the perception of the opportunity itself. I have previously applied this perspective, grounded in 'social exchange theory' (e.g. Homans, 1950), to classroom learning (e.g. Claxton, 1989, 1991), and shown how it provides a more constructive way of approaching the issue of pupil engagement with lessons than the traditional 'teacher talk' vocabulary of 'effort', 'laziness', 'motivation' and so on. But it is equally applicable to the world of adult and professional learning; and trainers or providers of education at this level will be able to maximise attendance, engagement and the quality of learning itself, if they understand something of the learners' soft, intuitive underbelly, so to speak. Let me illustrate what some of the considerations that enter in to this decision-making process might be.

Which of my valued goals may be advanced by engaging with this learning opportunity? Will it enhance my security, status or prospects for advancement in my current employment? Will it make the execution of my job more pleasurable, efficient or productive? Will it make me more attractive to other employers (of the same kind)? Will it open up the possibility of a career change? Is it intrinsically interesting? Will it act as a stepping stone towards the achievement of other learning goals? Am I feeling stale and in need of some stimulation?

What other priorities do I have at present, and how would accepting this learning invitation impact upon them? Do I feel as though I already have too much on my plate? Should I postpone this one for a while (until I have finished my MEd, or until the baby is a bit older)? Is this a continuing option, or is it a 'once in a lifetime' opportunity (in which case I might have to take a year out from the degree)? What sacrifices might be required (time with the family; holidays; fishing at weekends . . .)? Are there ways of advancing any of my other priorities by taking this on? Will it give me the opportunity for time away from school/the family, which I badly need?

What kinds of support and external resources are there likely to be? And how likely? Will there be enough time to integrate the learning thoroughly, or will it be another botch job? What sorts of books will I need, and can I borrow them from the local university library? Will my family give me the space I need to study? Are there any grants I might apply for to help with the costs? Is there anyone else from the school who might be interested, and with whom I could study/practise/share books and car journeys?

What possible (emotional) costs and risks are there? How would I feel if I found I wasn't up to it? If I had to drop out (because of other pressures) could I do so without feeling a failure? Am I willing to risk looking stupid by admitting I don't understand (or do I need to try to bluff my way through)? Are there ways in which my image of myself (as 'shy', 'practical', 'bright') might be challenged?

These questions are not all considered consciously, of course. Some of them may be, but it is often the case that the cost–benefit analysis proceeds unconsciously, issuing into consciousness simply as a feeling or an impulse, whose antecedents may not be recoverable into awareness (see, for example, Noddings and Shore, 1984). One may only be conscious of an intimation that this is 'not for me' or 'not right now', or of a feeling of being overwhelmed or excited by the prospect. As we shall see later on in this chapter, however, the identification of this decision-making process, and of some of the major ingredients of it, opens up the possibility that trainers and managers of professional learning could provide teachers with the opportunity to make better learning choices by *making* the process more conscious and deliberate. One of the advantages of doing so is that the intuitive weights given to different considerations, and the beliefs and assumptions that underpin these weightings, can be scrutinised and questioned. As we shall see both in this chapter and in Chapter 4, it is often the fact that these considerations weigh in the learning balance unreflectively that leads to self-defeating learning choices being made.

Nor is it the case that this personal appraisal of the learning situation takes place only at the point of potential entry. It may be the case that, once the decision to engage has been taken, this is implemented as a commitment to follow the course of learning wherever it may lead, and through thick and thin. But it is also possible that the decision to engage is one that is sporadically, or even continually, reconsidered as learning proceeds, so that unexpected demands or set-backs may lead to a flip from engagement into self-protection. Whether they physically disappear or not, it is always open to learners, if they judge it to be desirable, to withdraw their internal commitment and become passive passengers of the learning experience rather than active drivers of it. Thus continual attention to the motivational state of course participants is, as any adult educator knows, an important aspect of his or her role as a facilitator of learning.

THE VARIETIES OF LEARNING

One of the cornerstones of the ILT approach is that 'learning' cannot be seen as a homogeneous activity that can be characterised simply as 'more' or 'less', 'better' or 'worse', 'superficial' or 'deep'. One of the problems with many existing approaches to learning is that they assume that the kind of learning they are interested in represents learning as a whole. They start from what George Kelly referred to as a particular 'focus of convenience' (Kelly, 1955), such as management decision making, technical problem solving, self-actualisation or the acquisition of physical skill; develop a conceptualisation that seems to offer some understanding of (or at least some way of talking fruitfully about) the issues within that domain; and then present these characterisations as if their '*range* of convenience' – the domain of phenomena to which they actually apply – were **all** learning situations. There is now an abundance of evidence that learning and performance are to a large extent situation specific and context dependent (e.g. Brown *et al.*, 1989).

Instead let us start from the position that 'learning' is a broad umbrella term that covers a whole range of different types of learning challenge, different kinds of learning outcome, and different learning modes or strategies that a learner can engage or adopt. So once learners have 'passed Go', and decided that a particular learning challenge is one that they are going (albeit provisionally) to accept, they then have to select the learning mode that seems to them to afford the best chance of achieving the desired outcome in terms either of practical accomplishment, or of new competency, or both. Following a positive answer to the question of whether to learn, they have to make an initial choice of how to go about it. And again this choice must potentially reflect a whole host of influences. For example, two of the considerations that may go into this learning-mode selection are:

Which mode seems most likely to deliver the outcome or the competency that I want? Do I need more hands-on experience? Will I have to get my brain round some difficult material? Is it a matter of critical reflection on past performance? Shall I just sit and watch for a while?

What is the match (or mismatch) between the anticipated learning demands and my perceived learning styles and resources? Am I the right kind of person for this course? Have I got what it takes? Will there be much statistics (which I'm terrified of)? Will there be role-plays and simulations (which I always get a lot out of)? Will I have to present my ideas in front of a group (which is a fear that I really think it's time to overcome)? Will I be able to succeed by mugging things up at the last minute (which I've always managed to do before)? Will I have to remember lots of data (I've got a hopeless memory)?

THE CONSTRUCTIVIST PERSPECTIVE

The framework I am proposing falls within the psychological tradition that has come to be known as 'social constructivism'. This means that the sense that people make of their experience is a function of the knowledge, beliefs, schemas and attitudes, derived from previous, culturally situated, experiences, that they bring with them to the new event. Those knowledge structures which are brought to bear are the source of the personal meaning that that experience has. Meaning is constructed by the person, and attributed to experience; it is not recovered from it in any direct way. This view has a number of implications for the way in which learning is seen. The one that arises in the context of the present discussion is that what enters into the cost–benefit analyses determining whether, and if so how, to learn is not any *direct* apprehension of the risks, resources, etc., but subjective estimates of their value and significance that are attributed to them by learners on the basis of their past experience.

Thus it is not the actual, 'objective' risk of being thought foolish by one's fellow learners if one admits one's ignorance that is fed into the decision-making process, but the individual's own sense of the likelihood, and the personal cost, of such an eventuality. And this estimate may be an accurate one, or it may be wide of the mark. So, for example, a person who is particularly prone to see the world in terms of opportunities for humiliation, and who evaluates such occurrences in highly negative terms, is likely to exaggerate the personal cost of any learning experience where there is the possibility of public failure, and to avoid such experiences – even though they may also offer opportunities to pursue personal goals that are highly valued. Learners can be effectively blocked from taking up learning opportunities, or, if forced into them, will engage with them in a way that is designed to defend against the anticipated or imagined risks, rather than to maximise their learning. Their learning can be constrained or subverted by these exaggerated estimates of threat, or by failures to credit themselves with personal learning resources that they may in fact possess. In such cases we may reasonably refer to learning as 'blocked' or 'inhibited'. A major goal for learning support then becomes the dissolution of these blocks, or the presentation and construction of learning programmes that address the need for learning to be disinhibited as well as facilitated.

THE VALUE OF DEFENCE

I shall leave a more detailed discussion of the range of different learning modes or strategies that people may possess until Chapter 4. However, it will be useful to introduce here a general distinction between those responses to novelty or uncertainty that are designed to produce learning – what we might call 'enhancement strategies' – and those whose intention is to produce protection or defence of the people as they are – 'maintenance strategies'. The primary decision as to whether to engage with a learning opportunity or not is basically, therefore, one of selecting between enhancement mode and maintenance mode. Put crudely: if the apparent benefits and 'hope of success' outweigh the perceived costs and 'fear of failure', then one is inclined to sign up for enhancement. If not, then one opts for maintenance.

Thus learning has to be seen as one of two general stances we can adopt towards the unknown, each of which has value when deployed appropriately, and each of which has costs when misapplied. The ability to protect oneself from that which is too threatening, or to disengage when the investment of time and effort becomes disproportionate to the potential value of the understanding or skill to be acquired, is as valuable a component of our overall survival strategy as the ability to learn. The error comes when learners feel compelled to turn down learning invitations that are in fact valuable, accessible and (relatively) safe; or to engage recklessly or doggedly with learning opportunities that are in fact dangerous or a waste of time. It is essential to remember that learning is not always the smart choice; and that whether it is smart or not can only be assessed by the learners themselves. No teacher, however well intentioned, can get inside someone else's head and see what his or her idiosyncratic and evanescent portfolio of hopes, fears and expectations looks like. The present analysis suggests that even learners themselves are not necessarily privy to all the considerations that affect their choices, and that some of these choices may be skewed in ways that are not ultimately in their own best interests. Yet it is possible that an increase in this particular variety of self-awareness can be facilitated.

Just as with learning strategies, the ways of protecting oneself from physical or psychological harm are many and various, and each has its appropriate domain of application. It may be possible simply to decline the invitation and walk (or if needs be run) away. But, as we saw earlier in this chapter, this option is increasingly problematic for adult and professional learners, as the economic and social pressures on them to engage with learning mount. It is astute to select the learning battles that one wishes to fight; but it is becoming more and more self-defeating to decline all such invitations on principle. It is when physical 'fight and flight' are not available as options – when attendance, at least sometimes, is required – that one may have to adopt more subtle, psychological forms of defence.

Surprisingly these have been little investigated in the context of adult learning and professional development. In one classic paper Menzies (1959) analysed the practices, rituals and role relationships commonly encountered in nurse training in terms of their value as defences against the many strong sources of anxiety and distress to which both student nurses and their teachers are prey. It used to be habitual in such contexts, for example, to structure the course so that the group of peers with which any one student was working would be changed every few weeks – thus ensuring that the level of trust and intimacy between peers, which would have allowed their distress to be revealed, was never, or rarely, achieved. Though the professional development of teachers does not expose them routinely to serious sickness, the presence of death, and the need to make vital medical decisions often on the basis of inadequate information, nevertheless learning for mature adults is frequently, and undeniably, a stressful business, and the risks of learning being subverted, if these emotional and personal issues are not addressed, are clearly present.

One of the strategies that Menzies identified as a defence against the anxiety of responsibility she called 'upward delegation', or, more generally, regression. One of the ways in which professionals can ease the fear of inadequacy is by tactical underachievement: choosing (usually unconsciously) to operate well within their limits, and forcing managers or more experienced colleagues to take on those responsibilities which feel threatening. In some circumstances these senior colleagues are more than willing to collude with this upward delegation, because it furnishes them with the perfect excuse to do the same thing with the aspects of *their* jobs that they find stressful. In a learning situation, such a self-protective ploy will, of necessity, reduce the rate and depth of the learning that accrues.

A recent paper by Thompson (1993) explores the related tactic of withholding effort. Where learning is perceived as being difficult, and the person doubts his or her ability to complete it successfully, 'a tension arises between a motive to secure the glory [and rewards] of success by trying hard and a motive to avoid the ignominy [and inconvenience] of defeat by withdrawing effort'. The dreaded inference of inability can be avoided if engagement is deliberately half-hearted. If one can claim that failure to master a new task or competency reflects a lack of effort, rather than of ability, face can be saved. Thompson's study of undergraduates reveals the intricacies of this pattern, and the implications for teachers who are keen to minimise the defensiveness that their teaching may induce. For example, 'the performance of students who are particularly afraid of failing is improved when a task is described as "very difficult" . . . . With a ready-made attribution [of possible failure] to task difficulty rather than to [the] person, the threat to self-esteem is removed' (p. 470). There are, in the mature as well as in the young adult arena, a number of ways in which this withdrawal of effort may manifest itself: denigration of the teacher or the learning task, cynicism, or larking about may all mask self-protection.

INDIVIDUAL DIFFERENCES IN LEARNING

This kind of analysis, preliminary and somewhat impressionistic though it is, offers a more differentiated way of approaching individual differences in learning than many of the more familiar attempts such as those of Kolb (1984). These efforts to reduce learning styles to two, or four, or sixteen predetermined categories may be useful in stimulating reflection and self-awareness, but they are simply too crude to do justice to the qualitative differences between learners. Learners differ not just in the dominant disposition they bring with them to learning in general. They possess different repertoires of learning strategies: different both in the nature and the range of strategies that are potentially available. They differ in the extent to which they are locked into one style, as opposed to selecting a strategy to meet the perceived needs of a particular situation. They differ in the ways they interpret and give weight to the perceived rewards and risks of engagement. They differ in the sophistication and the availability of the knowledge and skill base that relates to the learning task. And they differ in their ability (and their disposition) to maintain a reflective or metacognitive self-awareness as learning proceeds, so that strategic changes of tack can be made when current strategies are failing to deliver the anticipated learning outcomes.

In particular the present emphasis on choice and strategy acknowledges the *situatedness* of cognition and learning (Brown *et al.*, 1989; Lave and Wenger, 1991). As I have already mentioned, there is abundant evidence that the cognitive resources, and the affective stance, that are deployed are heavily dependent on aspects of the immediate situation that may seem, to the teacher, to be quite peripheral to the central demands of the learning task. Physical location, or the person's mood, for example, may have a significant influence on how the task is approached, what is attended to, the kind of learning strategy that is selected, the degree of reflection in action, as opposed to unreflective automatism, and the nature and transferability of the learning outcome. The way in which teachers or trainers present both themselves and the learning tasks, the vocabulary they use, and so on, may have a dramatic effect on the stances that different learners adopt.

The recognition of the importance of all these influences makes it all the harder, of course, to design a learning programme that will be sure to meet the needs and dispositions of a heterogeneous group. What it indicates is a shift in emphasis from a premeditated approach, in which all the effort for ensuring a successful programme goes into the planning and design, to *an ongoing attention, throughout the learning experience itself, to the choices and reactions that individual learners are experiencing.* The on-line facilitation of reflection about learning becomes at least as important as the attempt to second-guess the styles and needs of a particular client group.

LEARNING TO LEARN

The constructivist underpinnings of integrated learning theory lead inexorably to a recognition that every opportunity to learn is also an opportunity to learn how to learn: to learn about oneself as a learner, and to develop, if one will, one's learning acumen. And concomitantly *every opportunity to teach is also, at least potentially, an opportunity to focus on the development of the attitudes and qualities of a 'good learner'*, at the same time as one aims to achieve a more specific learning goal. While a mentor is working with a beginning teacher on the preparation of lesson plans, or discussing a lesson that has just taken place, for example, the mentor may, through his or her demeanour and interactions, either be helping the student teacher to develop his or her autonomy and ability to become **self**-correcting, **self**-organising and **self**-aware; or actually be inhibiting the development of these qualities.

Likewise an 'expert' on mentor training, when working with a group of experienced teachers, may be either supporting or impeding the development of their ability to become critically reflective about their own practice. And whether this is a good thing or a bad thing depends not on some kind of blanket ideology, but on a clear appraisal of the specific needs of the situation, and on an understanding of how a set of educational values bears on learning goals and contexts. In the current social climate, which I outlined at the start of this chapter, attention to the development of learning to learn is rapidly becoming a vital concern for individual learners and their teachers right across the educational spectrum.

I shall have much more to say about 'learning to learn' in Chapter 4, when I shall discuss the implicit theories about learning and teaching that effectively control what an educational culture perceives as possible and desirable. When the concept of 'learning ability' becomes abbreviated simply to 'ability', and when ability is conceived of as a more or less fixed, general-purpose ceiling on possible achievement, for example, then the idea of 'learning to learn' lacks power, conviction and substance. Meanwhile this chapter has set out a framework for looking at adult learning and professional development, one that opens up some interesting practical possibilities for training, and at the same time offers a critical perspective on current practice.

NOTE

1 I am very grateful to those contributors who commented on the draft of this chapter, in particular to Mike Wallace for his supportive yet penetrating observations.

REFERENCES

Ball, Sir C. (1993) *Towards a Learning Society*, London: Royal Society of Arts.

Brown, J. S., Collins, A. and Duguid, P. (1989) 'Situated learning and the culture of cognition'. *Educational Researcher*, Vol. 18, No. 1, pp. 32–42.

Claxton, G. L. (1989) *Classroom Learning*, Open University course E208, Exploring Educational Issues, Unit 13. Milton Keynes: Open University.

Claxton, G. L. (1990) *Teaching to Learn: A Direction for Education*, London: Cassell.

Homans, G. C. (1950) *The Human Group*, London: Routledge and Kegan Paul.

Husen, T. (1986) *The Learning Society Revisited*, Oxford: Pergamon.

Keeton, M. (ed.) (1994) *Perspectives on Experiential Learning*, Chicago: Council for Adult and Experiential Learning.

Kelly, G. A. (1955) *The Psychology of Personal Constructs*, New York: W. W. Norton.

Kolb, D. A. (1984) *Experiential Learning: Experience as the Source of Learning and Development*, Englewood Cliffs, NJ: Prentice Hall.

Lave, J. and Wenger, E. (1991) *Situated Learning: Legitimate Peripheral Participation*, Cambridge: Cambridge University Press.

Menzies, I. E. P. (1959) 'The functioning of social systems as a defence against anxiety: a report on a study of the nursing service of a general hospital'. *Human Relations*, Vol. 13, pp. 95–121.

Neisser, U. (1984) *Cognition and Reality*, Oxford: W. H. Freeman.

Noddings, N. and Shore, P. J. (1984) *Awakening the Inner Eye: Intuition in Education*, Columbia, NY: Teachers College Press.

Ross, D. (1994) 'Workforce development policy: next steps'. Closing address, International Experiential Learning Conference, Washington, DC, November.

Thompson, T. (1993) 'Characteristics of self-worth protection in achievement behaviour'. *British Journal of Educational Psychology*, Vol. 63, pp. 469–88.

Chapter 2

When is experiential learning not experiential learning?

Mike Wallace

In this second chapter, Mike Wallace offers a theoretical deconstruction of 'the myth of automatic transfer': the assumption, underlying many so-called 'experiential' training courses in professional learning, that simulations are valid ways of conveying skills, and that what is developed and practised in the simulation context will, or should, naturally transfer back to the real-life professional setting without much or any additional attention to learning. Starting with his own experience of one such course, Wallace proceeds to show that this assumption seems to be motivated more by considerations of economy and 'neatness' than by any understanding of the nature of learning. In the course of this he develops a timely critique of the fashionable approaches of both David Kolb and Donald Schon, and presents a more comprehensive model of professional learning that does better justice to the complexities. The chapter makes a strong case that practice driven by impoverished models which rest on untenable implicit theories of learning is bound to be ineffective. Wallace's contention that effective professional learning requires verisimilitude rather than vicarious experience, and ongoing on-the-job support, is borne out by later chapters such as those by Agnes McMahon (Chapter 12) and Jan Winter (Chapter 13).

INTRODUCTION

A few years ago I experienced an intensive outdoor management training course at a venue deep in the country. I was placed in a team for five and a half days, together with a colleague I had known for a couple of weeks, and six managers from different walks of life whom I had never met before. We spent packed days and evenings tackling time-limited tasks in competition with other teams. After each task there was a reflective team review. A facilitator weaned us away from our concern with our frustrations over the task to examine our feelings and our team performance. These sessions were supplemented with lectures which drew eclectically on theories and research in offering us guidance for improving our performance as managers. We also learned rudiments of a sport which was designed to be challenging for us as individuals. I learned how to do a 'ferry glide', traversing a two-person canoe up a series of rapids, and how to come down them without ending up in the drink.

Our team had been bottom of the league all week, failing dismally to achieve our tasks. Each could be solved only if we achieved synergy as a team, whether the task was a treasure hunt (we were too busy arguing about who should look for what), a simulation where we had to manoeuvre a container of nuclear fuel into safe storage (we blew up the world), or, on the penultimate evening, a short comic drama (we failed to get enough laughs).

As we were about to pack up for the night, exhausted and resigned to our failure, the final task was announced. It was to last sixteen hours and whichever team won on this occasion would be declared the course winner. Every type of task we had already undertaken was included, so I had to shoot those rapids yet again. It was a highly charged experience, and my crowning glory was to crack the code which was the key to our team's success. We won.

What did all these powerful experiences do for me as a manager back in my university workplace? The short answer is not a lot, because I was inhibited from transferring what I learned about teamwork into my work setting. Yet the disinhibition required for me to make the most of my experience was not simply a matter of adopting a more positive attitude towards learning.

I was asked at the outset to suspend any disbelief and enter into the spirit of the course. Accordingly I took the decision to learn, and my engagement with the learning opportunity remained strong throughout. While most of the experiences cost me dear in terms of frustration, failure and, at times, fear, the strength of these emotions was far outweighed by the benefits of excitement, challenging tasks and ever tighter bonding within the team. At the low point after flunking each task, the facilitator asked participants whether they wanted to 'go for the keys' (to their car) so that they could drive off into the sunset, thereby shifting from an enhancement to a maintenance learning strategy which would be terminal as far as the course was concerned. We all admitted that the thought had crossed our minds, but nobody did it because of our strengthening motivation to 'go the extra mile' with our team mates and come out winners.

Our final triumph had left me with a feel-good factor that favoured my enduring effort to maximise the learning opportunity – but try conveying that to colleagues who don't know what you've been up to, don't share the matey feelings you have generated within your course team, and whom you are not supposed to tell about it. For the organisers had asked us not to divulge the secrets of our experience, claiming that the success of the course depended on participants being blissfully unaware about what they were in for at the start of the programme; many companies sent different managers each year, and amongst middle managers the training was surrounded in mystique which contributed to its desirability as a perk.

My transfer problem was rooted in the way the team tasks and setting were (sadly perhaps!) far removed by design from my routine managerial work and its context. Yet the course organisers had stated the assumption that we would be able to transfer what we had learned from one group, one set of tasks and one setting into another. This article of faith is open to question since it ignores the possibility noted by Eraut (1994) that additional learning is required of participants, and their workplace colleagues who have not attended an off the job course, if the desired transfer of learning into the workplace is to be made. No support was offered for transfer beyond encouraging participants to refer back to principles articulated during the course.

SIGNIFICANCE OF DIFFERENT EXPERIENCES

My – contentious – answer to the riddle posed in the title of this chapter is: when experiential learning for job performance is based on 'vicarious' experience (Bailey, 1987). The further a learning experience departs from the tasks that are the object of training and the situation in which they have to be performed, the more vicarious it becomes, and the more additional learning has still to take place in the real context of these tasks.

My problem over transfer of learning from off the job course to on the job practice is, perhaps, no more than we would expect according to research in fields as diverse as cognitive psychology and the training of teachers. The latter research will be discussed later; the former has contributed to an on-going debate over the degree to which knowledge employed in practice is situation specific, a product of the activity, context and culture in which it is developed and used.

The theory of 'situated cognition' articulated by Brown *et al.* (1989) was based on research into how people go about learning when free to do so in their own way. They argued that knowledge required for action is intricately linked to the context in which it is learned. A new context implies new learning in which old cognitive schemata become modified. On this account, I had more to learn and the conditions were not favourable for my induction, since the culture of the course which I had absorbed was anathema to the culture of the workplace. Others have argued that there are generic skills which can be transferred to different situations but their application entails picking up detailed contextual knowledge (Perkins and Salomon, 1989) – in other words, transfer entails additional, context-specific learning.

Present definitions of experiential learning appear to cover too much ground. Wutzdorff (1994, p. 2), for example, argues that diverse approaches to experiential learning share common assumptions:

this commitment to experiential learning is grounded in a philosophy that engages the learner actively in whatever is being learned. It is a philosophy that asserts that the development of knowledge and the acquisition of skills belong as partners in education, where each can transform the other. Therefore experiential learning necessarily goes beyond reading and listening as the primary routes to effective learning.

By directly engaging the learner in what is being studied, experiential learning then also re-shapes the teacher-learner relationship. Often this change means that the teacher steps out of the role of authority figure and possessor of knowledge and moves into a facilitator role. Experience itself becomes the teacher. The emphasis then is placed on the reflective process, where teachers and peers join the learner in making meaning out of whatever has been experienced.

The emphasis is on active engagement of learners, the primacy of their learning experience, facilitation (as opposed to transmitting knowledge), and making sense of experience through reflective dialogue between facilitator and learner. However, no distinction is made between different kinds of experience and the degree to which they relate to the context in which the learning is designed to be used.

Although the learning experience I went through was real enough – both demanding and exciting – and I certainly learned a great deal, it was not the same experience as learning to do my job more effectively. The training achieved all that it could do: provide me with generic principles which I had yet to learn how to put into practice at work.

In recent years, the popularity and diversity of activities labelled as experiential learning have increased dramatically within the realms of initial and in-service teacher training (the latter including management training for senior staff). It is striking how many of these activities are based on vicarious experiences such as role-play exercises and simulation games; but where the aim is to improve job performance, any old experience will surely not do. The purposes of this chapter are therefore twofold: to question some of the theoretical underpinnings of the experiential learning movement; and to make a case for liberating learners from the transfer problem associated with vicarious training experiences by focusing learning support for beginning teachers, experienced teachers and senior managers firmly on the real job in its real setting. The remaining sections will explore the theoretical base of experiential learning; consider evidence which points to the importance of learning support in the context of use; and employ a model developed in the light of this evidence to consider how to make the most of experiential learning within training design.

CONCEPTIONS OF EXPERIENTIAL LEARNING

Two of the most influential accounts of learning through experience will be examined. Advocates of training methods based on participants' experience (e.g. Dennison and Kirk, 1990; Hobbs, 1992), including outdoor management training (e.g. Beeby and Rathborn, 1983; Bank 1985), have made widespread reference to the theory of experiential learning put forward by Kolb (1984). The process of learning is conceived as a four-stage cycle (see Figure 2.1). Immersion in immediate concrete experience is viewed as the basis for observation and reflection. Observations are assimilated into an idea, image or theory from which implications for future action may be derived. These implications, hunches or hypotheses then guide planning and implementation of experimental action to create new experiences. Learners require the skills of learning how to learn in this way: the ability to immerse themselves openly in new experiences (CE), to reflect on these experiences (RO), to integrate observations into more abstract conceptual schemes or theories (AC), and to use these theories to guide decision-making and experimental action to solve problems (AE), leading to new concrete experiences.

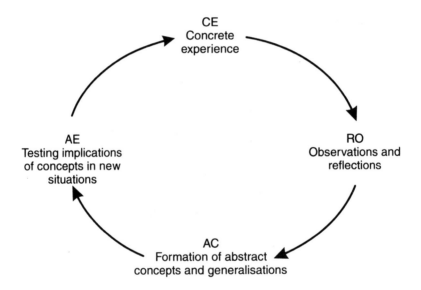

Figure 2.1 Kolb's experiential learning model

Different learning situations foster different skills. An affective environment highlights experiencing of concrete events; a symbolic environment emphasises abstract conceptualisation; a perceptual environment encourages observation; and a behavioural environment stresses taking experimental action. Tasks within my experience of management training provided a range of environments which fostered most experiential learning skills. The simulation exercise, for example, provided affective, perceptual and behavioural elements of a learning environment. It was strong on concrete experience, the opportunity to observe the consequences of our actions, and repeated chances (until we dropped the container of nuclear fuel) to experiment with new ways of solving the problem which the team had been set. While it was weak on abstract conceptualisation, the lecture sessions provided a complementary symbolic environment where we were presented with a range of concepts which we could apply to our more active tasks.

Kolb's research into how far the cycle was reflected in individuals' learning behaviour revealed wide variation, commonly being biased towards one or more elements. He claims that individuals' preferred learning styles become more effective the more they reflect the complete cycle. My management training experience quickly revealed such differences in behaviour: some team members were keen to leap before they looked, moving into action almost as soon as the task had been set (a bias towards active experimentation and concrete experience). Others wanted to look before they leaped, taking more time to explore the parameters of the problem and to employ problem-solving strategies in coming up with a plan of campaign (a bias towards reflective observation and abstract conceptualisation). In my team, some arguments arose because each type of learner could see the negative consequences of the other's approach: concrete experience junkies wondered if the abstract conceptualisers would ever let them get started, while the latter despaired of the way the former wasted time rushing down blind alleys because they had not thought through the problem.

So far so good, but does the theory go far enough? It certainly captures aspects of learning experience and points to practical implications, including the desirability of maximising the opportunity of any experience to support learning and the need to diagnose the bias in individuals' learning styles and foster balanced learning habits.

However, there remains an important gap in the argument. Any experience may indeed offer potential for learning, but Kolb does not address the transferability of what has been learned from one experience into another. The theory explains how learning through a particular experience takes place. I certainly learned from the treasure hunt how to work with my team of that week in doing treasure hunts. The point of the exercise, however, was not to train me as a treasure seeker, but as a member and leader of a different workplace team with very different tasks. The trainers assumed that I could automatically transfer this learning. It follows from Kolb's theory that a second set of experiential learning cycles would be required for the additional learning in my everyday environment that was necessary for the course to impact on my job performance.

While the theory holds good as far as it goes, lack of attention to the new learning that performance of tasks in each new setting entails appears ironically to have allowed many trainers, in the name of experiential learning, to assume that the vicarious experience of off the job training is sufficient preparation for the real experience of the job itself. The more vicarious the experiential learning experience, the more additional learning is required for transfer into the context of use and the greater the need for learning support with transfer. Conversely, the closer the experiential learning experience becomes to the context of use, the less additional learning is required and the easier transfer becomes.

Kolb himself has endorsed a wide range of activities as offering experiential learning, including case studies, computer simulations, the use of video, theatrical techniques, internships (which approximate to teaching practice in initial training), management role-play exercises, and even educational travel (see Lewis, 1986). According to his theory, each lies within the parameters of experiential learning. All experiences are real in the sense that they engage participants in cycles of action and reflection and draw on their past experiences but, where the aim is to train for performance elsewhere, a training experience which is divorced from the job can never be more than a valuable supplement to the vital experience of learning to do the real thing.

An alternative conceptualisation, compatible with the theory of experiential learning, is the notion of the 'reflective practitioner' developed by Schon (1983, 1987). He notes how individuals display competence in the uncertain, unique and complex situations of practice, yet their awareness of how they perform their tasks so skilfully is limited. In taking action they employ knowledge which is primarily tacit and intuitive. Most action is routine but when confronted with problems, they respond in one of two ways. They may either stand back and reflect on their action or 'reflect in action', a largely intuitive process of questioning tacit assumptions that failed to lead to the anticipated results. Such assumptions might include needlessly inhibiting implicit theories about themselves as learners (see Chapter 4). They then employ other knowledge in experimenting to solve the problem. The theory helps to explain how Kolb's experiential learning cycle may operate, suggesting that intuitive reflection in action may take place continually during concrete experience as well as the reflection on that action entailed in standing back and observing, conceptualising and planning experimental action.

Yet Schon also stops short of distinguishing between preparatory and real job experiences. He suggests that initial training for professionals should include a 'practicum' where problematic situations are tackled – an idea developed by Peter John in Chapter 16. Students are encouraged by a coach to think and talk as they work, so developing their capacity to reflect in action:

A practicum is a setting designed for the task of learning a practice. In a context that approximates a practice world, students learn by doing, although their doing usually falls short of real-world work. They learn by undertaking projects that simulate and simplify practice; or they take on real-world projects under close supervision. The practicum is a virtual world, relatively free of the pressures, distractions, and risks of the real one, to which, nevertheless, it refers. It stands in an intermediate space between the practice world, the 'lay' world of ordinary life, and the esoteric world of the academy.

(Schon, 1987, p. 37)

The 'virtual world' of the practicum is related to the real work situation, but offers students the opportunity to practise their performance without having to cope with the full complexity and risks of the job. A practicum may be designed to approximate more closely to the job situation over time as students gain in confidence and competence but, even in such a case, it still offers a qualitatively different experience from the actual job where mistakes really matter. The question remains over how students learn to become competent job performers once they emerge from the protected world of the practicum to undertake 'real-world work' without further support. Schon's version of a practicum offers a vicarious experience in that it is designed to simulate the job situation, leaving the beginning professional with the additional learning task of building on what has been learned in the practicum in order to become a competent practitioner.

If the additional learning were automatic, my concern would amount to mere conceptual nitpicking. Clearly, it is not impossible for some learners to make the transfer for themselves, but the more vicarious the training experience, the more support is likely to be needed to facilitate transfer (as in my case). Evidence from extensive research and professional experience indicates that the effectiveness of off the job training can be greatly enhanced if support is given for the integration of what has been learned into job performance. This is arguably the most important – yet so often neglected – component of training design.

TRAINING FOR TRANSFER OF LEARNING BETWEEN EXPERIENCES

Let us look at a key example of such research. Joyce and Showers (1988) carried out a rigorous study of in-service training for teachers that suggests how transfer of learning may be promoted. The focus of the training was complex teaching methods, such as enabling pupils to enhance their critical thinking skills. The researchers identified different components of training and their combinations which led to different outcomes for trainees. Table 2.1 summarises their findings.

A combination of all five training components favours effective integration of new skills or the refinement of existing ones within trainees' repertoire. Presentation of the theory or rationale for a new teaching method raises trainees' awareness and an additional demonstration of the method in use, by such means as a video, gives them the more detailed understanding necessary

Table 2.1 Training components, their combinations and impact on job performance

Training components and the combinations	Impact on job performance		
	Knowledge	*Skill*	*Transfer of Training*
Theory	Low	Low	Nil
Theory, demonstration	Medium	Medium	Nil
Theory, demonstration and practice	High	Medium	Nil
Theory, demonstration, practice and feedback	High	Medium	Low
Theory, demonstration, practice, feedback and coaching	High	High	High

Source: Based on Joyce and Showers (1988).

to perform the skills involved. Opportunities to practise the method in the training setting, possibly through a simulation, enhance skill performance in the training situation itself. Yet there is little transfer of what has been learned into trainees' practice as teachers. The skills may be employed mechanically but are unlikely to be deployed creatively and appropriately. Skills are soon lost as few trainees practise them regularly without provision of further support. When opportunities for constructive, factual feedback are given on trainees' performance while practising the method in the training session, there is generally some transfer: new skills are often eventually used in the classroom, they are deployed appropriately for the situation at hand and they are integrated with the existing repertoire.

The additional training component of on the job coaching by colleagues who have also received training is particularly powerful in promoting transfer. Coaching implies that teachers observe each other in the classroom and give mutual feedback to see how far the skills are being practised; they examine how far the use of the teaching strategy is appropriate; and they participate in collaborative problem-solving and action-planning sessions.

The combination of didactic and practical training activities that Joyce and Showers demonstrated to promote the learning of complex teaching skills is congruent with Kolb's experiential learning model. Presentation of theory and demonstration of good teaching according to this rationale give a basis for initial conceptualising and observation while practice, feedback and coaching provide opportunities for experimentation, concrete experience and reflective observation, using the concepts of the theory. The five components together require at least two experiential learning cycles: one for presentation of theory, demonstration, practice and feedback in the training setting; the other for practice, feedback and coaching in the job. Both contexts require reflection in action (as trainees practise off the job or attempt to implement new teaching strategies on the job) and reflection on action (prompted by presentation of theory and demonstration off the job, and provision of feedback and coaching on the job).

The finding that transfer was very limited when only off the job components of theory presentation, demonstration, and practice and feedback in the training session were included backs my contention that off the job experiential learning activities alone are inadequate where training is for job performance. Support is needed equally for the on the job experiential learning that transfer entails. My experience of management training was entirely off the job, consisting mainly of practice and feedback (in a team with most of whose members I would never have to work again), together with some presentation of theory but little demonstration of good teamwork practice.

LEARNING AND LEARNING SUPPORT FOR JOB PERFORMANCE

In designing training programmes for teaching staff, how may we realise the potential contribution of experiential learning while avoiding the pitfalls of over-reliance on vicarious experience? A model of learning and learning support developed elsewhere (Wallace 1991), which draws on the theories and research discussed above, provides a suitable framework for tackling this issue.

Learning for performance of management tasks (and, by extrapolation, teaching tasks) is conceived as a series of stages, linked to the contribution various forms of learning support can make to the transition from one stage to the next. The key stages of learning and the sequence in which they may occur are summarised on the left-hand side of Figure 2.2. The diagram indicates that the starting point for learning, consistent with experiential learning theories, is the concrete experience of learners' existing performance. A challenge to performance may be followed by several possibilities. Learning may entail some or all of the intermediate stages which lie between the original challenge and development of the ability to integrate new information and skills into skilful performance of teaching and management tasks in the job.

I will take the example of teachers who are required to implement curriculum changes entailed in central government reforms. The challenge to existing performance may be stimulated by official documents or accounts in the media, signalling the required changes. Teachers' awareness may increase further as they are forced to compare their educational beliefs and values with those underpinning the reforms in thinking through how they may respond in a way that they can justify. Greater awareness may lead to the development of a rationale for changes to be made in teachers' existing performance of tasks associated with particular curriculum areas. More specific, practical ideas on how to make changes, by, for example, redesigning curriculum

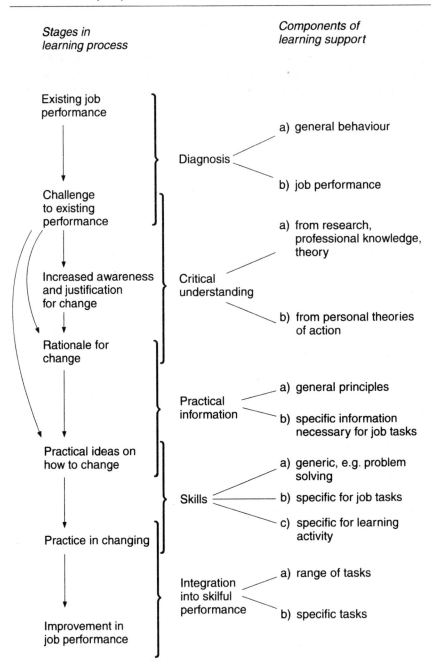

*Stages in
learning process*

*Components of
learning support*

Existing job
performance

Challenge
to existing
performance

Increased awareness
and justification
for change

Rationale for
change

Practical ideas on
how to change

Practice in changing

Improvement in
job performance

Diagnosis
a) general behaviour
b) job performance

Critical
understanding
a) from research,
professional knowledge,
theory
b) from personal theories
of action

Practical
information
a) general principles
b) specific information
necessary for job tasks

Skills
a) generic, e.g. problem
solving
b) specific for job tasks
c) specific for learning
activity

Integration
into skilful
performance
a) range of tasks
b) specific tasks

Figure 2.2 Linking the learning process with learning support

activities and reorganising resources, may follow from the rationale for change. These ideas may lead to practice in making changes by guiding actions to change, resource, teach and assess the curriculum. Improvement in job performance may result from gradual integration of these experimental actions into teachers' approach to the tasks of curriculum development and implementation.

Critical awareness relating to educational and managerial beliefs and values and having a rationale are not a necessary part of job performance itself. The only necessity is to have the know-how to do the job; developing critical awareness and a rationale are not essential for action (hence the bypass arrows in the diagram). In the example, it is plausible for teachers to proceed from a challenge to their existing performance either to the rationale for changes in the curriculum or direct to practical ideas on how to go about making them. Reflection may be confined to monitoring learning how to implement the new practical ideas. Even so, it is surely desirable that teachers are encouraged to consider why they are doing things so that the performance of teaching and management tasks is both informed rather than critically unreflective and justified rather than perceived as merely technical. Raising awareness and justifying action, together with a rationale for change, may be necessary for making informed and justifiable judgements about changes in task performance.

Similarly, teachers may conceivably have implicit theories about themselves as learners that are entirely supportive of their engagement in learning. Awareness raising is not a necessary condition for performance. Yet it is important for learning support to facilitate bringing these theories to the surface, since many learners are likely to hold ones that are unnecessarily self-inhibiting. If you don't look you won't find out.

The sequence of stages in the model of learning may be matched with different components of learning support which activities within a training programme may offer. Transition between each stage and the next may be promoted by one, or for most intermediate stages two, components of learning support. These components are subdivided to highlight variation in the type of support they provide.

Some form of diagnosis helps individuals or groups to bring present behaviour into question and identify a need for change. The focus may vary widely from their general behaviour as adults both inside and outside work to very specific aspects of their job performance. This challenge to existing performance may lead to the attempt to develop awareness and to justify proposed changes according to educational and managerial beliefs and values. The development of critical understanding about the job and its wider context is brought about by exploring the beliefs and values that inform learners' actions in the job. Since this process is essentially cognitive, learners may explore the perspective through which they interpret their performance by drawing on a range of concepts and ways of interpreting practical experience. These concepts and perspectives may be more or less abstract and more or less directly linked to the job. They inform the choice of actions and therefore are reflected in but are not a necessary component of job performance itself.

Critical understanding may be promoted by exploring concepts and perspectives from two main sources which are not completely distinct. One source is research, professional knowledge and theory, the stuff of books and educational courses, which constitute a distillation of practical experience interpreted through various concepts. Promoting critical understanding from this source is a powerful means of encouraging learners to question the assumptions of which, as Schon argues, they may otherwise remain largely unaware. The second source is practitioners' personal theories of action, the interpretation of their experience of the performance in question and of being a learner which may, of course, embody concepts and generalisations drawn from research, professional knowledge and theory, often unrigorously.

However, a limitation of reliance on practitioners' personal theories lies in the probability that they may share unquestioned assumptions which go unchallenged. Experiential learning as widely practised makes strong use of personal theories of action but very limited use of sources of abstract conceptualisation originating outside learners' experience, which could profitably embrace considerations to do with their approach to learning.

Increased awareness and the attempt to justify a change in performance leads to the development of a more specific rationale, usually embodying concepts within a perspective reflecting a particular set of educational and managerial beliefs and values. Equally, as discussed earlier, it is possible that a challenge to existing performance may lead directly to a rationale from within the learners' existing theory of action or from the perspective offered by a trainer, without a major effort to increase awareness and justify the change through development of critical understanding.

A rationale informing the change to be made links with more specific practical ideas on how to bring about this change in performance. Alternatively, the challenge to existing performance may lead directly to provision of practical ideas which guide the performance. Moving from a rationale for action to specific ideas on the steps to take in making a change may be promoted by the provision of practical information which varies in scope from general principles to detailed, specific information necessary for job tasks.

The transition from thinking about action to practice in making a change in performance, whether in a training institution or in the job, is promoted through support with the learning of skills. The degree of specificity of these skills varies from the generic, especially approaches to problem solving, to those that are specific for job tasks. Additionally, support may be given with developing skills which are specific for the learning activity, such as study skills, and those that assist more generically with learning to learn, like using intuition to solve problems.

Finally, support may be given for the process of integration of what has been learned into a skilful performance within the job context. The focus of this support varies from the general, covering the approach to a broad range of tasks, to the particular, referring to specific tasks embodied in the job.

The model helps to explain why my management training experience remained vicarious. Which components of learning support were offered, and which were missing? Reflective reviews encouraged us to diagnose where we needed to improve our teamwork for the kind of tasks we were facing; lectures gave us concepts designed to inform our actions; simulations helped us to articulate general principles about teamwork; specific information about tasks such as using a radio telephone enabled us to use the tools we were given; and detailed instruction in the skills of handling a canoe helped me to ferry-glide up the rapids. On the other hand, as we have seen, virtually no support was offered for integration of what we had learned into skilful performance in our workplace.

CONCLUSION: REALITY CHECK

The design of training programmes entails selection of learning support activities from a range of possibilities, each of which promotes the transition between particular stages of the learning process. The model encourages designers to ensure that learning support activities cover the transition between all the different stages of learning implied by the aims of the programme. Table 2.2 summarises the main focus of activities which tend to come under the banner of experiential learning. In designing training programmes for job performance, the key to successful use of activities which focus on participants' experience is to ensure that support is included for the key transition to improved performance in the job.

Some of the power of the more vicarious experiential learning activities lies in their very unreality. Outdoor experiences can be highly stimulating simply because participants are freed from their everyday world of office or classroom work and are given completely fresh challenges to meet. Simulations can provide a safe environment for modelling aspects of the job situation where risks can be taken without fear of real consequences, and processes that take months in real time can be compressed into minutes or hours. Activities based on vicarious experience clearly have a rightful place in trainers' learning support repertoire, but pride of place must be given to the more mundane but potentially more powerful activities which focus on participants' normal job experience.

So as to make the most of the range of activities which have been given the experiential learning label, it is essential to consider, first, what a programme is intended to achieve. Where anticipated outcomes are diffuse,

Table 2.2 The major focus of some experiential learning activities

Component of learning support forming major focus		*Examples of activities often labelled as experiential learning*
Diagnosis	(a) General behaviour	Counselling, learning styles analysis, personal journal, outdoor training, team building with strangers
	(b) Job performance	Critical friendship, job enrichment, being shadowed with feedback, personal journal, team building with a working team, training courses and workshops, mentoring
Critical understanding	(a) Research, professional knowledge, theory	
	(b) Personal theories of action	Critical friendship, mutual support group, networking, personal journal, counselling, action learning, shadowing with feedback, visits, mentoring
Practical information	(a) General principles	Case studies, simulations, training courses and workshops
	(b) Specific information for job tasks	Mutual support group, networking, shadowing, visits to schools, training courses and workshops
Skills	(a) Generic problem solving	Action learning
	(b) Specific for job tasks	Simulations, skills training, outdoor training for workshop teams, training courses and workshops
	(c) Specific for learning activity	Action learning
Integration into skilful performance	(a) Range of job tasks	Job enrichment, job rotation (especially with mentor), being shadowed with feedback, team building with working group
	(b) Specific job tasks	Peer coaching, expert coaching

as in personal development programmes which feature outdoor adventure activities, there is no specific performance target. By contrast, a key aim in training for job performance is to enhance that performance in some way. Second, the various stages in the learning process that participants will have to go through in order to achieve the programme aims should be identified. Third, activities (whether carrying the experiential label or not) should be selected that are likely to facilitate the transition between these stages of learning. Especially important for training programmes is the reality check: ensuring that the final transition into skilful performance in the job is covered! Fourth, consideration should be given to how effective learning strategies may be fostered through these chosen activities.

It seems clear that, in the design of effective training programmes, vicarious experiential learning activities are a more or less valuable luxury; real experiential learning activities which get to the heart of enhancing job performance are not. Beginning and experienced teachers and senior managers undergoing training will be disinhibited as learners to the extent that support activities reach the parts of their learning process that vicarious experiences don't reach.

REFERENCES

Bailey, A. (1987) *Support for School Management*, London: Croom Helm.

Bank, J. (1985) *Outdoor Development for Managers*, Aldershot: Gower.

Beeby, M. and Rathborn, S. (1983) 'Development training – using the outdoors in management development'. In *Management Education and Development*, Vol. 14, No. 3, 170–81.

Brown, J. S., Collins, A. and Duguid, P. (1989) 'Situated cognition and the culture of learning'. In *Educational Researcher*, Vol. 18, No. 1, 32–42.

Dennison, B. and Kirk, R. (1990) *Do, Review, Learn, Apply: A Simple Guide to Experiential Learning*, Oxford: Blackwell.

Eraut, M. (1994) *Developing Professional Knowledge and Competence*, London: Falmer Press.

Hobbs, T. (ed.) (1992) *Experiential Training: Practical Guidelines*, London: Tavistock/Routledge.

Joyce, B. and Showers, B. (1988) *Student Achievement through Staff Development*, London: Longman.

Kolb, D. (1984) *Experiential Learning*, London: Prentice Hall.

Lewis, L. (ed.) (1986) *Experiential and Simulation Techniques for Teaching Adults*, London: Jossey-Bass.

Perkins, D. and Salomon, G. (1989) 'Are cognitive skills context-bound?'. In *Educational Researcher*, Vol. 18, No. 1, 16–25.

Schon, D. (1983) *The Reflective Practitioner*, New York: Basic Books.

Schon, D. (1987) *Educating the Reflective Practitioner*, London: Jossey-Bass.

Wallace, M. (1991) *School Centred Management Training*, London: Paul Chapman.

Wutzdorff, A. (1994) Foreword, in M. Keeton (ed.) *Perspectives on Experiential Learning: Prelude to a Global Conversation about Learning*, Chicago: International Experiential Learning Conference Committee.

Chapter 3

Liberating the learner through assessment

Patricia Broadfoot

In this chapter, Patricia Broadfoot applies her experience in the area of assessment to the problem of 'liberating the learner'. She starts by reviewing the largely school-based literature on assessment, and concludes that the implicit theories that drive current practice are grounded in a historical tradition that is no longer either socially relevant nor psychologically defensible. Whether we like it or not, assessment drives learning, and therefore the type of assessment we use will play a large part in determining the learning attitudes and strategies that learners adopt, and also in influencing the extent to which learning, whether in school or in professional settings, offers the opportunity to develop learning ability itself. She argues that, while changes are taking place in a variety of other professional learning contexts, there are reasons why they have been slower to take hold in the sphere of education. If we are to stand any chance of shifting the attitude to assessment in schools, we have first to tackle the issues in the context of teachers' own professional development.

Since the earliest days of mass educational provision, terminal assessment procedures have largely governed the content of the curriculum, the way in which schools are organised, the approach to teaching and the learning priorities of students. Assessment has become both the vehicle and the engine that drive the delivery of education as we currently know it in schools and colleges. Because of this, it is arguably assessment that has been, for most students, the single most significant influence on the quality and shape of their educational experience, on their motivation and hence on their learning. The central role played by assessment in shaping the way in which education is delivered has come into increasingly sharp focus in recent years as governments have shown a growing awareness of the capacity of assessment policies to effect desired changes in the education system. Thus unless there is some fundamental breakdown in the long-standing link between education and employment, or governments are persuaded that accountability does not need formally to be provided for, the results of educational assessment are likely to continue to constitute the language by which the achievements of individuals, institutions and even whole education systems are judged.

But what model of learning do these powerful assessment traditions assume? How far are the assumptions that underpin their use appropriate for today's 'learning society'? Do traditional forms of assessment 'liberate the learner', in the sense that this book is exploring, or do they rather inhibit the pursuit of more and better learning? These are the questions which this chapter will address. In seeking an answer to them the chapter will first of all consider briefly the reasons why we have inherited the particular assessment traditions which are currently so pervasive. Second it will argue for an approach to assessment which is rooted in what we know about *learning* – especially the kind of learning needed for today's society – rather than what we know about *measurement*. Third it will consider the extraordinary resilience of the measurement paradigm. In offering this analysis, the chapter concludes with some suggestions for possible ways forward in assessment that do offer the potential for liberating, rather than locking up, the learner.

THE SOCIAL AND HISTORICAL CONTEXT

The assumptions on which most educational activity is based are rooted in notions of 'measurement' that date back to the changes that started to take place in Europe during the seventeenth century: to the growing beliefs in the power of science and of rational forms of organisation which are the cornerstones of the 'Enlightenment' (Broadfoot, 1996). New types of test were invented to provide a 'scientific' – and hence apparently rational – basis of determining individual levels of competence, which could thus provide a fair basis for selection. The long-standing emphasis on the demonstration of practical competence in a trade or craft, which had been until this time virtually the only formal assessment practised, gave way to tests and examinations which were designed as much for selection as they were for attesting competence, and so had to provide for the ranking of candidates *against each other* rather than against some set and explicit standard. To this end the content of the test, its conduct and its subsequent grading all had to be standardised, if the tests were to be a truly equitable, and hence rational, basis for selection. Thus entered the formal syllabus with its emphasis on content to be covered; the written test that lent itself to controlled conditions of administration; and the language of marks and grades that provided some common basis for interpreting the results so produced.

Associated with this change, as Claxton points out in Chapter 4, was a transformation in theories of learning. Claxton contrasts the 'psycho-mythology' of the pre-Enlightenment, pre-Cartesian era, in which learning was seen as involving many different types of activity and outcome, to the current situation in which learning is closely associated with the deliberate application of the concept of 'intelligence', and in which assessment, consequently, is based on 'the ability to describe and explain what one knows, rather than to reveal it spontaneously under appropriate real-life conditions'. Thus new types of test were invented that reflected the new emphasis on candidates' *relative* achievement, rather than the previous emphasis on standards.

Particularly significant in this respect was the advent of intelligence testing. This represented a move away from the assessment of some kind of achievement towards the assessment of *innate ability*. The assumption that individual potential could be measured in an objective, scientific way underpinned the growth of a pervasive and powerful belief that, among other things, educational assessment could somehow be detached from its context of operation and like, a ruler, be used in an absolute way to produce measurements of both achievement *and potential*. At the time, there was little substantial critique of this notion either in terms of principle or in terms of the techniques which were developed to operationalise it. Perhaps more surprising still is the fact that, although many such critiques have subsequently emerged concerning both the accuracy of the measures used and their impact on the processes of teaching and learning, they have yet seriously to dent the assumptions which underpin the measurement paradigm in general and notions of intelligence in particular.

Yet the model of learning that informs this book – integrated learning theory – makes such a view of assessment untenable. This theory argues that learning takes many forms, some of which are more measurable than others. It maintains that whether, and to what extent, learning occurs is a function of individuals' strategic judgement, their cost-benefit analysis concerning the risk-reward ratio of their investing effort aimed at achieving a given goal. Social constructivism, of which integrated learning theory is a variant, suggests that learning is a messy business which is influenced in idiosyncratic ways for any given individual by the complex mixture of understanding, beliefs and attitudes which is the product of past learning experience. Such a view is simply not compatible with any of the unidimensional or even fixed notions of ability which have for so long informed educational thinking and practice.

Nor are such conceptions of assessment compatible with the knowledge and skills that will be needed by tomorrow's citizens. Just as a shift in employment patterns provoked the emphasis on measurement for the purposes of selection with which we have become familiar over the last hundred years, so advances in technology and management practices are now prompting employers to call for educational systems in developed countries which equip the workers of tomorrow with transferable skills, a high level of adaptability and, above all, the commitment to go on learning. Thus Resnick (1994) is typical of many in emphasising the need for a more 'pragmatic epistemology' which conceives learning as rooted in interactive cognition.

Describing the influential 'New Standards Project' in the United States,

Resnick stresses the need to challenge several centuries of tradition in which the conception of knowledge has been theoretical rather than interactionist, and has therefore not, of itself, led to the capacity actually to perform. By contrast, the New Standards Project, with its emphasis on projects and portfolios, large-scale investigations and idiosyncratic learning goals, emphasises a variety of ways of interpreting quality and defining achievement. It recognises that learning can involve many different 'genres' of both activity and outcome. The power of new priorities, and hence practices, to challenge the domination of the measurement paradigm and its associated epistemology of learning is evidenced by the rapid growth of the movement in the United States. Nineteen states are now involved in the initiative which in consequence has begun to achieve the status of a quasi-governmental body (Resnick, 1994). Similar testimony to such changing priorities is evident at the present time in many other countries which are seeking to introduce assessment practices that support the full range of learning goals.

Yet these initiatives, which include the move to introduce records of achievement and student self-assessment in the United Kingdom during the 1980s, have still seriously to challenge the prevailing orthodoxy in the minds of politicians and public. It is still a reliable vote-catcher for politicians to talk of increasing the level of testing as part of a bid to raise standards (Airasian, 1988) . In England, the government's retreat since 1993 from continuous assessment in favour of traditional unseen exams, despite a chorus of protest from many of the communities involved – teachers, employers and even parents – provides a telling example.

Thus while it may be true to say that there is a growing acceptance of more learning-centred theories of assessment among educational professionals around the world, such novel perspectives have done little, as yet, to challenge the power of traditional forms of assessment, and the way in which they in turn influence conceptions of learning and teaching. In countries where the selection imperative is still overwhelmingly important – where, in effect, education has to be rationed – this is hardly surprising. In such contexts, examinations and especially multiple-choice tests provide the 'least worst' means of rationing educational opportunity: that is, both cheap and accepted as broadly fair, in that they are based on demonstrated merit and therefore seen as legitimate (Heynemann, 1993). But the assessment problems facing *developing* countries are more akin to those which originally gave rise in the West to the current assessment orthodoxy during the nineteenth century than they are to the assessment problems which post-industrial countries now face.

The measurement paradigm in assessment developed, as we have seen, as a specific response to the pressing need for a trustworthy and widely acceptable means of rationing educational opportunity according to some idea of 'merit'. Despite the inevitable technical limitations of any such device, the advent of a measure of professionalism and technical expertise to assist in the important business of deciding life chances was, on the whole, a step forward. And it is no doubt for this reason that the examination and testing industry is one of the most lasting legacies of colonial influence. Indeed it has now developed into one of the most successful international industries, which, like Coca-Cola, touches the life of almost everyone on the planet. Activity on this scale implies many entrenched interests, as well as a good deal of inertia and the sheer impossibility of even conceiving of forms of educational provision which have not been shaped by the discourse of measurement.

Nevertheless such new conceptions must be not only realised but implemented if we are to 'liberate the learner' in the way that is now required. Whilst it may have been reasonable to turn a blind eye to some of the well-documented shortcomings of traditional forms of assessment when, on the whole, they were doing their job well, it makes very little sense to allow such practices to continue when the limitations lie not only in their technical characteristics but much more fundamentally in their capacity to inhibit urgently needed change in education, and to obscure the real imperative facing education for the twenty-first century, which is the creation of committed and effective learners. The following sections elaborate this argument.

TESTING TESTING

It is being argued in this book that learning, and hence, by implication, performance, is the result of feelings, values and other learned attitudinal responses, as well as of cognitive processes. If this is so it should not be seen as surprising that so much research exists demonstrating the inaccuracies of conventional assessment techniques (see, for example, reviews by Satterly (1994) and Ingenkamp (1977)). Apart from the possible sources of error in the measurement itself – for example, the teacher may not have taught what is tested in the examination; students may guess, if the format is a multiple-choice one; the test may be incorrectly normed for a given population of students; and so on (Lee Smith (1991) provides a comprehensive list of these flaws) – performance itself has been shown to be neither constant nor a necessarily true reflection of learning.

At the most obvious level, the test may measure performance on a given day which has no connection with long-term retention by the student. Students may be bored or disaffected and not engage to the best of their ability with the test or examination. They may find the questions confusing or ambiguous. They may not be able to apply their knowledge because of the limitations of handwriting or other mechanical abilities. Many achievement tests merely measure endurance or persistence rather than learning. Some students who are divergent thinkers may read too much into the question. Some students become frightened and 'freeze up' in the testing situation, especially those who have little self-confidence or some kind of emotional or family disturbance. Furthermore, research in the psychology of assessment has consistently demonstrated that small changes in task-presentation, in response mode, in the conditions under which assessment takes place, in the relations between assessor and assessed, and within students on different occasions – all can affect performance (Black, 1993; Wolf and Silver, 1993).

Thus the measurement paradigm offers us what is, at best, only a rough and ready tool for identifying achievement. It offers us even less as a basis for predicting potential – which now is widely recognised as being neither innate nor fixed (Vernon, 1957; Karier, 1972). The increasingly extensive research literature on assessment in operation shows quite clearly that assessment is an essentially social process. That is to say, it is to a greater or lesser extent an interactive operation, in which a whole range of circumstances will affect the outcome: who the assessor is (even in an apparently objective multiple-choice test) or where the assessment takes place; (Gipps and Murphy, 1994). Clearly this does not mean there is no place for measurement techniques in the tool-cupboard of educational activity. Indeed there are many situations in which it is important to try to generate an accurate picture of individual or indeed group achievement – for diagnosis of a learner's strengths and weaknesses; to gauge the success of a particular course in achieving its objectives; to provide information on the overall performance of an education system; and, not least, the certification of achievement. Rather what it does mean is that it is time to challenge the 'sacred cows' of assessment, the concepts and preoccupations that have for too long inhibited the educational community from engaging with the quite different, but potentially much more important, assessment agenda which concerns its role in promoting learning.

The work of the French philosopher Michel Foucault traces the power to control the way reality is defined which is embodied in the evolution of particular discourses. One such discourse, he suggests, legitimates the 'hierarchical authority' and 'normalising judgement' which are the defining characteristics of the traditional examination. Students can be located, according to their demonstrated success, in an evaluative framework in which the whole territory of the development of learning has already been mapped out. External assessment represents the imposition of these standardised norms of progression according to the criteria of worth already laid down by the hierarchical authority (Broadfoot, 1996). Whether or not one is disposed to accept the finer points of Foucault's structuralist analysis, it is difficult not to accept its central tenet, namely that the language we use to articulate a particular subject has built into it particular concepts and assumptions that tend to delimit the arena of debate, and hence to preclude other ways of theorising experience, for which an equivalent language, and hence conceptual base, is lacking. Thus what we think assessment is, what it can do and how it might be improved, have all been questions that, until recently, could only be raised in terms of the dominant assessment paradigm.

To a great extent this remains the case. Despite a growing international obsession with assessing quality, this does not seem to have prompted an equivalent measure of development in assessment thinking. Indeed the opposite is the case, as the obsession with league tables, performance indicators and standards reinforces the preoccupation with measurement, while questions which focus on how such performance can most effectively be encouraged go not only unheard but even *unthought*. One explanation for the persistence of an assessment status quo which is increasingly out of step with the priority of raising and broadening learning thresholds is doubtless the inertia of habit, and the tendency to fall back on the tried and tested. Among politicians – who play a key role in perpetuating such thinking – traditional approaches to assessment have acquired a legitimacy which makes them invaluable, both as a rhetorical device and as a means of managing the aspirations of individuals. For the last hundred years or so, traditional forms of assessment have proved themselves to be vital tools in the hands of those responsible for managing the priorities and procedures of the education system.

But if, historically, educational assessment has been driven by a perceived need to measure individual capacity, it now needs to be driven by the need to develop that capacity – and to create new kinds of capacity in people of all ages, in short, to 'liberate the learner'. Problem-solving capacity, personal effectiveness, thinking skills and a willingness to accept change are typical of the general competencies straddling both cognitive and affective domains that are now being sought by employers. It is becoming increasingly apparent, however, that until we develop new kinds of assessment procedures that can relate to this wide range of skills and attitudes, not only will it be impossible to produce valid judgements about the success of the educational enterprise as a whole in terms of its goals; it will also help to ensure that certain desired learning outcomes will be neglected in practice. Not surprisingly perhaps, this is a lesson which is rapidly being learned in those areas of education which are most closely connected with the world of employment. In many countries, including the United Kingdom, Australia, New Zealand, Canada and the United States, efforts are under way to introduce more flexible and meaningful systems of vocational qualifications based on demonstrated, rather than inferred, competence (Curtain and Hayton, 1995). Characteristic of such frameworks is the inclusion of competencies which break down the inevitably artificial division between the *capacity* to perform a task at a given level and the *attitudes* that predispose an individual so to do. But if the English National Vocational Qualifications (NVQs) and those of other countries with similar characteristics represent a significant attempt to break out of the straitjacket of marks and grades, formal examinations, set sylla-buses and built-in failure levels – in short of the whole paraphernalia of traditional assessment thinking and practice – they nevertheless stop well short of fulfilling the criterion of an approach to assessment that has the capacity to 'liberate the learner'.

The emphasis on pre-specified, standardised learning outcomes that is embodied in the language of 'Elements of Competence' and 'Range Criteria' suggests a somewhat mechanistic view of performance. Indeed, as Nuttall (1993) suggests, the problem of lack of specificity in criteria is endemic to criterion-referenced assessment of this kind and has led many, including the National Council for Vocational Qualifications in England, to provide more and more detail in a fruitless attempt to eliminate ambiguity. Moreover, it is increasingly clear that where attempts are being made to include less explicitly vocational courses of study in such frameworks – for example, in Scotland and New Zealand – there appears to be an incompatibility between an assessment model based on pre-specified learning outcomes and courses of study in which such detailed pre-specification of desired competencies is inappropriate.

The recently introduced General National Vocational Qualifications (GNVQs) in England represent a brave, and currently popular, attempt to bridge the two approaches by combining a criterion-referenced approach to assessment, which emphasises the demonstration of particular competencies as defined by range statements within a broadly prescribed course of study in relation to which students can achieve 'pass', 'merit' or 'distinction', according to the level at which they are deemed to have fulfilled the criteria. Whilst the rapid growth in uptake of GNVQ courses (Wolf, 1994) is testimony to the motivational power of new approaches to both course provision and assessment, there is little evidence as yet to suggest how far the impact of this attempt to break the shackles of traditional assessment and its associated patterns of teaching and learning has gone, beyond the level of the attraction for students of something that seems both more relevant and more achievable, to a point at which it impacts on students' actual capacity to learn.

It is appropriate at this point to examine what this might mean in a little more detail. In Chapter 4 Claxton argues for the critically important role of motivation – and of non-cognitive factors generally – in promoting or inhibiting learning. Assessment is perhaps the most powerful influence on such drives and feelings. Although some students are motivated by the spur of competition and the glitter of potential reward, many more learn not to try for fear of failing. Claxton cites Dweck's work concerning students whose self-esteem is progressively eroded by negative assessment results and who frequently, in consequence, become what Dweck terms 'helpless prone' (see Chaper 4). Indeed research by Bandura (1977) and others shows that the amount of persistence exhibited by students is a function of how successful they expect to be. In short, students who have an image of themselves as successful learners are likely to be more motivated than those who have formed a more negative view of themselves in this respect.

A moment's thought confirms that it is assessment that is the purveyor of such messages. For students, the daily diet of evaluative language which is an inescapable, and probably essential, part of teaching is regularly reinforced by more formal evaluative communications in the form of marks and grades, and still further reinforced by the weighty messages of reports and parents' evenings, a process that ultimately culminates in the 'summing up' (Harlen, 1994) of the formal examination. Given that in this latter respect at least, failure is built into the system by definition, in that a given proportion of candidates is expected (and often required) to fail, it is unlikely that many learners will be liberated by such assessment.

Ironically perhaps, it was in an attempt to address directly the demotivating effects of such built-in failure that the educational community began to stumble on far more significant insights concerning how assessment might be used to transform the process of teaching and learning itself. In the United Kingdom, the Records of Achievement movement started with the idea that by broadening the range of achievements that could be formally acknowledged in a school-leaving document, this would improve the motivation of students who could not hope to succeed in public examinations. Gradually, however, the teachers committed to these initiatives came to realise that what was really making a difference in students' motivation and in the quality of their learning were the changes they were introducing actually in the classroom. These changes included sharing and discussing curriculum goals with students; encouraging students to set their own learning targets and to draw up more general 'action plans'; involving students in assessing their own work so that they were both more willing and more able to monitor their own learning; and teacher and student reviewing progress together. The opportunity for one-to-one discussion in particular made an enormous impact on many students who had never before had the chance of an individual conversation with a teacher about their learning on a regular basis.

Elsewhere I have argued that the educational community in general, and students in particular, have paid a heavy price for the failure to locate this ferment of activity in a scientific rationale that was capable of being every bit as convincing as that on which the previous assessment orthodoxy had been based (Broadfoot, 1993). In Crooks' (1988) comprehensive review of the psychological literature concerning the impact of assessment on learning is all the ammunition required to construct such a case. Caught up in their enthusiasm for the exciting things that were happening in their classrooms, however, teachers were content to trust their own experience, and to seek for no further explanation for the changes in motivation and capacity to learn that they were witnessing in their students (Broadfoot et al., 1988). In other countries the pattern has been essentially similar. Thus, in each case, when the politicians have begun to huff and puff they have apparently succeeded, with relatively little difficulty, in blowing down a house that lacks solid theoretical foundations. As the 'standards' agenda has become increasingly dominant internationally; as many governments have sought to create a market in education using a currency of test results and league tables; as 'performance indicators', quality assessment and inspection have come to define the *Zeitgeist* of the 1990s, so schools have had to revert to a very different set of enthusiasms and imposed priorities.

It is one of the odd ironies of educational research, however that, as Nisbet and Broadfoot (1981) argue, its impact is rarely direct. Rather ideas gather momentum – sometimes quite indirectly – until the time comes when conditions are right for them to make a specific impact. So it has been with new assessment thinking. Ideas that were forged out of the more obvious shortcomings of traditional assessment practices, as these impacted on schools, have been taken up and developed in circumstances where the combination of needs and constraints has been more auspicious for their growth. It is in the arena of professional learning in particular that there has been a recognised need to engage learners with developing the full range of professional skills, and a rapid realisation of the value of the new approaches to assessment, involving student learning, diaries, target setting, self-assessment, regular reviews of progress on an individual basis, the collection of portfolios of evidence, and so on – approaches which were often developed in rather different learning contexts (Gonczi, 1994). Doctors, police trainees, nurses and teachers – even lawyers and accountants – are now finding themselves taking part in training programmes which involve assessment techniques that are explicitly designed to *promote*, rather than to *measure*, learning. Figure 3.1 provides a typical illustration of such an approach to professional training. It emphasises the mixture of knowledge, skills, attitudes and values involved in such learning and the necessarily central role that reflection and self-evaluation play in promoting it.

It is not hard to find other, similarly-inspired examples of this trend. While schools have been drawing back from implementing the more radical aspects of the new assessment thinking as far as pupils are concerned, the implementation of its rationale has become commonplace in the context of teacher appraisal. Here again the emphasis is typically on using assessment – in the shape of personal review, discussion and target setting – to promote professional learning. In initial teacher education too, as Figure 3.2 illustrates, the new concern with identifying competencies is frequently integrated into a more formative assessment design, aimed at encouraging the learner teacher to develop skills of self-reflection and review.

Such approaches are rapidly approaching the status of a received orthodoxy in this kind of learning context, where there is an obvious necessity for professionals to be broadly equipped with a mixture of both cognitive and affective skills. The rapid spread of such practices in the arena of professional and vocational training has also helped to establish notions such as self-assessment and action planning as mainstream educational concepts, despite their relatively recent origins. Thus although the battle to 'liberate the learner' through assessment may temporarily have been lost in schools, the

**ASSET Programme
Core Assessment Criteria**

CRITERION NO. 1: 'Commitment to Professional Values'

Demonstrates self-awareness and commitment in implementing professional values in practice.
This involves demonstrating:

1 ability to understand and to implement anti-discriminatory, anti-racist principles;

2 awareness of the need to counteract one's own tendency (both as a person and as a professional worker endowed with specific powers) to behave oppressively;

3 respect for clients' dignity, privacy, autonomy, and rights as service users;

4 ability to manage complex ethical responsibilities and value conflicts;

5 ability to empower others.

CRITERION NO. 2: 'Continuous Professional Learning'

Demonstrates a commitment to and capacity for reflection on practice, leading to progressive deepening of professional understanding.
This involves demonstrating willingness and capacity:

1 to learn from others, including clients;

2 to recognise that professional judgments are always open to question;

3 to engage in self-evaluation, recognising and analysing one's strengths and limitations.

CRITERION NO. 3: 'Affective Awareness'

Demonstrates understanding and effective management of emotional responses in relation to others.
This involves:

1 demonstrating sensitivity to the unique complexity of difference situations;

2 developing effective collaborative relationships with others.

Figure 3.1 ASSET Programme Core Assessment Criteria
Source: Department of Employment (1994) *Competence and Assessment Compendium No. 3*, Cambridge: Pendragon Press.

war continues. The beginnings of a new assessment discourse, of concepts which reflect a preoccupation with learning, rather than with dependable measurement, suggest that we are witnessing a genuine paradigm shift; that the tyranny of testing is at last being challenged. To measure or to learn: that is the question.

Comments by PGCE student.		Staff assessment of the student's level of achievement. Please incorporate future development comments.
	SUBJECT KNOWLEDGE • Understand the knowledge concepts and skills of the main teaching subject. • Know and understand the NCATs and PoS for the main subject if applicable.	
	SUBJECT APPLICATION **1. *Lesson Planning*** • Plan both indiviual, and a series of, lessons setting appropriate aims and allowing for differing abilities in your students. • Foster a range of learning styles and use a variety of teaching strategies appropriate to the age, ability and attainment level of pupils.	
	SUBJECT APPLICATION **2. *Communications*** • Communicate clearly and suitably with students, both orally and in writing.	
	SUBJECT APPLICATION **3. *Information Technology*** • Select and make appropriate use of a range of equipment and resources.	

Figure 3.2 Part of the University of Bristol PGCE Professional Practice Student Profile Record

REFERENCES

Airasian, P. (1988) 'Symbolic validation: the case of state-mandated High Stakes Testing'. *Educational Evaluation and Policy Analysis*, Vol. 10, No. 4, Winter, pp. 301–15.

Bandura, A. (1977) *Social Learning Theory*, Englewood cliffs, NJ: Prentice Hall.

Black, P. (1993) 'Conference Paper – Association of Assessment Inspectors and Advisers'. Reported in *Times Educational Supplement*, 1 October.

Broadfoot, P. (1993) 'Exploring the forgotten continent: a traveller's tale'. *Scottish Educational Review*, Vol 26, No. 2, pp. 88–96.

Broadfoot, P. (1996) *Education, Assessment and Society*, Milton Keynes: Open University Press (forthcoming).

Broadfoot, P., James, M., McMeeking, S., Nuttall, D. and Stierer, B. (1988) *Records of Achievement. Report of the National Evaluation of Pilot Scheme*, London: HMSO.

Crooks, T. J. (1988) 'The impact of classroom evaluation practices on students'. *Review of Educational Research*, Vol. 58, No. 4, pp. 438–81.

Curtain, R. and Hayton, G. (1995) 'The use and abuse of a competency standards framework in Australia: a comparative perspective'. *Assessment in Education*, Vol. 2, No. 2, pp. 205–25

Gipps, C. and Murphy, P. (1994) *Fair Test? Assessment, Achievement and Equity*, Milton Keynes: Open University Press.

Gonczi, A. (1994) 'Competency based assessment in the professions in Australia'. *Assessment in Education*, Vol. 1, No. 1, pp. 27–44.

Harlen, W. (ed.) (1994) *Enhancing Quality in Assessment*, London: Paul Chapman.

Heynemann, S. (1993) Keynote lecture to the World Congress of Comparative Education Societies, Prague.

Ingenkamp, K. (1977) *Educational Assessment*, Slough: NFER.

Karier, C. (1972) 'Testing for order and control in the corporate liberal state', *Educational Theory*, Vol. 22, No.2.

Lee Smith, M. (1991) 'The meanings of test preparation'. *American Educational Research Journal*, Vol. 28, No. 3, pp. 521–42.

Nisbet, J. and Broadfoot, P. (1981) *The Impact of Research on Policy and Practice in Education*, Aberdeen: Aberdeen University Press.

Nuttall, D. (1993) Presentation at Conference organised by Centre for Policy Studies on the Dearing Review of the National Curriculum in England, 21 September 1993, London.

Resnick, L. (1994) 'The New Standards Project'. Seminar given at University of London Institute of Education, June 1994.

Satterly, D. (1994) 'Quality in external assessment'. In W. Harlen, (ed.) *Enhancing Quality in Assessment*, London: Paul Chapman.

Vernon, P. (1957) *Secondary School Selection*, London: Methuen.

Wolf, A. (1994) 'GNVQs 1993–4: a national survey'. FEU/Institute of Education/The Nuffield Foundation (available from the FEU, London).

Wolf. A, and Silver, R. (1993) 'The reliability of test candidates and the implications for one-shot testing'. *Educational Review*, Vol. 45, No. 3, pp. 263–78.

Chapter 4

Implicit theories of learning

Guy Claxton

This chapter explores and illustrates in more detail the notion of implicit theories of learning. It argues that they are indeed 'implicit' because many preconceptions about learning have themselves been picked up tacitly, and are only partially, if at all, available to conscious scrutiny. Some of these belief systems concern the nature of 'self', especially the way people see themselves as learners. Such beliefs often reduce learners' tolerance for the uncomfortableness of learning, causing them to get upset, become self-critical and lose heart. Other beliefs concern the nature of mind and of knowledge. Some prevalent views of the mind disallow certain valuable learning strategies, such as those that rely on cognitive processes that are slower, less conscious and less capable of being controlled or assessed. Implicit theories of learning itself – what resources it takes, what kind of time course it follows, what kinds of products it generates – can also misguide both the recipients and the designers of professional education. The effect of such tacit beliefs on both the theory and practice of adult professional learning has been well illustrated by the two preceding chapters.

In Chapter 1 I outlined an approach to adult professional learning that I called integrated learning theory, ILT. The goal of this theory is to provide a framework, and a language, within which one can look at all the psychological aspects of professional learning as a whole. ILT makes possible a discourse about learning within which the learner's feelings, values, hopes and beliefs, as well as his or her cultural and ideological setting, form a necessary context for any discussion of more cognitive aspects of learning. Learners are seen as possessing a repertoire of ways of learning, and ways of defending – elaboration and maintenance strategies – which are deployed as the result of a partially, often predominantly, unconscious decision-making process within which all kinds of cultural and personal factors, as subjectively interpreted, may play a role. The conceptual key to understanding these interpretive processes, the fifth cornerstone of ILT, is, I argued, a person's store of *implicit theories*: the residual schemata, or unconscious belief systems, left behind in the mind by previous experiences of all kinds, and which are brought to bear on current events in order to attribute significance and meaning to them. It is on the nature and the psychological dynamics of these implicit theories that this chapter now focuses.

The significant costs and benefits, risks and rewards, which weigh in the balance of a person's learning decisions, are themselves underpinned by a host of views-of-the-world that are the distillates of past experiences and teachings. Whether something shows up on the learning balance sheet as a debit or a credit, an asset or a liability, and how much weight it is given, is a matter of interpretation; and these interpretations are based in the intuitive analogies that learners draw between a new, unprecedented situation, and past experiences which they judge (again, for the most part, implicitly) to be similar. (As Samuel Butler said, 'Though analogy is often misleading, it is the least misleading thing we have.')

It is, we might say, the fundamental nature of the mind to register and store experiences in such a way that they can be used as the basis on which to build skilful action in the future. We distil the past, bottle it, and add it to the present, like a tincture, to give to bare events their significance and their meaning. The essential process of cognitive psychology is to investigate the storage of past experience, and its influence on present perception, action and thought, and by doing so to create models of what is going on, behind the scenes, as one fabricates experiences and crafts courses of action. The particular concern of a cognitive educationist (like myself) is to approach this task in such a way that the models and theories that are developed are not only predictive of human performance, but also of practical use to those whose job it is to design and deliver educational experiences. An educational theory is of no value unless it offers planners and practitioners, in C. H. Waddington's famous phrase, 'tools for thought'.

There are many ways in which these records of the past, and the ways in which the brain-mind brings them to bear on the demands of the present, have been conceptualised. We might see them as books in a reference library – but this image leaves us with the problem of accounting for the activities of a homuncular librarian. It does not help us to understand the *intelligence* of the system. A more fruitful model is that of a computer which possesses thousands of files and subprograms, each of which can be accessed and activated by its own call sign or 'calling pattern' (Morton *et al.*, 1985). Once retrieved and 'loaded', a particular file then enables the system as a whole to interpret what is currently going on, to assign significance to it, and to anticipate the consequences of various courses of action. These files have been given a range of different names by different theorists: schemas, scripts, frames, headed records, cell assemblies and minitheories are some of the labels that have been used.

Here I shall use the term *implicit theories*: 'implicit' because the vast majority of these files are not open to conscious inspection – we can say very little about *how* we walk, talk, recognise faces or learn new things – and 'theories' because these mental models of the world, and of ourselves, are similar in some ways to the theories of scientists. Though they are not explicit, as a scientist's are, they embody assumptions, beliefs and hypotheses, and their value depends on their ability to generate successful predictions. A footballer's implicit theory of ball, pitch, muscles and teammates enables him to compute, in the twinkling of an eye, a delicate pass for the winger to run on to. A skilled cook's implicit theory tells her when it is time to put the broccoli on, even though she may not be able to tell you how she knows. An experienced teacher's implicit theory leads him or her to go easy on a noisy class, one of whose members has just fallen from a rope in the gym, where a beginning teacher might have misinterpreted their anxiety as disobedience or hostility, and intervened in a heavy-handed way. In fact it is precisely when our implicit theories lead us into error, or are mute when we need them to speak, that learning occurs. By collecting data and information, as a scientist does, a crude theory is refined and developed to the point where, if all goes well, it makes available reliable, flexible expertise.

However, it is not learning as the refining of implicit theories that I wish to focus on in this chapter: I have developed that idea elsewhere (Claxton, 1989, 1990). Rather I want to explore the effect on learning of a particular cluster of implicit theories that people may hold about themselves and their ability, about the nature of knowledge, and about learning itself. I shall argue that there are a number of such theories that commonly lead people, at all levels and phases of education, to interpret perfectly natural aspects of the learning process as threats or aberrations, and thus to bias the cost–benefit analysis towards defence and avoidance, and against learning and engagement. If adult learners unconsciously or semiconsciously make an analogy between a current learning context and their own (unhappy) experience of school, for example, then a whole raft of anachronistic apprehensions and assumptions may be activated which lead them to become invisible, or play the fool, in just the way they did when they were 15, to the detriment of their own learning, and in defiance of all the evidence of their ability to meet this new challenge resourcefully and, eventually, successfully.

IMPLICIT THEORIES OF SELF

Learning is what one does to transmute incompetence into competence, ignorance into knowledge. By definition, learning starts in the zone of the unknown, and attempts, via a whole variety of activities, mental and physical, to discover comprehension and expertise. Learning at its most general therefore requires that learners be able to tolerate, up to a point, certain concomitant states and feelings that may inevitably arise along the way. One may well make mistakes, for example, as one experiments. As one searches for effective ways of getting along with a new spreadsheet, a new syllabus, a new head of department, so one discovers what does not work, as well as what does. One may well pass through states of mental confusion, in which one does not know what to do, and may even not know, yet, how to conceptualise what it is that one does not know. Comprehension often emerges gradually from a fog, and unless one can tolerate being fogged for a while, that process of 'coming into focus' may be subverted. One may also experience some variant of anxiety: apprehension, tentativeness, uncertainty, timidity. In fact one might define 'anxiety' as the way learning *feels*; the necessary affective corollary of not knowing how your actions are going to affect the situation (Levitt, 1980). And finally, in this short litany of tolerances, there may be the need to accept a shift, as one learns, in one's self-image (Burns, 1982). A beginning teacher, or a new headteacher, may both feel a change in the way they see themselves as a result of their growing into new roles and new forms of expertise.

What then happens when a person's implicit theory of self contains beliefs about conduct, standards and worth that are at odds with the required tolerances for learning? Suppose that this person tacitly believes that his or her acceptability as a colleague, or even as a person, depends on being right, or competent, or successful. In this case, the fact – or even the possibility – of making mistakes, or being found wanting, must be experienced as aversive, a breach of the conditions under which self-worth or self-esteem can be maintained. One cannot be 'wrong' without also feeling that one is wrong for being wrong. Or suppose that one implicitly believes that mental clarity is a valid indicator of one's competence and intelligence. Again, one cannot then be confused without also having one's claim to maturity, or even in the extreme sanity, being jeopardised. Confusion, like error, is thus transmuted by an implicit theory of self into a condition that one must work to avoid.

Or suppose that the very experience of anxiety has come to be seen as a symptom of not being up to the mark. Instead of taking anxiety as a useful visceral indicator of the need to learn, signalling a delicate blend of the tendencies to engage and to disengage, one now has to take it is a signal of personal inadequacy. And as this is a state to be avoided, so anxiety itself becomes a trigger for avoidance or defence. Or suppose more generally that any of the set of descriptors of self, which comprise a person's self-image, has become mandatory rather than provisional, a constraint on how one is permitted to be rather than a cumulative summary of observed tendencies and dispositions. Under this condition, any learning experience which threatens to reveal oneself as other than this prescription is bound to be construed as an assault on the integrity of self, and is thus to be rejected (Greenwald, 1980). Assumptions about one's own talents and aptitudes, for example, can easily become self-fulfilling prophecies: 'I'm hopeless at maths', 'I can't draw', 'I just know I could never master that computer/write poetry/see those stupid 3-D pictures', and so on create patterns of avoidance, distress or half-hearted engagement which serve only to validate the belief. As we saw in the discussion of the study by Thompson (1993) in Chapter 1, one common way of protecting one's self against the experience of inadequacy is to withhold effort.

Taken together, these core assumptions about the nature of one's personality, or the conditions of personal worth, are capable of transforming those states that naturally arise in the course of learning into valid and necessary reasons for avoiding learning.

IMPLICIT THEORIES ABOUT MIND AND KNOWLEDGE

In the previous section I illustrated a number of beliefs that contribute to what might be called our personal ontology, and our personal system of ethics. But these are also accompanied by a personal epistemology: a collection of beliefs about the nature of mind, of knowledge and of knowing. Again I can do no more here than provide some illustrations.

Every culture includes as part of its collective mythology a view of mind, a kind of psychomythology, we might call it. Since the seventeenth century, and the shift in the view of human nature commonly attributed to Descartes, European culture has associated rationality and intelligence closely with consciousness. Prior to this shift, people experienced a much greater continuity between conscious and unconscious, and were happy to embrace within their sense of identity a recognition of non-pathological unconscious forces and processes (Whyte, 1979). Education, within pre-Cartesian Europe, as well as within many non-European cultures, could draw on activities that were not explicit, not articulable, and not necessarily associated with a clear sense of conscious will or intention. One could learn 'through osmosis', as well as through rational deliberation. Our contemporary education, on the other hand, being based on a view of mind in which, if the unconscious has any role, it is as an emotional disruptor of learning rather than as a cognitive resource, has come to rely predominantly, if not exclusively, on learning modes in which one can 'show one's working', and in which the assessment of learning is based on the ability to describe and explain what one knows, rather than to reveal it spontaneously under appropriate real-life conditions. Our implicit psychology of mind has marginalised processes of learning that cannot be premeditated, and which rely on the 'education of intuition' (Bruner, 1967), or simply on a mindful (but not intellectual) immersion in experience.

Recent work in cognitive psychology, however, is reminding us of the value of unconscious learning. Lewicki et al. (1992), Seger (1994) and others have reviewed a host of contemporary studies that show that unconscious learning is not only a valuable component of the 'learning tool-kit' but is actually capable of achieving learning goals that conscious strategies are unable to achieve. Berry and Broadbent (1984), for example, have shown that learning to manage complex industrial or technical situations proceeds much faster through a kind of unfocused trial and error than it does through a deliberate attempt to figure out and 'understand' what is going on. Furthermore, giving explicit tuition at the start of the learning process can actually interfere with this unconscious learning and impede it. If either an educational system as a whole, or individuals within it, succumb to an implicit theory of mind that disallows the unconscious, and the intuitive learning modes with which it is associated, then they are going to ignore the existence and the value of part of their natural learning endowment, and are destined to struggle vainly to apply deliberate strategies to situations where they are inappropriate.

A more familiar aspect of our implicit educational epistemology concerns the assumption that 'knowledge is manufactured by people called scientists or intellectuals who do something called research in places called universities, and it is then cut up and packaged, like supermarket meat, into syllabuses and textbooks which convey this knowledge to distribution points called schools where it is dished out to and ingested by involuntary consumers called pupils or students, under the supervision, and with the assistance, of people called teachers'. The problems with this as a foundation for schooling are too well known to rehearse here. That this view creates passivity in learners, narrows yet again the range of learning strategies that are brought to bear, and causes much confusion in teachers about whose responsibility it is to make sure that learning happens, is familiar territory. More pertinent to the present discussion is the possibility that teachers, to the extent that they have imbibed this philosophy of knowledge and learning, will carry it forward into their own lives and activities as learners. One could see much of the recent work in the psychology of adult learning (Brookfield, 1986; Kolb, 1984) as an attempt to undo these constraints – an effort that has borne much fruit in industrial and business contexts, but which yet has to percolate fully into the world of formal professional development within education. One could argue that teachers (in some subjects at least), being perpetually steeped in this receptive epistemology, will be the last to recognise its limitations when it comes to their own learning.

A further illustration of the effect of epistemological beliefs is provided by Langer et al. (1989). Knowledge can be presented by a teacher to a learner in two rather different ways. It can be presented 'absolutely', as if it were established to be universally and incontrovertibly true. Or it can be presented conditionally, as if this were one position or viewpoint amongst several, which could be taken to apply within certain domains but not others, and/or which was quite likely to be overturned or superseded as understanding developed. The former mode would be typified by a teacher saying 'Mentoring *is* an activity that requires critical reflection'; the latter by saying 'Mentoring *could be* an activity that requires critical reflection'. In Langer et al.'s study, college students were taught the same information in the two ways, and were then tested for the creativity and flexibility with which they were able to deploy the information. Those taught conditionally were significantly more creative and flexible that those taught absolutely. We might account for this by saying that, when knowledge is presented as cut and dried universals, learners are implicitly led to engage learning strategies that simply record it. After all, what else is there to be done? Conversely when an element of doubt or conditionality is introduced into the situation by the teacher's choice of language, one is invited to engage with it in a more questioning and intelligent fashion. The implicit epistemology embedded in the presentation influences the learning strategies that people select, and this in turn influences the kind of knowledge base that is established in the learner's mind.

IMPLICIT THEORIES ABOUT LEARNING

We could summarise the foregoing discussion in terms of a number of tacit assumptions about what learning *is*, or how it *should be*, or what it *could be*, each of which implicitly prescribes what learning isn't, or shouldn't be, or couldn't be. Learning should be error free, confusion free and anxiety free. Learning is passive. Learning is a rational and intellectual process. When you've learnt something properly, you should be able to explain it. The appropriate way to test (all) learning is to ask someone to talk/write/think *about* it.

We could add to this list a number of other implicit theories about learning that may create unnecessary distress and avoidance. Suppose someone holds the implicit view that learning is (and therefore should be) a process of fitting small, well-defined bits of understanding together, rather like making a watch, so that when the whole is properly assembled it will automatically result in a new competency. Such a person will expect his or her grasp to proceed in a series of manageable steps, each of which preserves, and builds upon, what has previously been understood. For some learning tasks, these expectations may turn out to be realistic; but there may well be other domains which simply do not function in this way. In these domains, as I mentioned above, a more appropriate metaphor may be that of photographic printing, where the image gradually appears as a whole, without any of the parts being clearly discernible in advance. Those whose expectations of learning are based solely on the former analogy will be 'thrown' when they find themselves obliged to grapple with learning material that cannot be assembled in this way, and which requires a more prolonged period of tolerance for confusion.

If, in addition to the effort to adhere to their inappropriate template for learning, they are also threatened by confusion (as I discussed above), then their learning is going to be doubly uncomfortable, and their tendency to throw in the towel prematurely will be all the greater. The obvious cost of this is that competence is less likely to be reached, or reached more slowly.

But a more subtle price is paid in terms of the development of concentration. If there is no point in continuing to engage with something that refuses to reveal itself quickly – because the model implies that something has gone *wrong* with learning when this happens – then one is deprived of the opportunity to practise the art of maintaining concentration and focus, and to discover its value. Premature abandonment of learning means that certain important 'mental muscles' do not get developed.

Similarly someone who assumes that learning proceeds as a smooth, monotonically increasing straight line of competence will be unprepared for the possibility that learning can just as well proceed through a series of waves and troughs, or with plateau periods where no visible progress is being made. Karmiloff-Smith (1984), for example, has demonstrated the vital importance in child development of what she calls 'learning beyond success', in which children take a competency which they have already established, and play with it, testing it to destruction in various ways, experimenting with ways of tying it in with other domains of expertise, of increasing conceptual coherence, which may lead to a temporary drop in apparent competence. Though it may look from the outside as if the children have regressed, losing a fluency that they seemed to have established, from the inside this is no developmental hiccup, but a vital further stage of deepening understanding. There is no reason to suppose that adults, at least in certain domains of learning, outgrow the need for this kind of learning. Yet their implicit theory of learning may preclude it, and thereby cut the learner off again from a valuable component of his or her potential learning repertoire.

The idea that one should always be able to articulate, at least to oneself, what it is that one has learnt, means that, when one does not know what one has learnt, one is inclined to assume that one has not learnt, or has not learnt 'properly'. This idea may be linked to another which assumes that 'real learning' is hard work: deliberate, effortful and often 'boring'. Thus *play* – that which is easy, convivial, fun, and from which no discernible (never mind *measurable*) outcome accrues – has to be defined as 'not learning', and treated as an activity of less educational value and lower status. Despite many teachers' valid intuitions to the contrary, pre-school and primary education continue to struggle with the judgements that these implicit theories of learning arouse. And exactly the same tendencies towards ambivalence or disdain may be seen in the teachers' centre and hotel conference rooms when activities are introduced for which adult learners 'can't see the point'. Their willingness to 'take learning seriously' – note the emphasis on seriousness – is filtered through a set of implicit and often archaic theories which may lead them to withdraw commitment from potentially valuable activities.

The prevalence of this implicit theory of learning as 'hard work' and defined by its outcome was demonstrated by Bereiter and Scardamalia (1989). In a study that investigated people's beliefs about learning, they found that both children and adults alike view learning as predominantly a matter of *problem solving* and *memorisation*. One knows that learning has occurred when one can either solve a new problem, or remember what has been 'taught'. The major difference between adults and children is that the adults are more caught in a view of learning as a path to a predetermined goal, whereas the children often focus more on the activity of learning than its outcome. The development of an instrumental view of learning is, of course, important and valid. There are many occasions in which learning is rightly conceived of as a means to a preconceived end. All I wish to point out here is the risk that, if this view of learning is tacitly installed in someone's mind as the only view, then it precludes other possibilities and activities from also being treated as valid forms of learning.

The view that learning is quintessentially intellectual leads to a neglect of the imaginative, the emotional, the intuitive and the contemplative as paths to valid knowing. While there is a rapidly increasing interest amongst adult and professional educators in these alternative modes of learning, they commonly have to overcome a barrier of incredulity before gaining acceptance. Imagination and fantasy are still treated within education as rather primitive forms of learning, suitable to the primary school, but something out of which one should be encouraged to grow as one progresses towards Key Stage 4 and GCSE. Emotions are still treated as interruptions to learning, rather than (sometimes) vital topics of and resources for learning. Primary schools strive to create an atmosphere of perfect and perpetual happiness, thus depriving children of opportunities to learn how to deal skilfully with their anger or distress. It can even be the case that any other attitude towards 'negative' feelings than denial or suppression is treated as 'dangerous': a kind of unlicensed playing with fire that should only be attempted by skilled professionals like counsellors and psychologists wearing protective clothing. While the idea that learning demands continual busyness, and that therefore if you are not visibly doing something you cannot be learning anything of significance, disables those vital learning modes that require stillness, reverie, inwardness and reflection. It is widely known that creativity demands 'incubation' as well as 'preparation' and 'verification' (Wallas, 1926) – but not, apparently, by those who design educational programmes for either young people or their teachers.

IMPLICIT THEORIES ABOUT ABILITY

One of the areas in which the influence of implicit theories on learning has been investigated in most detail concerns people's conceptions of *ability*. Carol Dweck and her associates (Dweck, 1986; Dweck and Leggett, 1988; Chiu *et al.*, 1994) have identified two contrasting patterns of response to the experience of being frustrated or blocked in learning which she calls 'mastery orientated' (MO) and 'helpless prone' (HP). She presents these as if they were predominant characteristics of different groups of learners, whereas they may more commonly be different modes of response which an individual may display in differing domains or under different circumstances. In MO mode frustration leads to a heightened commitment to the task, an increase of 'effort' and a creative exploration of cognitive resources and learning strategies. You 'go for it'. In HP mode, on the other hand, frustration leads to a withdrawal of commitment, an increase in distractibility, a regression to more primitive and ineffective strategies, and a feeling of emotional upset and comparative inadequacy. In MO mode you feel challenged; in HP mode you feel threatened. In MO mode your self-esteem stands to gain through an increase in competence and ingenuity; in HP mode your self-esteem stands to lose through a sense of incompetence and failure.

Interestingly, Dweck's research shows that the predominance of these two patterns is unrelated to any measure of a person's actual ability. 'Bright' students, though they meet difficulty less often than less bright ones – that is what it means to be 'bright' – are as likely to fall into the HP response when they do get blocked as those who meet difficulty more regularly. However, what she has discovered is that the tendency to helpless proneness is underpinned by a particular implicit theory of ability: not of the learner's level of ability, but of ability itself, what kind of thing it is. Again she identifies two contrasting implicit theories, which she calls the 'incremental' and the 'entity' theory. The incremental view sees ability as a malleable, inflatable quality, capable of expansion; whereas the entity view sees ability as a fixed trait, an invariant, frequently innately determined or 'God-given' quality that characterises you, and follows you from context to context, in the same way as your 'blue eyes' or your 'black hair' do.

Dweck's discovery is that tacitly holding the entity theory of ability is what predisposes a person to helpless proneness. As she says, if you believe that ability is capable of expansion, you are free to try to *improve* it. But if you believe that ability is fixed, then the best you can do is try to *prove* that you have as much of it as you would like to. Thus when learning gets hard, it has two quite different meanings for the two groups. In MO mode, it is an opportunity to learn how to learn: to discover new strategies and develop new resources. In HP mode, it is an opportunity to demonstrate to yourself and others that your resources are inadequate, and this is, as we have seen, an eventuality that many people seek to avoid.

These findings have been demonstrated in age groups from 5-year-olds to undergraduate students. Though they have not yet been investigated in the context of adult professional development, there is no reason to suppose that they would be very different, at least for learning that takes place in formal settings that remind learners, consciously or unconsciously, of school-like settings within which their tendencies to helpless proneness, if they exist, have been situated. In fact it would be interesting to see to what extent the effects of implicit theories, such as those of 'ability', *are* dependent on certain kinds of content, task demand and context. There is now a great deal of evidence to show that people's cognitive resources may appear surprisingly variable across different domains. It is quite possible that this reflects in part the domain-specificity of their implicit theories.

LEARNING TO LEARN

Let me conclude this review of implicit theories by saying a little more about the possibility and the nature of 'learning to learn', for this is of considerable relevance to adult and professional learning, especially if those adult learners are teachers of the young. As I argued in Chapter 1, the establishing of attitudes and competencies that are conducive of good learning is a central concern of schoolteachers, and if they are to facilitate this development it is important that they exhibit them themselves. It is therefore important that professional learning in education should convey an understanding of learning to learn, and help to develop it.

The idea that 'ability', or 'intelligence', is some kind of mental capacity which people possess in varying degrees, and which partly determines their level of success at cognitive tasks, is no longer tenable (Howe, 1990). Wagner and Sternberg (1985) have shown that performance in a variety of practical, real-life situations is not predicted by conventional tests of 'intelligence', but rather reflects the specific, and largely tacit, knowledge base that people possess about the particular domain. Ceci (1990) has shown that the complexity of a person's reasoning processes may be unrelated to measures of his or her general 'ability'. Psychologists are coming to the view that 'ability' is often highly situation specific, and is better seen as a learnable tool-kit of cognitive strategies and resources (Claxton, 1990; Howe, 1990).

This tool-kit comprises intellectual strategies, of course. But if it is to be as effective as possible, it also needs to include the ability to attend carefully to the evidence of the senses; to utilise fantasy and imagination; to practise and 'play' with practical solutions even when the immediate problem has been solved; and to access quieter, more contemplative modes of mind within which intuition can emerge. Each of these needs to be connected to an accurate specification of when, where, how and for what purpose it is to be appropriately used. And powers of self-awareness, reflection and meta-cognition need to be developed which can 'oversee' the deployment of these variable resources, and ensure that they are capable of being refined in the light of experience. This is a complex set of skills and qualities which we are only just beginning to articulate (Claxton, 1990). One of the most important preliminary tasks for educators, in their roles both as learners and teachers, is to engage in a process of critical reflection upon their outmoded implicit theories of learning, for while these remain tacitly installed in their minds, neither the necessity nor the possibility of a different view of learning can be seriously entertained.

REFERENCES

Bereiter, C. and Scardamalia, M. (1989) 'Intentional learning as a goal of instruction'. In L. B. Resnick (ed.) *Knowing, Learning and Instruction: Essays in Honor of Robert Glaser*, Hillsdale, NJ: Lawrence Erlbaum.

Berry, D. and Broadbent, D. E. (1984) 'On the relationship between task performance and associated verbalizable knowledge'. *Quarterly Journal of Experimental Psychology*, Vol. 35A, pp. 39–49.

Brookfield, S. (1986) *Understanding and Facilitating Adult Learning: A Comprehensive Analysis of Principles and Effective Practices*, Milton Keynes: Open University Press.

Bruner, J. S. (1967) *Towards a Theory of Instruction*, Cambridge, MA: Belknap Press.

Burns, R. B. (1982) *Self-Concept Development and Education*, London: Holt, Rinehart and Winston.

Ceci, S. J. (1990) *On Intelligence ... More or Less: A Bio-ecological Theory of Intellectual Development*, Englewood Cliffs, NJ: Prentice Hall.

Chiu, C., Hong, Y. and Dweck, C. S. (1994) 'Toward an integrative model of personality and intelligence: a general framework and some preliminary steps'. In R. J. Sternberg and P. Ruzgis (eds) *Personality and Intelligence*, Cambridge: Cambridge University Press.

Claxton, G. L. (1989) *Classroom Learning*, Open University course E208, Exploring Educational Issues, Unit 13. Milton Keynes: Open University.

Claxton, G. L. (1990) *Teaching to Learn: A Direction for Education*, London: Cassell.

Dweck, C. S. (1986) 'Motivational processes affecting learning'. *American Psychologist*, Vol. 41, pp. 1040–8.

Dweck, C. S. and Leggett, E. L. (1988) 'A social-cognitive approach to motivation and personality'. *Psychological Review*, Vol. 95, 256–73.

Greenwald, A. G. (1980) 'The totalitarian ego'. *American Psychologist*, Vol. 35, pp. 603–18.

Howe, M. J. A. (1990) 'Does intelligence exist?'. *The Psychologist*, Vol. 3, pp. 490–3.

Karmiloff-Smith, A. (1984) 'Children's problem-solving'. In M. E. Lamb, A. L. Brown and B. Ragoff (eds) *Advances in Developmental Psychology*, Vol. 3, Hillsdale, NJ: Lawrence Erlbaum.

Kolb, D. A. (1984) *Experiential Learning: Experience as the Source of Learning and Development*, Englewood Cliffs, NJ: Prentice Hall.

Langer, E., Hatem, M., Joss, J. and Howell, M. (1989) 'Conditional teaching and mindful learning'. *Creativity Research Journal*, Vol. 2, pp. 139–50.

Levitt, E. E. (1980) *The Psychology of Anxiety, 2nd edition*, Hillsdale, NJ: Lawrence Erlbaum.

Lewicki, P., Hill, T. and Czyzewska, M. (1992) 'Non-conscious acquisition of information'. *American Psychologist*, Vol. 47, pp. 796–801.

Morton, J., Hammersley, R. H. and Bekerian, D. A. (1985) 'Headed records: a model for memory and its failures'. *Cognition*, Vol. 20, pp. 1–23.

Seger, C. A. (1994) 'Implicit learning'. *Psychological Review*, Vol. 115, pp. 163–96.

Thompson, T. (1993) 'Characteristics of self-worth protection in achievement behaviour'. *British Journal of Educational Psychology*, Vol. 63, pp. 469–88.

Wagner, R. K. and Sternberg, R. J. (1985) 'Practical intelligence for real-world pursuits: the role of tacit knowledge'. *Journal of Personality and Social Psychology*, Vol. 49, pp. 436–58.

Wallas, G. (1926) *The Art of Thought*, New York: Harcourt.

Whyte, L. L. (1979) *The Unconscious before Freud*, London: Friedmann.

Part II

Cultural perspectives

The six chapters in the second part of the book present data that illuminates the culturally embedded nature of implicit theories about learning. In the first two, Chapters 5 and 6, the emphasis is on the assumptions that underlie practice in contrasting cultures. Chapter 5, by Marilyn Osborn, contrasts the attitudes to their own learning of primary school teachers in England and France, and explores the effect on those attitudes of recent national policy changes in both countries. Chapter 6, by Elisabeth Lazarus, focuses on the implicit theories of learning that new entrants to the teaching profession bring with them in England and Sweden, and the way those attitudes change over the early weeks of their encounter with rather different teacher training courses. In Chapter 7, Peter John explores the way in which student teachers' own experience of learning leaves them with implicit theories that may hinder their development as teachers. In the latter trio of chapters in this part, the emphasis shifts even more to the process of unearthing and challenging implicit theories of learning, by exposing teachers to different cultures. In Chapter 8 John Hayter and Paul Weeden recount the impact on their PGCE students' views of learning of a trip to The Gambia. In Chapter 9 Terry Atkinson charts a similar voyage of discovery undertaken by Modern Languages student teachers during their teaching practice in different countries of continental Europe. Chapter 10, by John Hayter, continues the exploration of cross-cultural experience on beliefs about learning, but focuses on the sometimes rather disorientating experience of overseas students coming to the UK to study for higher degrees.

Chapter 5

Teachers as adult learners

The influence of the national context and policy change

Marilyn Osborn

This chapter draws upon questionnaires, semi-structured interviews, and observation of primary school teachers in England and France. It investigates some of the factors influencing their readiness to develop as learners, to take on new ideas and to respond to them, particularly in the context of policy change, as well as examining teachers' implicit beliefs about what is appropriate in order to facilitate children's learning. Previous research on primary teachers in England and France suggests that the national context of the two education systems, and national cultural traditions may have an important influence on what is seen as possible by teachers and may act as a further barrier to, or a facilitator of learning. Of particular interest are the comparisons of data collected before and after recent educational reforms in both countries. One aspect of cultural difference, influenced by the policy changes in both countries, is the extent to which teachers see themselves as collaborative, as opposed to solitary, learners. In general, Osborn shows how the policy changes have led to change in teachers' implicit theories of knowledge, teaching and learning, leading in turn to a shift in their attitude to their own professional development. The chapter has clear links with the other contributions to the book that have a cross-cultural dimension: Chapter 6 by Elisabeth Lazarus and Chapter 9 by Terry Atkinson especially.

INTRODUCTION

Teachers as professionals have always been deeply involved in developing their learning – not only in institutional settings or in the context of accreditation, but also as independent, self-directed learners (Tough, 1978; Brookfield, 1988). Teachers who update their own knowledge in order to develop new topics in their own teaching, or those who deliberately choose a particular topic because it is something they want to learn about, are good examples of such self-directed learning (Fair, 1973; Denys, 1973). For most teachers, however, the process of learning and professional development is partly self-directed and partly directed by others, undertaken both within and outside formal in-service training courses.

In the context of the current rapid changes in education policy faced by many education systems in Europe and elsewhere, there is a particularly pressing need for such involvement in learning and professional development by teachers. As Guy Claxton's opening chapter suggests, the decision on whether or not to engage in learning may depend upon many different influences such as the teacher's own experiences as a learner, the pressure of other commitments, the strength of the perceived need for learning, and an intuitive cost–benefit analysis of the rewards and risks inherent in the situation. This chapter considers two other kinds of influence whose importance is often underestimated: those of the national context and national educational policy change.

Through an examination of primary teachers who have been faced with imposed change in two different national contexts it poses two related questions. First, what is the influence of the national context or the national education system on teachers' perception of themselves as continuing learners with responsibility for their own professional development? Second, when policy changes are imposed from above in these different national contexts, what effect do *they* have on teachers' readiness to engage in learning and to take on new ideas? In particular, to what extent do such policy changes act as facilitators of or barriers to learning so that teachers may decide to engage in change, to resist it, or simply to try to ignore it.

To explore these issues, I will draw upon data from several different studies undertaken by myself in collaboration with colleagues, in which teachers have talked about their own learning in the context of wider issues of educational change. The earliest of these studies (referred to here as the Bristaix study) was carried out in the mid 1980s in England and France before important educational reforms in both countries which aimed to change the nature of teachers' work (Broadfoot and Osborn, 1988, 1993; Osborn and Broadfoot, 1992, 1993). This included a questionnaire survey to 360 primary teachers in England and France followed by interviews and observation of a selected subsample. The chapter also draws upon two recent studies carried out after the educational reforms (the PACE study and the STEP study) with comparable samples of primary teachers in both countries (Pollard *et al.*, 1994; Broadfoot *et al.*, 1995), and a third, smaller study of how English primary teachers learned new roles in the wake of the reforms (the NASUWT study (Osborn and Black, 1994)).

THE INFLUENCE OF THE NATIONAL CONTEXT

Findings from the Bristaix study carried out in the 1980s suggested that the national context in which teachers work deeply influences their views of their professional responsibility in relation to their own learning as well as that of their pupils. In both questionnaires and interviews with primary teachers in England and France before recent educational reforms, we found major differences in the extent to which teachers in the two countries saw themselves as having a responsibility for continuing their own learning and professional development, and even in the extent to which they felt free to develop and change their teaching styles and skills (Broadfoot and Osborn, 1988). A detailed description of the research design can be found elsewhere (e.g. Broadfoot and Osborn, 1993).

In England, although constrained in many ways by sometimes conflicting obligations to colleagues, parents, headteachers and governors, teachers saw themselves as relatively free to develop their own teaching styles, curriculum and teaching topics. They saw themselves as having the possibility of change and experimentation. However, some teachers expressed an anxiety about the sheer open-endedness of their task and felt a lack of structure and guidelines.

In contrast, French teachers' conception of their role was narrower and centred more closely on carrying out their contractual responsibility for meeting curriculum objectives. Although less constrained in many ways by a strong sense of accountability to parents, headteachers and colleagues, they did not see themselves as having the possibility of professional development, of choosing their own teaching approaches, or of developing original topics which encapsulated the objectives of the French national curriculum. Many perceived themselves as simply carrying out directives from above.

When we analysed the responses of this representative sample of teachers in both countries to the question 'What does professional responsibility mean to you?' one distinct dimension of difference which emerged was in relation to the extent to which teachers adopted what might be called a 'meta-professional' stance, a tendency to think about the nature of teaching as a profession, its importance and its meaning. There was also a difference in the extent to which teachers in each country 'reflected' about the nature of their own teaching and saw their work as problematic and subject to question (Van Manen, 1977; Zerchner and Liston, 1987; Day, 1993). When we coded their responses looking for evidence of this dimension, English teachers emerged as significantly more likely than their colleagues in France to adopt a reflective stance in considering the nature of their role and how to carry it out. For example, they saw themselves as having a responsibility for their own professional development, for improving their knowledge and training and keeping abreast of new ideas, for collaborating with colleagues as well as 'upholding the profession and acting in a professional capacity'. As one English deputy head put it:

> I need to always be aware of new techniques by going on courses, reading educational publications etc. I try to bring these to the attention of my colleagues by discussion and, once again, example .... I need to feel satisfied with my teaching – and to do this I have put into my work a lot

of thought and planning. I thoroughly enjoy the interaction with other teachers I meet on courses – I find the necessary 'drug' to bring enthusiasm and enjoyment into my teaching.

French teachers, while focusing more intensively on the importance of their classroom teaching in terms of meeting objectives for each child by the end of the year, were much less likely to have a conception of themselves as continuous learners with a responsibility for their own professional development. A typical response to the question about professional responsibility which lacked this reflective dimension was:

> Professional responsibility means to work as carefully and as conscientiously as possible, but also enthusiastically, to encourage the learning of the children who are entrusted to us for six hours of the day.

or

> It means making sure that my pupils acquire the knowledge and skills necessary for their passage to the next class, avoiding error in the evaluation of my pupils, remaining as far as possible attentive to their needs and expectations while at the same time remaining objective and unassuming in my role as teacher.

It was clear from observation and subsequent discussion with teachers that these differences stemmed at least in part from the historical legacy of the two national cultural traditions as well as from more immediate features of the two education systems which included differences in initial teacher training, in the degree of centralisation of the curriculum, and in the employment status of the teachers.

Since the late 1980s when the above data was gathered, there have been major education policy reforms in both countries which have challenged the fundamental professional perspectives of the teachers concerned. In France the substance of the reforms (*loi d'orientation sur l'éducation* 1989) has been pressure towards a more collaborative way of working and a more individualised, child-centred pedagogy, while in England the emphasis has been rather different, moving towards the imposition of a centralised national curriculum with objectives to be met for each child (Education Reform Act 1988). The result of the English reforms has also been to emphasise even more the collaborative nature of teachers' work which was already evident in the 1980s relative to teachers' work in France.

In the 1990s further research has been carried out to document the response of teachers in both countries to educational policy change. The following section will draw upon these studies to investigate the extent to which these reforms have influenced teachers' readiness to adopt new learning roles or to see themselves as having responsibility for their own professional development.

THE INFLUENCE OF RECENT POLICY CHANGES IN ENGLAND AND FRANCE

Since the educational reforms in both countries, two recent studies carried out with colleagues at the University of Bristol and the University of the West of England, the PACE (Primary Assessment, Curriculum and Experience) and STEP (Systems, Teachers and Educational Policy) studies, have posed the same question about professional responsibility to representative samples of teachers in both countries. In England a stratified random sample of teachers (of Years 3 and 4 children) in eight regions completed questionnaires; in France, a comparable sample drawn from four regions completed similar questionnaires. A subsample of teachers in both countries was also interviewed. (For more details of the samples and how they were drawn, see Broadfoot *et al.* (1995).) When these responses were analysed, it became apparent that, since the reforms, whereas there had only been a slight increase in the proportion of French teachers describing a 'reflective' or 'meta-professional' dimension to their conception of their work (from 59 to 63 per cent), the proportion of English teachers who mentioned this aspect of their role had increased dramatically from 68 per cent in the 1980s to 93 per cent in 1994.

For example, within this overall 'reflective' dimension, 34 per cent of teachers in England now made specific mention of the importance of continuing training, learning and updating their knowledge, compared with 8 per cent of French teachers. In the 1980s, the proportion of teachers mentioning this had been 7 per cent of French teachers and 15 per cent of English teachers. In contrast, since the reforms French teachers were more likely than English teachers to describe themselves as needing constantly to re-evaluate and reassess their own work (14 per cent of French compared with 1 per cent of English; before the reforms, this had been important to only a minority of teachers in both countries (6 per cent)).

A typical French response still concentrated on the importance of the children's educational success and of working within the prescribed directives. As one teacher put it:

> To be professionally responsible is to achieve the goals set out by the end of the year, to make sure that children can read, write, and count correctly; to develop children's full potential, make them independent, and give them a desire to learn and to work hard; to respect the law, and the established authorities.

Although they were still a minority, an increasing number of French teachers, compared with the 1980s, talked in terms of what we coded as a metaprofessional or a reflective dimension. For example, one teacher talked in terms of a personal need to 'do my work responsibly, with reflection, to be aware of the effect of my actions, of my way of presenting myself'.

Another whose response was on the level of personal reflection talked of:

> being able to evolve, to put one's work into question, to be able to justify what I have done, and to present the reasons for my choices.

While a third said:

> For me it's fixing an objective, a target, following it to the end with an approach in which one believes, and when it is achieved, to re-examine it, reflect upon it and evaluate the outcome.

Another argued:

> It's to ask oneself questions about one's role, one's usefulness, and one's efficiency.

Others talked on a more metaprofessional, societal level of the importance of the teachers' role. For example, one said:

> My personal view is that the teacher must be above all someone who is always evolving. She must try to evolve in herself: in terms of updating her knowledge, in terms of her relationships with the children . . . . Quite apart from all the reforms, this type of teacher is always trying to enrich her teaching.

Others argued:

> It's the difficulty of reconciling accountability to the authorities, who have invested the teacher with an impossible task, with being a professional in one's contact with pupils. It's having convictions that one is sometimes being asked to ignore.
> The teacher has a duty to keep up-to-date after initial training, through continuing education, in-service training, personal reading, courses etc. to the highest possible level, and to try to become cultivated, to become open to the world and to society.

In both countries there had been a striking increase in collaboration between teachers as a result of the reforms. For English teachers this was not a complete change but more a further development of the relatively collaborative culture which had existed already in English primary classrooms in the 1980s (Nias *et al.*, 1989; Acker, 1995). They were now planning and working together in a more formal and structured way, whereas before their collaboration had been more informal and relatively unstructured.

However, for French teachers the increase in collaboration represented a relatively new way of working. Previously in French primary schools teachers had seen themselves as isolated and autonomous civil servants responsible only to the ministry of education. There had been very little sense of a school ethos or of working as a team. In the recent interviews, however, teachers referred frequently to *l'équipe pedagogique* (the teaching team) and talked of how they had to learn to work closely in collaboration with colleagues as well as the pleasure this new collaborative role had brought them.

As one teacher put it:

The introduction of the cycles (part of the reforms in France) has forced teachers to meet together, to exchange ideas, to try to work together.

Another argued that as part of her professional responsibility:

The teacher has a duty towards colleagues, to work together, to exchange ideas and help, to fit the content of one's teaching in with that of the rest of the team.

Another pointed out that she now needed to:

respect a programme of work planned as a team, profiting from the experience of each individual and sharing one's knowledge.

Although such collaboration was seen as a legal obligation, for most teachers it also represented a very positive move forward. Such expressions of co-operation were very rare indeed before the reforms, when the only reference to colleagues was in relation to the teacher's 'duty' to send them children at the end of the year who were capable of passing to the next class.

Many French teachers also expressed a new conception of the needs of children and of the way in which they expected to work with children. Many of these were certainly influenced by the emphasis placed by the reforms of 'centring education on the child', although such legislation may simply have legitimated what many teachers in France were beginning to do anyway. Such was the view of a number of teachers in our study who also ascribed the changes to changes in society, personalities of teaching staff and suggested that some of these changes had pre-dated the Jospin reforms.

It seems then, that although French teachers had not changed anything like as dramatically as teachers in England, there had nevertheless been a shift for many in how they saw themselves, in their 'implicit theories of self', as Claxton put it in the previous chapter, and hence in the extent to which they perceived a need for continuing learning. Some teachers in France had changed very little, however, and saw little reason for questioning or re-examining their existing practice. It was suggested by some of their colleagues that the main barrier to learning might be fear. As suggested in Chapter 1, opportunities may well be perceived as threats. As one teacher argued:

Those who wanted to open their eyes (to the possibility of change) did so, those who were afraid . . . because it's also that – to break away from using textbooks and a prescribed curriculum is difficult. I think those who were afraid haven't dared to try new ideas. For them, nothing has changed.

Although there were many exceptions, it was noticeable that amongst those who were reluctant to change were many older teachers who had invested years of effort in teaching in a way which was now being called into question. For some of them the losses involved in investing time and energy in change might well be seen as outweighing the gains.

Certainly a number of French teachers who were reluctant to consider changing their pedagogy felt a lack of confidence as well as a lack of the necessary training. In addition, they confessed an incomplete understanding of child-centred methods and felt that there were insufficient resources and inadequate training to support an attempt to change. Some of those who wanted to concentrate more on individual children and small groups felt frustrated by what they perceived as large classes and lack of extra adult help. Nevertheless, class sizes in France were considerably smaller than in England (an average of twenty-eight compared with thirty-three in England). In some schools, where several of the teachers felt this way, the general perception was that the reforms had had very little effect, because there was no check on whether change had been implemented: 'If teachers don't choose to change, if they don't do it, nothing happens to correct them.' These teachers felt that their existing methods of teaching worked relatively well.

In England, of course, the situation was quite different as teachers had less choice over whether to change. However, although it would have been possible simply to go through the motions in a superficial way, very few had taken this option. The increase in the perceived need to continue learning and updating knowledge was clearly linked to the constant need for teachers to acquaint themselves with new areas of the National Curriculum as they came on-stream, to master new forms of assessment, and to devise ways in which it was possible to cover the attainment targets now set out for each year group and to incorporate them into their teaching in an interesting and creative way.

One teacher's response exemplified the wide-ranging nature of the role she perceived for herself, with a particular emphasis on taking into account her colleagues' as well as her own academic development:

Being responsible as a professional means to give of my best at all times both socially, personally, and academically to the life of the school. To show care and consideration for my colleagues' well-being and educational development. To be thoughtful in my organisation and innovative in academic development. To foster care and understanding in the children's social interactions and provide the means by which they can achieve their true potential with pride and enjoyment.

The English reforms also involved teachers in learning many new roles. For example, they had to plan more extensively with colleagues, and to become co-ordinators with responsibility for a particular area of the curriculum. These roles ranged from simply being responsible for the ordering, storage and allocation of resource materials for their curricular area, to, at the other end of the spectrum, becoming a specialist in a particular curricular area with time spent supporting other teachers in their classrooms, usually teaching alongside them.

A separate recent study by the author (NASUWT study) based on interviews with teachers in the upper years of primary school identified several barriers to the successful learning of these new roles (Osborn and Black, 1994). Some of these obstacles were structural, such as the lack of non-contact time within the school day for curriculum co-ordinators, who were nearly always class teachers in addition, actually to work with colleagues. However, some were partly self-imposed as well as structural, such as a reluctance to threaten the autonomy of colleagues by suggesting the possibility of entering their classroom in order to work with them.

As one teacher put it:

> Initially I would prefer them to come to me for help because it's better that they come to me rather than I go to them because they then feel ownership of it . . . . It's no good forcing them otherwise they won't take it on board.

Most primary teachers felt that a very sensitive approach was needed to work with colleagues in this way, yet little or no in-service training had been provided in order to help teachers focus on new roles and relationships with colleagues and on effective ways of working together inside as well as outside the classroom.

THE NEED FOR IN-SERVICE TRAINING

In both countries then, it was noticeable that teachers expressed a strong need for in-service training and at the same time an anxiety that so little was provided. While an individual has to overcome self-imposed barriers to learning in order to make a decision to engage, there are also structural and institutional barriers such as lack of in-service training which can seem to be just as insuperable.

In England, many teachers in the upper years of the primary school saw in-service training as almost unavailable (Osborn and Black, 1994). Most of the support they had received in adapting to change had come from within the school itself, mainly from colleagues and from the headteacher. Provision varied from one Local Education Authority to another, but in the least well provided, there were few courses or adviser-related support available. A further obstacle was that even where courses were available, many schools managing their own budgets had been forced to give a low priority to INSET as opposed to other demands on their funds. Indeed, in some schools, teachers had funded themselves in order to attend one of the few available out-of-school INSET courses. As one teacher described it:

> There is virtually no money in the budget now for courses. It is a drastic change from a few years ago.

In France also, teachers frequently mentioned their need for a more structured programme of training in how to deal with the new teaching approaches required, arguing that the occasional days which were provided were 'too light to be real training', 'there is a need for a more structured approach', 'they (the authorities) have asked us to adopt a more child-centred approach, but they have given us no guidance in how to do it'.

As one committed teacher described it:

> There is no funding for change. You have to change by yourself. There is no training, no extra equipment, not even a library with books about teaching. So you have to keep asking to go on courses, to go to conferences at your own expense, to buy books. I think some people just don't change because of that.

Even where funding was available, this teacher did not think that the in-service courses had adapted to the reform's requirements. In order to be able to go on a course herself, she had had to be very insistent and to go on it during sick leave. 'So they stun us with brilliant changes and afterwards we just have to make the best of it unaided.' This is exactly the short-sighted, hit-and-run approach to professional training that Mike Wallace exposed so effectively in Chapter 2.

Clearly, for teachers in both countries, the lack of support and training for change was a major obstacle to continued professional development. However, in addition to the need for structural support, a more self-directed process of learning was necessary as the following section suggests.

LEARNING TO MEDIATE

Learning to adapt to change without feeling submerged or taken over is a necessary technique for survival. Teachers in both countries had to confront this problem and find solutions to it. In the PACE study of teachers' responses to change introduced by the English Education Reform Act we found that certain key qualities enabled teachers to make a creative response to change without losing their sense of professional identity. These could be summarised as learning to mediate the effects of policy change; in other words, the ability to feel confident enough about their own practice to be able to make choices and to be selective in how they implemented the programmes of study. These teachers often worked in a supportive school with a collaborative culture. They were able to avoid 'over-conscientiousness' (Campbell et al., 1991), and to benefit from the structure and guidelines offered by the National Curriculum without letting it drive them or destroy what they perceived to be good about their practice (Osborn et al., 1992; Pollard et al., 1994). They could be seen as active mediators, taking ownership and control of the innovations and working to integrate the best of the changes into what they knew to be good about their own practice.

For these teachers openness to change and learning was important, but so was preserving a sense of their own professionalism. One example of such a teacher in England was Sara, an experienced infant teacher who was interviewed three times over the course of several years. Although she found the pace and scale of the education reforms extremely demanding and difficult to keep up with, and had experienced a sense of loss of some of the things which were important to her in teaching (for example the opportunity to respond in a spontaneous way to ideas introduced by the children and to build her teaching around them), she remained open to the possibility of learning and change.

It was important to her to take control of the changes and find ways of making them part of her thinking rather than simply seeing them as external targets which had to be met. As she put it:

I think what I hope to do is to internalise myself as a teacher, internalise all this detail and to then be able to use it in good infant practice.

In a later interview she argued that her teaching had become far more focused and structured as a result of her response to change. She saw this as having both positive and negative results, but there was no doubt in her mind that she had improved her skills in some areas such as assessment. Even more importantly, she felt that her practice had evolved to the point where she now felt in control again.

I definitely feel when the National Curriculum was first implemented and all the orders came through – we took them all on board – I felt very restricted. I felt under so much pressure. I felt it was an impossible task. I couldn't do it.

As a result of rationing the new demands and being selective in what she chose to implement, she had evolved without losing what she felt to be most important in her teaching. She now argued 'I feel far more in control now, and I feel, "Yes, I can do this again" it *is* possible.'

Her response contrasted with that of a colleague in the same school who was an equally experienced and committed teacher, but who had not been able to adopt this approach of mediating external demands to her own professional ends. She had not found a way of rationing the demands and being selective about which she chose to carry out, nor did she see the changes as an opportunity for new learning. In contrast she now felt submerged and taken over and had lost confidence in her ability to be an effective teacher.

The teachers in France who felt most positive about the recent education reforms also talked of the need to internalise the changes, to be selective, and of the importance of integrating change into existing practice. Several of the teachers talked of being mediators, taking the best from the reforms, but using their own judgement in the end. As one put it:

> We need to be able to take the good aspects of the reforms imposed by the government and at the same time to be able to look at them critically.

Another talked of the need to 'immerse herself in the reforms' in order to make them a natural part of her teaching.

A headteacher in an inner-city school put the argument slightly more strongly:

> Ministerial decisions and circulars are far from my concerns. I select from the documents what is relevant and useful for the children. I leave the rest. We continue following our own beliefs without getting excited by circulars and reforms.

However, he emphasised that many of the recent official recommendations had already been implemented in his school some years ago. In an area where '80 per cent of families were illiterate in any language' they had found it necessary to adopt a more child-centred approach to meet the social and personal needs of the children even when this was not officially encouraged.

> By definition every educational minister who comes on the scene makes his reforms. When one looks closely it's what one is already doing. The reforms force open doors that are already open in our school.

Many of those French teachers who had learned to change their teaching to become more child responsive had considerably increased their enjoyment as a result. As one teacher put it 'It's more interesting to be a teacher now. More is expected of us but on the other hand it's more satisfying.' Another argued 'It's given me a boost. It's done me good.'

Isabelle, a teacher in a large inner-city school, had begun an extensive attempt to learn new skills and to update her knowledge. She had just finished a month's video-making course, and was involved in introducing the use of video and group work into her teaching of drama. She tried new ideas in the classroom every year. As she put it 'I'll never get tired of this job. I find it personally enriching learning and preparing new teaching. I adore it.' She also tried 'to get the other teachers to see the possibility of doing things differently and trying out different ideas each year'.

CONCLUSIONS

It is clear then, that in both national contexts policy change had acted to some extent as a catalyst, leading many teachers to seek to increase their involvement both in independent, self-directed learning and in structured learning opportunities such as those provided by in-service training. However, the substance of the policy changes in England and France was very different. Whereas in France some teachers argued that the reforms were simply legitimating changes which they themselves had already begun to introduce, in England, for most teachers the reforms represented a sharp break with present practice, and came into conflict with some fundamental beliefs about teaching. Nonetheless, it seems that in both countries policy change was influential in leading teachers to re-examine their practice, to develop new ways of working together, and to strive to update their knowledge and skills to meet new demands.

These teachers' responses suggest that barriers to learning can be both self-imposed and internal, and structural and systematic. Although relatively free in the past to develop new teaching styles, French teachers formerly saw themselves as constrained into simply carrying out directives from above. Since the reforms, it appears that the atmosphere of change in France has introduced increased reflectiveness and readiness to change amongst at least some teachers. Such teachers expressed a wish to learn, but were keenly aware of a lack of support for change, and a lack of in-service and advisory help.

How has the shift in some French teachers' attitudes come about? One important influence for change appears to be the considerable increase in collaborative working which has taken place. In the late 1980s in France, we found that few teachers discussed problems or difficulties in the classroom with colleagues. There seemed to be a tension between teachers being prepared to show themselves as uncertain and therefore as needing to learn, and the need to present a 'front' which required them to appear to colleagues as authoritative and competent teachers (a dilemma that seems to get bigger the more senior you are, as revealed by the studies reported of headteachers in Chapter 12 and senior education professionals in Chapter 11). This appeared to be closely related to the isolation of most French teachers in their own classrooms, with relatively little contact with colleagues, often no joint coffee breaks or informal discussion, and no staffrooms where such contact could take place. The lack of a school ethos or a collaborative culture meant that there was no supportive environment where anxieties and mistakes could be seen as acceptable.

In contrast, in England, where teachers had staffrooms and a relatively collaborative culture, it was far more common for them to talk together about their problems and their successes in the classroom and to provide mutual support. The emphasis on informal collaboration made it possible to relax, to some extent from the need to appear an 'expert teacher', and to admit a need for support and learning.

The recent reforms in France have placed far more emphasis on teachers working as part of a team with colleagues. On recent classroom observation visits, it was noticeable that most schools now had rooms set aside as staffrooms where staff met regularly at coffee and lunch times and where much discussion took place, which included sharing of problems of classroom management, ideas for teaching, as well as discussion of social events.

In interviews French teachers talked extensively about the ways in which they now planned together and with great enthusiasm about joint topic work between classes and outings organised together. It seems that collaboration meant less pressure to present an external image as an expert. Indeed, it is more difficult to maintain such a 'front' when one works more closely with colleagues as part of a team. Consequently, it is now easier for French teachers to see themselves as co-learners. Their 'implicit theories of self' may have shifted in response to the move towards greater collaboration and consequently some of the former barriers to learning and to professional development may have been broken down.

In England the pace and nature of the changes have led teachers to become even more collaborative than in the past and to plan together both in whole-school terms and with colleagues of the same year groups. The changes have also forced teachers to take on new roles such as that of curriculum co-ordinators. Here, too, collaboration seems to be linked with an increased readiness to learn. However, the nature of the reforms in the two countries is different. While the French reforms seemed to legitimate or encapsulate what some teachers were already feeling, in England the reforms often cut across teachers' most fundamental beliefs about children's needs and about what constitutes good teaching. Consequently, teachers who had not merely survived, but had come through the changes to be able to teach creatively, had learned to be mediators, taking the best from the changes and adapting them to fit their beliefs about teaching. In spite of the imposition of change from above against teachers' prevailing beliefs, there was a great willingness to learn, to keep up to date with all the documentation and to take on new roles.

The findings presented here suggest, however, that in both countries there was a lack of structural support for change in the form of training, a lack of in-service and advisory help for teachers of junior age children and a lack of non-contact time to help teachers to update their knowledge and skills by working in and observing in colleagues' classrooms.

It appears that in the context of rapid policy change in both countries, the structure and framework of the system had not adapted fast enough to meet new needs. The message is clear: the decision to engage and to become involved with the process of change is a necessary but not a sufficient condition for learning to take place. Structural support in the form of adequate resources and well-designed, relevant in-service training is also required.

REFERENCES

Acker, S. (1995) 'Carry on caring: the work of women teachers'. In *British Journal of Sociology of Education*, Vol. 16, No. 1.
Broadfoot, P. and Osborn, M. (1988) 'What professional responsibility means to teachers: national contexts and classroom constants'. In *British Journal of Sociology of Education*, Vol. 9, No. 3.
Broadfoot, P. and Osborn, M. (1993) *Perceptions of Teaching: A Comparative Study of Primary School Teachers in England and France*, London: Cassell.

Broadfoot, P., Osborn, M., Pollard, A. and Planel, C. (1995) *Primary Teachers and Policy Change*, final Report to the ESRC.

Brookfield, S. (1988) 'Individualised adult learning'. In *Lifelong Learning*, Vol. 1, No. 7.

Campbell, R. J., Evans, L., Neill, S. R. St. J. and Packwood, A. (1991) *The Use and Management of Infant Teachers' Time: Some Policy Issues*, Warwick: University of Warwick Policy Analysis Unit.

Day, C. (1993) 'Reflection: a necessary but not sufficient condition for professional development'. In *Teaching and Teacher Education*, Vol. 19, No. 1.

Denys, L. O. J. (1973) *The Major Learning Efforts of Two Groups of Accra Adults*. PhD Thesis, University of Toronto, unpublished, available by microfilm, National Library of Canada, Ottawa.

Fair, J. W. (1973) *Teachers as Learners: The Learning Projects of Beginning Elementary School Teachers*. PhD Thesis, University of Toronto, unpublished but available on microfilm.

Nias, J., Southworth, G. and Yeomans, R. (1989) *Staff Relationships in the Primary School: A Study of Organisational Cultures*, London: Cassell.

Osborn, M. and Black, E. (1994) *Developing the National Curriculum at Key Stage 2: The Changing Nature of Teachers' Work*. Report commissioned and published by NASUWT: Rednal, Birmingham.

Osborn, M. and Broadfoot, P. (1992) 'A lesson in progress? French and English classrooms compared'. In *Oxford Review of Education*, Vol. 18, No. 1.

Osborn, M. and Broadfoot, P. with Abbott, D., Croll, P. and Pollard, A. (1992) 'The impact of current changes in English primary schools on teacher professionalism'. In *Teachers' College Record*, Fall.

Osborn, M. and Broadfoot, P. (1993) 'Becoming and being a teacher: the influence of the national context'. In *European Journal of Education*, Vol. 28, No. 1.

Pollard, A., Broadfoot, P., Croll, P., Osborn, M. and Abbott, D. (1994) *Changing English Primary Schools: The Impact of the Education Reform Act at Key Stage One*, London: Cassell.

Tough, A. (1978) 'Major learning efforts: recent research and future directions'. In *Adult Education* (USA), Vol. XXVII, No. 4.

Van Manen, M. (1977) 'Linking ways of knowing with ways of being practical'. In *Curriculum Inquiry*, Vol. 6, No. 3.

Zerchner, K. and Liston, D. (1987) 'Teaching student teachers to reflect'. In *Harvard Educational Review*, Vol. 57, No. 1.

Chapter 6

Teacher trainer and student teacher: sources of divergence in perceptions of learning?

Some reflections on training in England and Sweden

Elisabeth Lazarus

In this chapter, Elisabeth Lazarus presents the results of a small-scale piece of action research. As a relatively new entrant to the ranks of teacher trainers, she is concerned to use the framework of the present book to throw light on her own practice: specifically on the barriers to learning that student teachers might experience as a result of any mismatch between their implicit theories of how they learn, and those of their tutors. As a Swede working in England, Elisabeth was also interested to explore this issue in both cultures. Some national differences did emerge in the attitudes and philosophies of tutors, and the experience of students. But it is the disparity between students' and tutors' implicit learning theories, regardless of national culture, that emerges most strongly. The question for teacher trainers of 'do we give them what they want, or what we think they need?' is clearly a crucial one in designing courses of initial teacher education.

INTRODUCTION

As a head of department in a multi-cultural, inner-city school I was involved in developing teaching and learning projects with colleagues to benefit our pupils and ourselves. We agreed with Claxton (1990) that we could no longer ignore the experiences and strategies that learners brought with them, and that we had to rethink what was happening in our classrooms. On changing institution, moving from school to university and into initial teacher education, it seemed natural and appropriate to question our teaching and learning styles here as well. A number of key questions emerged which provided the starting points for the exploration that this chapter reports. Do we adequately meet the challenge of training student teachers from varied backgrounds, offering a range of experiences and perceptions and with greatly varying needs? To what extent do the explicit and implicit beliefs held by teacher educators about the learning needs of their student teachers influence this learning? Are perceptions of learning influenced by a particular national, institutional or cultural setting, or can attitudes and beliefs be attributable only to individuals? What causes dissonance (as defined by Festinger (1959)) in the early phases of training and how does this motivate and affect learning? As someone relatively new to teacher training, and to working in universities, I was keen to undertake a small 'action research' project which would both support me in reflecting on my own practice and assumptions, and also perhaps reveal more clearly some of the implicit theories that my students brought into their training with them. And as a Swede, who was trained and has taught in England, it seemed particularly appropriate (and practical) to study these two countries, both to look for cultural differences in student and tutor beliefs, and to see if there were English and Swedish aspects to my own thinking. It seemed particularly interesting to investigate parallels in the student teachers' and tutors' perceptions during a phase of change, and to try to tease out some of the factors, both psychological and situational, that combine to influence a student teacher's performance. As Sjödahl (1990) points out 'human behaviour is as a rule regulated by multiple determinants . . . several attitudes may interact and strengthen or weaken the relation with overt behaviour'. This chapter particularly attempts to highlight some of the implicit and explicit theories of learning held by the interviewees, and to show how these views have influenced their teaching and learning.

BACKGROUND TO THE PROJECT

Teacher education has been subject to change in England and Sweden in recent times. In England, a competency model of initial teacher training with a large proportion of time spent in schools (66 per cent of the one-year postgraduate course) was introduced in 1994. In Sweden, teacher education was reformed in 1988, still maintaining three training programmes for future teachers: one for year groups 1–7, one for Years 4–9, and one for the non-compulsory upper secondary (*gymnasium*) sector lasting approximately four years. Further changes were introduced in 1992 when subject studies at university could be 'completed with one year of practical pedagogical training' (Swedish Ministry of Education and Science, 1993, p. 136), the so-called PPU course. This quite controversial move was in response to a teacher shortage (all gymnasium courses are being extended from two to three years, regardless of whether these follow the vocational or academic routes) and a political initiative to 'recruit people with different backgrounds and subject interests to the teaching profession' (ibid.). So far the uptake on the PPU programmes has been low. Although a political consensus in educational matters tends to exist in Sweden (an example of this would be the introduction of the National Curriculum in 1980), it remains to be seen whether the Swedish equivalent of the English postgraduate certificate in education will remain throughout the period in office of the recently elected social democratic government. The educational reforms were introduced by the previous conservative government with the objective of ensuring that 'conveying knowledge [would] be emphasised as the primary objective of the school' (ibid.).

In Sweden, 90 per cent of school students continue their education, beyond the compulsory nine years of grundskolan, at the *gymnasium* which combines traditionally academic and vocational routes of training. It has been argued in Sweden that 'formal education has increasingly become the main vehicle of social mobility and an individual career' (Husén, 1989) and that 'prolonged schooling with expanded enrolment has in recent years . . . been the main instrument in attempts to cope with youth unemployment' (ibid.). English is compulsory in Swedish schools, and entitlement to an optional second or third foreign language also exists. Pupils who speak a language other than Swedish at home are also entitled to mother-tongue teaching. This enhanced programme together with compulsory English from Year 4 onwards has put significant pressure on the modern languages teaching pool.

The changes in teacher training in both England and Sweden can also be seen as a response to shortcomings in the educational system perceived by politicians and sections of the public. The questions of 'what constitutes a good school?' and how schools can become 'learning organisations' have been investigated from a number of angles (cf. Dalin, 1993; Fullan, 1993; Hargreaves and Hopkins, 1991; Hopkins *et al.*, 1994; HMI, 1988). Factors such as a good school ethos, well-trained and motivated teachers, purposeful learning and adequate resources have all been implicated. Similarly the question of how teachers learn and develop has been a major focus for recent research in a number of countries (cf. Miller, 1993; Madsén, 1994; Elliott, 1993; Day *et al.*, 1993). Many schools in England and Sweden have approached the differing learning needs manifested by pupils through differentiation projects and by adopting varying teaching and learning styles. Worries have been expressed of a developing 'educational underclass . . . psychologically undernourished, verbally under-stimulated and disturbed by sheer neglect' (Husén, 1989). How can we counteract this trend in our schools and prepare future generations of teachers who 'cannot rely either on instinct alone or on pre-packaged sets of techniques? Instead, [the teacher] must think about what is taking place, what the options are . . . in a critical, analytical way' (Brubacher *et al.*, 1994). (Here we meet again the same issues raised by Marilyn Osborn in Chapter 5.) At a time of change, the dissonance between the beliefs and values of individual teachers, and those being imposed upon them structurally or politically, becomes especially strong. Hence the need to attempt to understand more fully just what those implicit theories are.

DATA COLLECTION

Three English student teachers (Suzy, Jennifer and Diana), on an initial teacher education course preparing to teach modern languages in the secondary school sector, were interviewed at crucial points in the early stages of training: prior to the commencement of the course; at the end of the first week of the official university course; prior to their autumn-term school experience and after this experience. The students were interviewed individually or in pairs. The semi-structured interviews explored their expectations of the course, what beliefs they held about how children learn and what perceptions and memories they had of their own learning. They focused on which aspects of the training were most helpful and how they preferred to learn. The interviews also tried to probe what kind of teacher they would like to become. Noticeable changes in perceptions were explored. What was really causing them difficulties in the early phases of training? Were their varied backgrounds and experiences taken into account? The interviews lasted two to three hours. The student teachers also kept personal diaries in which they recorded their experiences, and these were made available to me. One student withdrew from the course before the end of the project. All student teachers on the Bristol course complete written evaluations at the end of each term, and my target group also completed a questionnaire for this project.

Two university tutors (Edward and John) in Bristol were interviewed to explore the beliefs they held of the learning needs of their students. Their educational background and training were discussed, as well as their beliefs about support, the role of mentors, methodology, content and purpose of the course. Answers were sought to questions such as: what characterises 'good' student teachers and 'good' teacher educators? What is the essence of a 'good' learner'? These tutors were also observed working with the student teachers in seminars and tutorials. The tutors had varied experience of teaching in secondary schools and of mentoring.

In order to provide comparative data five student teachers from Sweden, at varying stages of their training, were interviewed after I had observed them teach (Ewa, Ingrid, Barbro, Kristina and Katrin). Only one student teacher (Ewa) was following the new practical pedagogical training programme. A further sample of three recently qualified teachers was interviewed (Bibi, Greta and Solveig). Two methodology tutors (Ulla and Lena) at the Lärarhögskolan (HLS, Institute of Education) in Stockholm were asked the same or similar questions as the tutors in Bristol. The Swedish participants were also asked to complete a questionnaire. The interviews were conducted in Swedish or English according to the preference of the person interviewed. As limited time was available for interviews, these lasted between forty-five and ninety minutes. All translations and transcriptions are the responsibility of the author. All names have been changed to preserve anonymity.

THE STUDENT TEACHERS' BIOGRAPHIES AS LEARNERS

To the question 'What sort of learner do you think you were at school?' the three English student teachers responded quite similarly. They all considered themselves to have been good or very good learners both at school and during undergraduate programmes. Suzy saw herself as 'a bit of a swot' who thrived in a comprehensive school where she associated with a close group of friends 'who liked to learn, liked school, liked to achieve academically'. Nevertheless, Suzy related how, at the age of 10, her headmaster had shaken her by the shoulders when she asked him for some help with mathematics problems. This left her feeling 'upset and confused', an experience she has not forgotten. She wanted to be reassured and hoped that a teacher would tell her 'Oh look, just believe in yourself a bit more – you're fine', but she never got to hear this. The strategy she developed to cope with subjects she found difficult (especially mathematics and chemistry) was to make a conscious decision to understand them and to learn for herself. She obtained grade 'A' at O-level in chemistry. When I expressed admiration at being able so accurately to recite grades from O-level (she is 32-years-old), Suzy retorted that during her 'formative years of academic study' she felt 'represented by [her] grades'. She knew that she gravitated towards things which were difficult. Jennifer, on the other hand felt that she learned 'despite the fact that the teacher was not particularly interesting, . . . and out of sheer rebelliousness'. She chose to work hard at subjects which her parents (who were teachers) were not interested in or could offer no help with, 'to prove I'm good . . . without help from them'. Diana 'enjoyed learning . . . and did not need much motivation'. She particularly enjoyed 'taking decisions for (herself)', and teachers 'who encouraged you to follow your own ideas', although she too found some difficulties in learning mathematics. All three interviewees obtained very good or excellent degrees at university.

Three of the Swedish interviewees seemed to have experienced difficulties at school. Barbro felt 'frightened at school' and cites her mathematics teacher as an example of someone who instilled fear. Katrin felt she could empathise with her pupils on teaching practice as she 'had difficulties at school' herself; a similar view is expressed by Greta ('I can understand how my pupils feel when they find English difficult'), who also experienced problems with mathematics. Ingrid and Kristina seemed to find it more difficult to think about themselves as learners and commented on their teachers and schools instead. Ingrid mentioned a bad English teacher who taught her 'how not to do it'. Bibi, Solveig and Ewa perceived themselves as good learners. The interviews highlighted a dilemma which I also experienced at school: the discrepancy between how we perceive ourselves and how we perform in examinations and are judged by the outside world. In the light of this it must be stressed that all the Swedish interviewees had had very successful school careers and had had to compete for strictly limited places on this teacher training course, where entry depends only on grades, and interviews are only given to prospective PPU students.

EXPECTATIONS OF THE TRAINING

Both groups of students had only vague expectations of the training they were to receive. When the English student teachers were asked before the course commenced what they expected from the year, not surprisingly the responses were hesitant. 'Hard work' was mentioned by all of them. Jennifer imagined that a large proportion of the training course would be delivered through lectures, similar to her undergraduate experience some time ago. Diana felt that the year would 'test' her and offer her:

> different teaching experiences: [I know] that it is only by going out there and dealing with thirty-five students and by a bit of trial and error, that [I am] going to know how to react when . . . you come across problems, but . . . also you can be told a little bit of psychology . . . that can be learnt.

She felt positive about the course and had discussed it with friends who had said they had liked it. Nevertheless, she admitted to feeling a mixture of anxiety and excitement and being 'prepared for it to go either way in the end'.

Suzy expressed herself very forcefully when she said:

> I was very lucky. I was one of the generation who was the last who got out before this intense analysis of education started . . . I want to see for myself what is happening. What you can do about it, see for myself and work from within.

Later in the interview she said she had 'no anxiety whatsoever'. In contrast to her rather solitary undergraduate experience she expected large amounts of time when she would 'have to be somewhere, listening to someone or doing something, which for me as a mature student . . . is quite a good way to start. It slams you into discipline.' Towards the end she claimed that in a professional course 'I would not expect to be spoon-fed . . . [however] this course, as I see it possibly happening, seems to be more spoon-fed'. She was nevertheless convinced: 'I will be learning so much'.

The one student who was able to articulate most clearly her expectations of the training course in Sweden was, not surprisingly, the mature PPU student who had only recently started her training. She knew that she would be attending twice as many seminars and talks on pedagogy as on methodology, and as she found this intellectually stimulating, she was looking forward to the year. The others could only remember having expectations of themselves and not of the training programme.

WHAT MAKES A GOOD TEACHER?

In the descriptions Diana gave about her English education, she expressed the following qualities. A 'good teacher' is someone who is 'creative and encouraging . . . lays down rules, knows their stuff [one step ahead], . . . is interested in their subject . . . a good communicator, makes you reflect, is patient and tolerant . . . [someone] who elicits answers from pupils, not just tells them'. Suzy described a good teacher she experienced as someone who 'constantly took us very seriously, [was] very concerned for our grades, prepared the lessons and was thorough . . . [had] a good sense of humour . . . [and encouraged] a spirit of competition'. Jennifer saw a good teacher as one who is 'sparking off interest and enthusiasm'. She can clearly remember a Latin teacher who 'walked around the classroom reciting Latin' bringing the language to life.

All the Swedes mentioned good subject knowledge as a prerequisite for a good teacher but also 'patience; must give pupils time to express themselves; imagination; ability to create a good atmosphere in the classroom, removing pupils' fears of making mistakes and helping them to dare to speak' (Greta, Bibi, Solveig). Kristina and Ingrid added cultural knowledge, flexibility, variety and sensitive use of target language (in other words the language being taught to the pupils) as well. Barbro, Katrin and Ewa interpreted a good teacher also as someone who could motivate pupils to learn for themselves, to develop their intrinsic motivation. I think that as the Swedish student teachers had already spent more time in schools, it is likely that this produced a somewhat more articulate and detailed description.

It is interesting to note that the two university tutors from England and the two Swedish tutors interviewed described good teachers in similar terms: 'Someone who demonstrates a great interest in all aspects of their future job with a willingness to try out new ideas' (Ulla); 'very interested in children . . . [someone] who sees [pupils'] learning from their point of view . . . not one single lesson without a moment of laughter . . . good subject knowledge . . . confident, who will do everything they can to develop themselves together with the children' (Lena). Edward felt that he initially thought more of the pupils and what type of teacher he wanted his students to become.

> I wanted to make sure that they would go out there and do the best for the children they taught and that children would get someone who was going to empower them and not dictate to them, so that any child would have the opportunity of learning from this person, rather than only those children who conformed to a set pattern of expectations of what a language learner was.

With time this view has changed to a greater awareness of the student teachers as learners, of them realising their potential and being:

> empowered to do whatever they want . . . . They have to work out for themselves what is best for them, whether they want to be a teacher or not. Then they have got to work out where they want to teach and what and how.

All four felt that the varied experiences and backgrounds of their student teachers should be taken into account in planning their training programme, but were not totally sure how successfully this was being done.

THE STUDENT TEACHERS AS LEARNERS

John agreed with his Swedish colleagues that most of the learning for student teachers takes place in schools 'at the cutting edge, in a much steeper learning curve than . . . here. That's where you meet the pupils head-on.' At the university he hoped student teachers would grow professionally, as autonomously as possible by 'providing them with support and advice and that expertise which I hope to have'. He wanted his students to 'gain insight into how children learn', to take 'reflections forward and apply them to situations they might encounter at school', but without providing concrete examples of how this could be achieved. Edward disagreed with many people in teacher education who:

> believe you've got to [be] a reflective practitioner . . . . I think that is a highly dogmatic view of how students are going to learn. I believe much more that a) all students will learn in their own individual ways and b) people will learn whatever you do to them . . . the biggest thing we can do is to get out of their way . . . and give them the space in order to learn, yet to come in at critical points and spice things up and either push them on a bit or say . . . you are getting too far in that direction.

Lena tried to engage her student teachers with their emotions when she carried out activities with them. She frequently asked the question 'what did it do to you when I did that or said that?'. She found it very important that the atmosphere in her seminar group, of up to eighteen students, has to be very caring (*kärleskfull* = full of love), but also critical. The language she used is interesting and reflected my own experience, where female educators more readily engaged and exploited emotions in training sessions. She developed sessions which modelled the classroom ('do here what we want them to do there'), but at their own level. Some students were active learners, whilst others were observers and fed observations about the learning situations back in discussions. She liked to provide her student teachers with practical ideas which they could use in their classrooms. Her sessions were of necessity intensive as she could only meet the PPU students for sixteen hours before they embarked on their first practice. Ulla wanted them to see teachers 'in action . . . in the very classroom' but also expected them to have held discussions with her first and 'use my ideas as well'.

THE INSTITUTIONS

There is no clearly articulated conceptual framework or philosophy of teacher education in either Bristol or Stockholm, although there are published course descriptions. The methodology employed is the responsibility of each tutor. At HLS the tutors do not observe each other nor is a culture of co-operative working encouraged by the institution (cf. Chapter 5), as the tutors have very heavy workloads. Ulla joined the institution recently after having been a school-based mentor for student teachers for over twenty years. She found it difficult at first as she was given very little guidance, 'so I use whatever method I find suitable based on my own teaching [twenty-five years]'. Lena, who had worked at HLS longer, has proven extremely helpful and has unofficially taken on the role of Ulla's mentor.

In contrast, John and Edward have planned and designed the modern languages course collaboratively with a third tutor, myself. 'Good planning, organisation and classroom management' (John) is fundamental to their teaching. Sessions try to incorporate clear aims and objectives, examples of good practice, pair and group tasks, student contributions based on reading or observation. We all formally observe each other at least once a term, but informal observation is more frequent as sessions sometimes involve team teaching. The four interviewed tutors held very strong beliefs about the use of the target language in the modern languages classroom, to which some of their students found it difficult to reconcile themselves. The four also ran some methodology sessions in the various target languages. They jointly professed that they had developed their methodologies from listening to student teachers. Ulla said 'the students influence me a lot. I listen to them and try to meet their demands.' Although the structure of support for the tutors was different in the two institutions I could not detect a national difference in the perceptions of the four tutors. The culture of the institution and how this was interpreted by the individual seemed of much greater significance, as were personal relationships.

THE TRAINING FROM THE LEARNERS' PERSPECTIVE: SATISFACTION OR DISCORD?

> Techniques used in schools with teachers listing facts, giving orders and often manipulating [pupils] with punishments and rewards are ineffective when it comes to educating adults. Experience shows that for most people teaching is best delivered through well-supported involvement in new activities – learning by doing. That's what training is all about.
>
> (Pritchard, 1995)

The deficiencies and misconceptions of this model of children's learning in schools seem glaring. It is even more disturbing when published in a respectable newspaper in a section entitled 'Training trainers – the future starts here' (ibid.). How true is this statement in the experience of mature student teachers embarking on professional training and development?

Jennifer felt that she learned by doing, although she thought that she needed:

> a fair amount of guidance to start with. I don't pick up new ideas very easily. So I'll probably be one of those who needs . . . very clear tasks 'this is what you are going to do, this is how you are going to set about doing it, now you'll get on and do it'.

During a later interview she mentioned that the practical sessions at the university had been most useful, as she did not see herself as 'a very creative person'. She mentioned a new language learning session where at the end she felt exhausted but also a 'feeling of exhilaration: I've learnt something!'. Jennifer tried to observe as many different teachers in action as possible and found this very helpful and 'reassuring'. The training, in her opinion, had not been too traumatic and she had not wanted to walk out. At the end of the first week she had been rather frustrated and felt she needed 'more to get my teeth into'. Her academic learning preference was not being fully met. She would have liked to have obtained a reading list much earlier. She was also worrying about assignments and her teaching placement, as she is a mother of three small children. When questioned about pair and group activities Jennifer clearly preferred pair work as she found this 'easier [and felt] less threatened . . . . I am not very good sometimes with other people.' At the end of the third interview her worries were no longer assignments or teaching practice. She felt very tired and had 'read more books in the last 10 weeks than in the last 10 years'. She found the course:

> very interesting . . . I started off not being sure if I was doing the right thing. I think that during the course of the term I felt a lot happier, particularly as a result of the first teaching practice. I did quite enjoy that, having not expected to.

In her diary the frustration she felt over a special-needs placement was evident: 'disappointed again that so much time seems to be wasted, also that tasks are not more relevant to individuals. My own inclination would be to "tailor make" projects much more around their obvious interests'. She decided to use her own initiative and resolved the situation to her satisfaction. Another instance where annoyance showed through in her diary was after a lecture on professional development: 'I found this very politically biased, was annoyed. I was amazed that most of the students seemed to swallow the line. Surely it is the lecturer's job to put forward facts, or both sides [of an argument] and let students decide for themselves?' It is interesting to note that Diana's reaction was radically different to the same session: 'the talk about the history of [the] teaching profession . . . was brilliant'.

Jennifer was very pleased that she had managed to discipline herself and organise her own learning. She was surprised that other, younger students have found this difficult. She acknowledged that previously 'having worked to deadlines and juggling commitments' must have been useful, as well as 'being used to having less time for yourself as a woman and a mother'. In this area she acknowledged that her prior experience had been most useful in supporting her learning. Occasionally her age (mid forties) has caused her to feel slightly excluded; at her teaching experience school she was the only student teacher over twenty-six years of age. She had not felt able to join in social activities to the same extent as others, although she was aware that her social relationships had developed. She perceived a self-evaluation question- naire, completed after the first school experience, as useful as it was 'good to accept that there were certain things that were good even if there are others that need work', as she tended to be 'overly critical' of herself.

During the interviews it became evident that Diana's experiences were quite different from Jennifer's. In her diary she clearly articulated which aspects of the training she found useful: practical sessions, tutorials, talks/ lectures (as long as these were not repetitive and gave practical examples) and IT sessions. She was critical of seminars where she was 'not sure what the purpose is, what we are aiming to do', or where she was not sure if the tutor was professing personal views or research findings. She similarly disliked the number of handbooks she had to refer to (one general handbook, one for modern languages and one for the educational and professional strands) as 'it's quite confusing having to refer to several booklets . . .'. 'In the lectures/seminars etc. it is the teachers' experiences they tell us about that have been most useful – something concrete to seize on'.

Both Diana and Jennifer felt that work in school was essential. Diana wrote that it was a 'new experience for me to see how a teacher approaches a class of non-academic pupils'. She was 'impressed that the school has organised . . . seminars so well'. She felt her learning and development was hindered by not being able to watch more teachers. 'I'm impatient to get into the classroom more'. At the same time she is finding 'some (not all!) of the lectures [and] seminars more frustrating as it now seems I've had lots of theory and not practice! (Although the practice also seems daunting, but I feel the longer I don't do any, the more daunting it will seem.)' The major area of discord in Diana's training, a feeling that she is being given too much theoretical foundation and not enough hands-on experience as the school is slow in organising this, became even more evident in her diary entry of 1 November:

found the theory side of things frustrating – especially when we are shown e.g. class management videos showing perfectly behaved pupils – this bears no relation to the classes I see at school X!! . . . I definitely find it frustrating that here at school X I don't feel I have the opportunity to witness the theory we've been talking about at university – e.g. class management, using the target language, putting work up on walls. And despite the fact that everything you read/hear says you shouldn't have low expectations of slower pupils it does seem to be the case here (teachers have overtly said this to me . . .) . . . . And I find that as I read through various books about good teaching practice I'm saying 'that's all very well but try that at school X!'

The university has evidently not prepared her for the 'reality' as she sees it.

There is a definite dichotomy in Bristol. Student teachers are unlikely to experience periods of autonomous learning and reflection, where tutors 'get out of their way', as the course timetable is so full of input. In contrast Swedish student teachers have few contact hours with their tutors and spend much time reading, researching and preparing model lessons, alone, in pairs or in small groups. Those who followed the traditional four-year training course felt that there were periods when they had little or no contact with their tutors at HLS. 'Does the HLS know that we exist? . . . Who is responsible for our training? I would not know whom to ask [for advice]' (Ingrid). Swedish student teachers do not have personal tutors as the Bristol students do.

The Swedish student teachers generally felt that there was too strong an emphasis on general pedagogic studies in Stockholm and not enough time spent on subject-specific methodology. They suggested that some methodology classes should be open to all students of modern languages, looking towards similarities in language teaching and learning rather than presenting a narrower perspective which each language could transmit. They articulated a strong uncertainty about the relationship between general pedagogy, methodology and didactics:

> In pedagogy we discussed frequently that there should be a 'red thread' which should underpin all our work. One should see work as a spiral and . . . avoid segmentation. . . . But then in methodology classes short spurts of activity, short moments in each lesson and variation [was] . . . what we learnt. That does not fit!
>
> (Bibi)

Not one was able to define the differences between methodology and didactics, but they held much clearer views about pedagogy. With hindsight the newly qualified teachers said that their training lacked 'overarching aims' and a debate which would raise questions such as 'What sort of pupils do we want? Why are we teaching them languages?' (Bibi). 'We hardly ever discussed learning or discipline problems during our training . . . it should have been discussed' (Solveig). Some of their tutors were firmly anchored in schools whilst others 'appear to have taught 30 years ago'.

The Swedish students articulated a sense of discord, lack of harmony between theory and practice, not dissimilar from Diana's views. They felt that there was a 'sense of a "right way of teaching" and organising a lesson' across Sweden, which was part of an implicit 'unwritten tradition of language teaching' (Greta). 'Lessons should be interesting . . . one should be bubbly, happy and full of initiatives in order to get pupils interested' (Bibi). 'And one has to fight with all the other problems students have – that they don't want to be there and that they have problems at home – and still get them very enthusiastic about English, German, French. . . . That makes me feel . . . oh, I'm a bad teacher . . . I think we need to change everything in schools'. The 'training lacks strategies . . . the message, which is not wrong, was "find your own way". The problem is: how long does this take?' (Greta).

In contrast to the English experience, school mentors (*handledare* = a person who leads you by the hand) in Stockholm have to observe every lesson the student teacher teaches. This can cause conflict and frustration when student teachers feel that they have to adapt to a particular teaching style in order to get good feedback (Ewa). Some also highlighted a sense of insecurity and incompetence in an earlier practice when they were expected to teach in the target language but their own subject knowledge was still limited.

In contrast to the other Swedes, Ewa felt that the strongest influences on her development had been her pedagogics tutors and the reading she had done for this course. She said that all assumptions, her own and those of her tutors, were subjective and needed 'to be carefully scrutinised and reassessed from time to time'. She further intimated that 'experienced teachers such as our tutors often are quick to categorise students' and that 'they form their views too quickly'. She saw herself as a 'quick and efficient learner' whose learning needs had been addressed to some degree. I would think it likely that her views reflected the fact that she had been trained by the practical pedagogical route, after many year's experience of working in different countries and environments. She presented a view which other mature students echo.

English student Suzy liked the participatory side of training sessions but mentioned that this is quite foreign to most people. She 'learns a lot from doing it . . . all the stuff we are doing (in college) is really valid but I have not got anything concrete from it'. It surprised her when a fellow student exclaimed 'I actually realised that they are not going to tell us how to do it!' She felt that some of the 'childish level of participation' was difficult, having 'to play games . . . someone comes in and throws a frog at you . . . can throw people off balance . . . [especially] mature students'. She found her language tutors 'not dogmatic . . . I recognise flexibility when I see it'.

In her last interview before a period of sick leave and deciding to abandon the course Suzy voiced the concern that working in a larger group was a challenge as was 'letting go of traditional notions of [a] teacher' – that is, unearthing and updating her implicit theories. If you are unhappy or lack confidence you are 'not open to learning' in her opinion. She was wondering whether she could cope and, in contradiction to previous statements, admitted to 'worry[ing] more than most'. She liked to be in control and found the course challenging because of a 'change in lifestyle'. She felt the course lacked direction, control and structure and would have liked the purpose of sessions emphasised. She also felt that there was a lack of time. She was uncomfortable in the main seminar room as it was quite small for the number of students. When directly questioned as to whether she perceived any dissonance between herself and her tutors, her answer was an emphatic 'no'. The fact that this was going to turn out to be Suzy's last day, that she felt unable to continue with the course, unable to come to terms with 'some dissonance [which] is the usual state of affairs' (Festinger 1959), will have to speak for itself. Claxton's assertion that 'we can no longer assume that learners' feelings are separable from their mental performance: rather, they are inextricably linked' (Claxton 1990) rang very true in her case.

SUMMARY AND CONCLUSIONS

What have I learnt from carrying out this project? In Bristol, where the tradition of co-operation and goodwill between schools and the university has been long standing, it was less problematic to develop, strengthen and formalise these relationships in a new partnership. A very successful initial training phase of school-based mentors has been described elsewhere (Lazarus, 1994). This closer collaboration probably accounts for the high rate of satisfaction of student teachers with their mentors. In order to ensure that the university-based element of the course continues to match the needs of our students we must continue to question the methodologies we employ, encourage co-operative working and mutual observation by tutors. It is crucial that we and our school mentors are aware of any conflicting implicit and explicit messages that we transmit.

The strongest message from the Swedish student teachers was that they felt that their learning and professional development needs were not supported enough because of the disjointed nature of the training programme. Their language development was supervised by the University of Stockholm, pedagogical sessions were run by one branch of the Institute of Education whilst methodology back-up was provided by another. The student teachers felt uncertain who was in charge of their training overall and felt the need for personal tutors. The methodology tutors, highly praised by the student teachers, were also aware of the isolated nature of their work. They are presently unable to change their programme, integrating pedagogics and methodology to a greater extent, without institutional change. Change in the practical pedagogical training is, however, already under way elsewhere in Sweden. In a paper to be published later this year, Owe Lindberg of the University College of Örebro advocates a training which should be conceptualised as 'teacher training as research, as a process for developing knowledge and as a public debate' (Lindberg, 1995). He presents a model of integrated pedagogical, methodological and didactic training which, I think, would satisfy all the student teachers I interviewed. He also advocates better training of mentors and stronger partnerships with schools.

I could detect no major or striking differences in the beliefs and perceptions by the four tutors which could be attributable to institution or country, rather than gender. They have similar backgrounds and experiences. They have considerable freedom to develop the teaching strategies that they consider most suited to the learning needs of their students. The amount of thought given to the learning needs of their students varied with experience and whether such a debate was encouraged within the institution. The very individual preferences for learning styles expressed by the student teachers I interviewed confirmed my own views, arising from observation of children in classrooms. In these early stages of training dissonance was most marked when messages emanating from the institutions contrasted sharply with realities experienced in schools. This seemed unrelated to cultural or national settings.

If we return to the original question 'to what extent do the explicit and implicit beliefs teacher trainers hold about the learning of their student teachers influence this learning?' I feel that we as teacher educators need to listen to the views and attitudes expressed by our student teachers. We have to adopt strategies and methodologies which allow and support the professional development of the individual. We must acknowledge that for some, in my case Suzy, the tension and stress inherent in the training programme and in our methodology can become too great and they may need to withdraw from the course. I learnt to my regret that my perception of Suzy as a highly intelligent and competent student teacher was at odds with her own view. I found it very hard to let her go and I have been wondering ever since, without being able to find an answer, whether it was our erroneous perception of her learning needs which contributed to her resigning from the course. I hope that I have started to develop strategies and methodologies in my own teaching which should be of benefit to future trainees, enabling them to learn and develop as professionals in a way that is most suited to their needs.

REFERENCES

Brubacher, J. W., Case, C. W. and Reagan T. G. (1994) *Becoming a Reflective Educator – How to Build a Culture of Inquiry in the Schools*, Thousand Oaks, CA: Corwin Press.

Claxton, G. (1990) *Teaching to Learn*, London: Cassell.

Dalin, P. with Rolff, H. G. (1993) *Changing the School Culture*, London: Cassell.

Day, C., Calderhead, J. and Denicolo, P. (eds) (1993) *Research on Teacher Thinking: Understanding Professional Development*, London and Washington, DC: Falmer Press.

Elliott, J. (ed.) (1993) *Reconstructing Teacher Education: Teacher Development*, London and Washington, DC: Falmer Press.

Festinger, L. (1959) *A Theory of Cognitive Dissonance*, London: Tavistock.

Fullan, M. (1993) *Change Forces – Probing the Depths of Educational Reform*, London: Falmer Press.

Hargreaves, D. H. and Hopkins, D. (1991) *The Empowered School*, London: Cassell.

HMI (1988) *Secondary Schools: An Appraisal*, London: HMSO.

Hopkins, D., Ainscow, M. and West, M. (1994) *School Improvement in an Era of Change*, London: Cassell.

Husén, T. (1989) 'Schools for the 1990s'. In *Scandinavian Journal of Educational Research*, Vol. 33, p. 1.

Lazarus, E. (1994) 'Partnership in initial teacher training between university and schools – some reflections on the training of school based mentors'. Paper given at the annual ATEE conference, Prague.

Lindberg, O. (1995) 'En möjlig lärarutbildning'. In *Lära till lärare*, Uppsala: Maud Jonsson Centrum för Didaktik.

Madsén, T. (ed.) (1994) *Lärares lärande*, Lund: Studentlitteratur.

Miller, R. (1993) *Lehrer lernen – ein pädagogisches Arbeitsbuch für Lehreranwärter, Referendare, Lehrer und Lehrergruppen*, Weinheim and Basel: Weltz.

Ministry of Education and Science (1993) 'The Swedish way towards a learning society – a review'.

Pritchard, S. (1995) 'Training trainers – the future starts here'. *The Guardian*, Careers Supplement, 7 January, p. 2.

Sjödahl, L. (1990) 'Are attitudes only of theoretical interest?'. *Scandinavian Journal of Educational Research*, Vol. 34, p. 4.

Chapter 7

Understanding the apprenticeship of observation in initial teacher education

Exploring student teachers' implicit theories of teaching and learning

Peter D. John

This chapter continues the concern of the last with the implicit theories of learning held by new entrants to the teaching profession, but it zooms in on one vital aspect of that concern, and tackles it in a more literature-based and qualitative research framework. Peter John's question is: where do student teachers' beliefs about learning come from? And his answer is that they derive, very largely, from students' own experience of teaching and learning at school. As pupils sit in classrooms, they are not just learning chemistry or French; they are developing intuitive models of what it is to be a teacher, and what, in their judgement, makes a 'good teacher' or a 'bad' one. These implicit theories channel the way students approach the business of learning to teach, and the kind of teacher they aspire to become. Peter draws on the life histories of PGCE students, and uncovers the effect on their views of teaching and learning that their own school experience has had – especially the teachers who have made a particular impact on them. These implicit views sometimes create barriers to their learning.

INTRODUCTION

Research on teacher thinking has highlighted the fact that teachers develop and hold implicit theories about their pupils, about the subject matter they teach and about their roles and responsibilities and about how they act (Bussis *et al.*, 1976; Ball, 1990; Olsen, 1981). These implicit theories are not neat constructions and complete reproductions of the educational theories found in academic texts; rather they tend to be eclectic rules of thumb and generalisations drawn from 'personal experience made up of beliefs, values, biases and prejudices' (Clarke, 1989, p. 309). However, despite quite extensive knowledge about the nature, structure and substance of experienced teachers' tacit knowledge very little time has been spent exploring the sorts of understandings and beliefs that prospective teachers bring with them to initial training. This chapter therefore examines the extent to which student teachers' experiences as pupils influence their developing conceptions of teaching and learning.

IMPLICIT THEORIES AND THE APPRENTICESHIP OF OBSERVATION

It is now widely accepted that when student teachers enter courses of professional training they are not *tabula rasa* but have imprinted upon their minds numerous images of teachers, teaching styles and learning processes which have been shaped by what they have witnessed as pupils. Thus conditioned they build up assumptions, expectations and schemata about teaching and learning which are often unconscious and unquestioned; these basic assumptions then shape their ability to absorb new models of teaching, adopt different attitudes or behave in fresh ways.

For Dan Lortie (1975) these predispositions and experiences are central to the on-going process of becoming a teacher. According to Lortie (1975), teacher socialisation begins not when students start their practicum but the day they enter school themselves as pupils. The folklore of teacher education attests to the continued and powerful influence of these latent models to affect the professional learning of new teachers. However, as Lortie (1975) is at pains to point out, this apprenticeship is not a true one in the literal sense of the word since it does not represent the acquisition of an occupation's technical knowledge. It is instead more a matter of imitation, which when generalised can form itself into a set teaching style. This process, claims Lortie, is enhanced by the fact that most of these imitative understandings are created from viewing the teacher from the pupil's perspective. He comments:

> It is improbable that many students learn to see teaching in an ends-means frame or that they normally take an analytic stance towards it. Students are undoubtedly impressed by some teacher actions and not by others, but one would not expect them to view the differences in a pedagogical, explanatory way. What students learn about teaching, then, is intuitive and imitative rather than explicit and analytical; it is based on individual personalities rather than pedagogical principles.
>
> (Lortie, 1975)

A number of studies have echoed Lortie's (1975) views and have shown the entering dispositions of student teachers to have had an influential effect on the professional learning that occurs in initial teacher training and beyond. Nias (1989) has indicated that teachers sometimes into their ninth year in the classroom still draw on these latent images, a factor which shows not only the longevity of such experiences but also attests to their depth and intensity. Other studies using biographical and life history methodologies have shown that the effect of these experiences is influential in two ways: first they provide clear positive and negative role models (Knowles, 1992) and second, as Ross (1987) argues, this informal modelling process is highly selective with student teachers using a mixture of approaches and styles culled from their own experiences as pupils.

According to other researchers the effect of the apprenticeship can also be felt at the subconscious intuitive level. Here the recurring symbols of authority combined with hierarchical methods of teaching encourage among students a dependency and deference towards authority and a belief in the 'jug and water' theory of learning (Zeichner *et al.*, 1987; Nias, 1989). In an attempt to trace the influences of these pre-training experiences, Amarel and Feiman-Nemser (1988) tracked a small number of students through their professional training courses and found that school experience, if anything, reinforced their earlier views and had a conservative effect on their thinking and practice. This 'wash-out' effect appears to be related to the power of the apprenticeship to guide and control what student teachers take from courses of initial training.

In contrast, two longitudinal studies by Hollingsworth (1989) and John (1991, 1992) found that student teachers' entering dispositions integrated dynamically with their experiences to produce professional learning and that their pre-programme beliefs served as filters for processing their experiences. In an earlier study, Calderhead (1987) similarly examined the interpretive frameworks student teachers used when undergoing professional training and found that students often entered courses with dysfunctional conceptions of teaching. And although courses helped them acquire utilitarian knowledge on planning and evaluation, students tended to plateau early and rarely acquired the kinds of pedagogical thinking needed to engage pupils in the detailed process of learning.

The outcome of much of this research suggests that the apprenticeship of observation is hugely influential in the professional learning process and plays a central role in shaping what student teachers take from their courses of training (Grossman, 1990). Yet despite some scholarly activity we still know very little about the nature of these pre-training influences and the sorts of variations that exist within and among different subject areas. The study described below draws on in-depth life history interviews with forty-two history PGCE students carried out during the initial weeks of the course. The results describe not only the nature of their experiences but also the ways in which their conceptions of their subject and their learning of it both influence and guide their own evolving beliefs and understandings about teaching. The chapter ends with a series of suggestions regarding the sorts of strategies that can be adopted by teacher educators and mentors to help students overcome the negative effects of this apprenticeship.

UNCOVERING BIOGRAPHY

Exploring the implicit theories of beginning teachers requires a journey into their biographical experiences so that one can understand something of the contexts that have shaped their beliefs and viewpoints. One such context is the historical experience of lives lived in classrooms, for it was there that prospective teachers first experienced the classroom life to which they will return as student teachers (Britzman, 1988).

The life-history-based interviews (Woods, 1987; Knowles, 1992; Troyna and Sykes, 1988) were semi-structured and comprised mainly open-ended questions aimed at eliciting information about the students' experiences at school, the teachers who had taught them and the influence they had had on their current thinking. In addition, they were asked about their own learning experiences and the sorts of teaching that appeared to enhance it. The interviews explored the nature of their current concerns. Prior to the interviews, the sample of students were asked to observe a number of teachers during their first serial visit to schools and further questions invited them to compare these observations with their own experiences. Finally, the sample of students were shown two video tapes of practising teachers – the first was regarded as embodying current notions of 'good practice' in history teaching; the second was a tape of what might be loosely regarded as 'traditional' teaching. The students were asked to view the tapes and comment freely on the lessons; their views were then explored in the formal interviews.

In analysing the data the aim was to render the material into a form which best described the experiences of the sample. The study was therefore guided by the principles of ethnographic semantics which makes the meaning the informants give to their verbal expression the major focus of the analysis (Spradley, 1979). In addition, a constant comparative analysis was used which allowed concepts and themes to be selected through a stepwise iterative analysis of the transcribed protocols (Miles and Hubermann, 1984). The themes were then clustered around broad labels which described the statements in terms of the subject's actual comments.

THE FINDINGS

The student teachers' initial conceptions of teaching were to a large extent dominated by their own experiences of teaching and learning. Their retrospective recollections were both vivid and diverse while at the same time being the lens through which they viewed current classrooms. Of crucial importance was the host of latent models their own experiences as pupils had provided them with. These tended to cluster around both positive and negative images. In terms of the former it was in the main a particular teacher, usually of history, who stood out. This 'significant other' not only provided the external motivation for the students to continue to study but also provided them with an informal quality control mechanism that helped shape their initial conceptions of teaching. One remarked: 'when I was in the third year I had an inspirational teacher. She knew what she was talking about and communicated the subject clearly and imaginatively.' While another did not really enjoy the subject until she studied at advanced level, 'it wasn't until I went to the local sixth form college that I really began to enjoy history. The teacher was excellent – she was caring and thoughtful and took time to explain things in detail if you didn't understand.'

One student was even able to trace her decision to become a teacher back to the experience of being a pupil in one teacher's class. The following extract (*S* is the student, *I* the interviewer) therefore shows the power and lasting intensity of these early role models,

> *S*: I want to be like Mr. Gatjik – he was one of the main reasons why I decided to teach – he was one of my gurus at school. His lessons were so stimulating and his room was full of the creative efforts of his pupils. There was always a different tone in his class, it was different to the others.
>
> *I*: In what ways?
>
> *S*: Well because he cared and took time over problems. He would explain things after the class and was always cheerful and enthusiastic about history. You could tell he cared and he knew his subject so well. I'm not sure I can live up to his example.

As indicated above, when describing good teachers, the students tended to concentrate heavily on personal characteristics such as enthusiasm, charisma, warmth, likeability and good subject knowledge. Similarly, when asked about the teacher they would like to become, they drew heavily on these character- istics and described themselves as wanting primarily to be liked and respected. This was reinforced in many of the interviews by the notion that teachers were born, not made, and that teaching was about being charismatic. The endogenous nature of teaching was continually seen as a reference point or a standard which sometimes created doubts in their minds about their own self-concept. One commented:

> A good teacher is one who shares their enthusiasms with the children, who knows what they're talking about and who is passionate about their subject. I want the children to like me – but not in a pally way but by being respected for my knowledge and for the interest I take in them. The good teachers I had, had powerful personalities – not in an evil sense – but had a sense of humour, were quick witted and lively. I'm not sure I have what it takes; I don't think I'll be able to improvise like they did.

This final point echoes across the data: the notion that teaching is an extemporary, unplanned, spontaneous performance. Such a reaction appears to reflect Lortie's (1975) view that the apprenticeship of observation provides only a limited view of teaching. As pupils these students had limited access to their teachers' actions and their pre-teaching thought processes. He comments:

> Students do not receive invitations to watch the teacher's performance

from the wings; they are not privy to the teacher's private intentions and personal reflections on classroom events. Students rarely participate in selecting goals, making preparations or post mortem analyses. Thus they are not pressed to place the teacher's actions in a pedagogically orientated framework.

This line of thinking is further exemplified in the following extract where the student compares her old teacher to one teacher she has just observed:

> My old history teacher wouldn't have let things slip like she did. He was liked and respected. We knew what we could and couldn't do; we knew the boundaries. But he was so enthusiastic and helpful. He taught tradition- ally but he was also a character with it – I'm not sure if I have such a persona – he was able to enthuse through the sheer force of his character.

While another felt that:

> A good teacher has to be enthusiastic and have a willingness to see history as being a whole subject as being linked to their personality. Good teachers also try to understand children's problems and are friendly and thoughtful not distant and remote.

In contrast to the positive images provided by these 'significant others', their descriptions of bad teachers tended to focus more on the poor quality of their pedagogical skills. Bad teachers were thus seen as overdidactic, badly organised, with poor communication skills and unable to control classes. The transcripts are littered with illustrations of these 'poor' teachers and the frustration felt by the students at their inabilty to learn in their lessons. The preponderance of textbooks and note taking as the primary teaching tech- niques was widespread and often the students contrasted their new ex- periences against this apprenticeship of observation and felt, somewhat ironically, that current or as some claimed 'more modern' practices seemed to have improved the quality of teaching.

One typical comment was:

> With my teachers, well it's difficult to remember – but they were always dominant and didn't really care that much about you as a person. They just delivered the material, usually badly and then left.

In the following extract one student shows her anger and concern at not being able to question or discuss an event:

> It's difficult remembering back but it was mostly didactic teaching – the teacher always stood at the front and delivered a lecture. There was very little teacher-pupil interaction we just scribbled down the notes as fast as we could. I remember questioning one teacher and daring to ask whether the Gunpowder Plot as it was presented in the text book was in fact accurate? I was told to be quiet and not to ask such questions. In my

classroom I would love such a question to be asked and would encourage debate and interaction.

Some compared their experiences of bad teaching to the positive teaching they had recently observed on the video:

> When I did history at school it was the exact opposite of what I've just seen. He fired the pupils up; he put so much of himself into it and the variety – we just sat down, took notes either from the text book or from dictation. It was all geared to passing exams. Here the children get a chance to think and to participate. It was so much better than the way I was taught. I was bored to tears.

Another recollected a bad teacher in considerable detail:

> We had one terrible teacher he dictated everything but we still couldn't understand what he said. He was a martial arts expert and had the sort of face that is reserved for those in the Mafia. But his lessons were dead lessons. To start with his classroom management was terrible he would shout at people and threaten them but it still didn't work. Sometimes he would grab somebody and make an example of them and call them his slave. Some of us found it funny but many were terrified. He had no teaching techniques – he babbled; he was badly organised and sometimes brought the wrong notes to the lesson. We didn't always tell him though we just pretended to write and had a rest.

Much of this poor teaching tended to come from the selective and fee-paying sector although a substantial amount was also evident in comprehensive schools. Paradoxically though, when asked about the origins of their passion for and continued interest in history, the respondents claimed that these were developed despite rather than because of much of the teaching they had received. For many the spark came from their family: visits to historical landmarks and museums from an early age often provided the motivation for the subject. For others it was an intense personal interest which began at a young age with stories and objects. For some the significant teacher provided the spark while for others it was a case of the teachers being marginalised in order to continue with the motivation. In the following extracts the reasons are exemplified:

> S: Most of our teachers just gave us the information and expected us to learn it.
> I: So why did you study history and how did you come to enjoy it?
> S: It's funny isn't it – yes I loved history and still do – I didn't know any different. I suppose although I was always interested in history for as long as I can remember. We – our family – always visited museums and historical sites you know the National Trust that sort of thing. I was always reading history books and stories about the past, so I

suppose my interest came before I went to school – I probably would have studied it regardless of the teachers.

I always enjoyed history. I loved visiting castles and churches and places like that. I used to imagine what it would have been like living there all those years ago. The interest has always been there and even when the teacher was boring me to death I still loved it. I used to go home and read the notes I'd made and think about things. I suppose I learned despite them.

I remember working in rows and answering questions from the text book. The teachers were very strict and I can't remember ever going on a visit.

I: If things were so bad why did you study history and why the continued interest?

S: Well I just enjoyed it I suppose. I loved reading about the Wars and I spent hours collecting details about famous people and events. I worked a lot in my own time and built up my interest that way.

These negative experiences, however, tended to inspire the students to want to compensate their pupils for the poor teaching they had received. Thus the idealism and enthusiasm for alternative teaching styles. Most were impressed by the small amount of 'good' teaching they had been exposed to in their limited observations; the desire to copy and to model themselves on these practices was evident in the urgency by which they expressed their views. And yet, in terms of their understanding of learning, their ideas were still very simplistic and straightforward. Despite expressing a desire to enthuse and engage pupils through the use of varied methodologies, the power and depth of their own previous learning experiences proved to be a constant barrier to the emergence of more powerful models of teaching and learning.

Time and time again the students maintained that enjoyment was bound to lead to learning and yet virtually all the sample equated learning with the acquisition of factual knowledge. Despite their enthusiasm for the alternative methods of teaching observed in schools these were still regarded as peripheral to the learning process which was in their eyes based firmly on the learning of events, dates, facts, places and people. Learning was therefore seen as predominantly teacher driven with the teacher deciding what and how things should be taught. In this conception learners had to be roasted not brought gently to the boil; the omnipresence of this view is supported by similar findings in other subjects (Ball, 1990; Wilson, 1990).

One student claimed: 'I was taught all about famous people, places and dates. It was hard going at times but these things are essential if children are going to go on to study history seriously'. While another felt that after observing a successful role-play he was decidedly 'positive about the method' but quickly qualified the initial enthusiasm by claiming that 'although the children were enjoying themselves and were clearly putting their knowledge to good use they surely can only do that at the end of a topic because there has to be such a lot of hard nosed learning of dates, events, places and people before they can go on to interpret those facts in the form of a role-play'.

Another, while attacking some of her own teachers' limited approaches, still maintained the primacy of rote learning as a necessary prerequisite to the use of what she called 'modern teaching methods:

> I don't really want to use the methods of teaching I was subjected to but children still need something akin to it. I know children need to see other points of view and teachers should treat their points of view with respect but they still need facts before they can explore the outer regions of history – or any subject for that matter. Perhaps the best approach is to lecture regularly but follow that up with quotes and discussions.

This belief in the primacy of factual knowledge as a basis for learning was closely related to a complex set of pedagogical beliefs. Here their limited and unproblematic view of teaching and learning contrasts markedly with their espoused belief in the need for alternative, more varied and interesting teaching methods. The early observations had clearly influenced their thoughts but had made few inroads into their more deeply held implicit theories. This view is supported by Reynolds (1989) who claims that student teachers maintain their own remembered experiences in order to question positions both presented and observed rather than to interrogate the pedagogical value of their own previous experiences. The following exchange illustrates this point:

> S: The teacher on the video was good, don't get me wrong, and he was different to my teachers but I would like to have seen more. What did the children know when they left the class? Okay, they may have understood a bit more about the horror of the war and the effect it had on families but what about the causes and the build up? It's easy to get carried away.
>
> I: So the causes and the events are more important than the human effects?
>
> S: No, of course not, but they have to know these things and really teaching them directly seems to me to be the only way. I wish we had seen that teacher teaching the causes using that more open ended method, now that would have been really instructive.

These initial conceptions are also supported by an intricate concern network. Of central importance is their anxiety about their own levels of expertise in their subject, a factor which seems to contradict earlier research which suggests that students feel they already have enough subject knowledge to begin teaching (Freeman and Kalaian, 1989). Perhaps this finding is a reflection of the subject and the nature of undergraduate degrees which are increasingly based on the 'cafeteria style' curriculum thus producing the historians' obsession with their period. Many talked at length about not knowing enough history and of lacking the breadth or depth needed to teach the National Curriculum adequately. This was closely linked to their on-going concerns about classroom management and discipline. Many of the positive role models mentioned were perceived as being good classroom managers but having spent hours on the receiving end of such approaches, the students were led to believe that such success is 'in-bred' and you either 'have it or you don't'. Such a view probably originates from seeing teaching from the pupils' point of view and yet when faced with the complexity of teaching such a simplified conception may be a hindrance to the learning and development of particular teaching and control strategies. One commented:

> You have to be in control in the class otherwise they will take control of you. Lessons have to be on the teacher's terms and if you don't know the topic you're teaching then you immediately have a problem. Good teachers know their subject and children know when you know your subject. Once they spot your weakness you're in trouble – how do I tell a class I don't know the answer – what will they think of me? The respect will just disappear.

Another felt he had forgotten all of his degree already:

> I can't remember a damn thing about it – it's a giant blur! What happens if they ask me an awkward question? I'm not confident as it is but if they kept asking me something obscure or even simple, well God knows what might happen! The thing is I probably won't have class control either to fall back on because I'm not the bold type, I don't have the charisma that some of my teachers had.

SUMMARY

It would appear from the above findings that student teachers enter courses of professional training with powerful images and deeply held beliefs about teaching and learning. These implicit theories may be inhibiting factors when they confront the realities of teaching and learning. They can be summarised thus:

- The students appear to assume that good teaching is closely linked to a positive set of personal and affective characteristics. Thus they see warmth, enthusiasm, commitment, humour and patience as being at the epicentre of exemplary teaching. Making pupils feel good and then being liked in return is seen as central to successful practice. Non-exemplary teachers, on the other hand, are seen as possessing poor pedagogical skills, lacking in imagination and badly organised.
- The feeling of having lost out in their own school days also appears to instil in the students a need to create in their classrooms and in their own teaching

those conditions that were missing from their own experience. However, these urges are balanced by the ingrained belief that content knowledge can only be transmitted through the use of such traditional methodologies.

- The apprenticeship of observation also seems to have influenced the students' understandings of how and what pupils should learn. These conceptions are based on the idea that learning is equal to knowledge extension, that the more pupils are exposed to knowledge, the more they will pick up, and the more practice they are given at handling data, the more they will eventually learn. Such beliefs may be a result of subject enculturation – a process which has been enhanced by a university experience that seemed to continue rather than challenge their underlying assumptions.
- If, as seems likely, student teachers assume that their own experiences of learning are generalizable across the wider school population, their recollections of their own interests and abilities may become the yardstick by which they judge the success or otherwise of the particular teaching strategies they have observed.
- The interviews revealed that the images these students have of teachers, teaching and learning are oversimplified mainly owing to the preponderance of a pupil-centred perspective. Such a position could limit their propensity to interrogate their own and others' teaching and may thus inhibit the emergence of more powerful alternative conceptions of teaching and learning.

DISCUSSION

The analysis of the data yields a number of interesting conjectures concerning the power and influence of the apprenticeship of observation. At the heart of their preconceptions is the belief that teachers are born, not made; this is a highly individualistic interpretation which reinforces the image of the natural teacher who somehow possesses talent, imagination, warmth, charisma and intuition.

Such a set of implicit theories has implications for teacher preparation in a number of ways. First, they serve not only to devalue educational theory but also to give rise to a stand-and-deliver conception of teaching. Second, since the teacher appears as a completed product, *the need to change or even to explain one's activity may seem relatively unimportant. In this world of the self-made teacher, pedagogy becomes a natural extension of one's character* and teaching style becomes all pervasive (Britzman, 1988). This is not necessarily bad since teaching style is bound to reflect something about the individual. However, what is worrying is the way in which such ideas, if not challenged, could lead to the continued mystification of the process whereby teaching style develops.

This self-made view of teachers is closely linked to the notion that teachers are experts. A common fear expressed by the interviewees was of not knowing enough to teach, a factor which may be linked to the specificities of their subject. Hidden behind this concern was the expectation that teachers must be certain in their knowledge and that 'teachers are supposed to know the answers'. This 'absolutist' view of teaching probably reflects deeper beliefs about the nature of knowledge and knowing, which are themselves not always open to inspection. It may also be that their 'intuitive epistemology' leads many to persist in the view that knowledge primarily consists of discrete units of understanding which have to be transmitted through teaching and acquired through learning.

This view of the teacher as the fount of all knowledge was shaped and internalised during their primary, secondary and undergraduate education with the result that by the time they entered teacher training, the expert image had become naturalised. Knowing the answers also appeared to influence their conceptions of the teacher's ability to think on his or her feet. Their own teachers appeared to know the material backwards; becoming an expert in their eyes therefore meant not only being confident in the subject matter but also being able to control the flow of knowledge from teacher to pupil. The teacher–pupil relationship was thus reduced to a conduit along which the flow of knowledge passed undisturbed from one to the other.

As a result of their anxieties the students often displayed a need for recipes to deal with classroom control and management because they were already familiar with the teacher being seen as a controller. In consequence, courses that appear not to deliver these 'tips for teachers' may appear as speculative idealism rather than concrete realism. This factor alone should make the critical analysis of teaching an even greater imperative. For unless these implicit theories and the concern network that supports them are 'outed' and put to the test, it is likely that their taken-for-granted assumptions may be reinforced and refined during their school-based experiences.

CHALLENGING ASSUMPTIONS

How can teacher educators address this apprenticeship of observation? How can student teachers be provoked into examining and then rethinking their own experiences and memories of teaching and learning? What strategies can be used to challenge these latent beliefs and implicit understandings?

Research in cognitive science has outlined the resistance encountered when attempts are made to alter deeply held beliefs (Allport, 1954; Nisbet and Ross, 1980). Similarly, research into conceptual change indicates that three pre-conditions are necessary before individuals can be encouraged to alter their values and beliefs: first, individuals must be dissatisfied with current understandings; second, they must be presented with compelling and practical alternatives; third, they must be offered ways in which they can graft new beliefs onto the old. It is therefore incumbent on teacher educators to create the necessary conditions so that these internalised beliefs and models can be effectively challenged (Grossman, 1991).

Unlike much of medical education, the professional preparation of teachers is not about presenting to the student teacher a large and complex body of knowledge, although many student teachers appear to believe that the learning of teaching will be something akin to the learning of other academic subjects (Calderhead, 1994). Instead it is more a process of preparing students to learn to adapt their emerging skills to changing environments and conditions, and even to initiate change by being inventive and creative; this can only be done, however, if many of their implicit assumptions are challenged from the outset.

Subject teacher educators are ideally placed to do much of the latter. Both Hargreaves (1988) and Lacey (1977) have claimed that patterns of social-isation into teaching are distinctly related to particular academic disciplines, while Bernstein (1971) and Becher (1985) have commented that induction into teaching also means being introduced to a particular subject subculture and community. Furthermore, method courses are by their very nature intensely practical and are ideal places to explore theoretical issues in a context that can provide student teachers with the opportunity to reflect upon classroom practices from a broader perspective (Grossman, 1991). The following five broad strategies are therefore suggested as foci for subject teacher educators to help their students address their initial beliefs and images of teaching.

First, subject teacher educators can help liberalise their students by ensuring that subject seminars mirror an open learning environment where values, feelings, beliefs, ideas and practices are presented, explored, ex-amined and evaluated in an open, relaxed and constructive manner. This permissive atmosphere (Abercrombie, 1953) may then act as an antidote to the students' own school and undergraduate education and is a vital first step in getting them to rethink their implicit understandings and beliefs.

Second, the findings of this study and others indicate that intending teachers need to rethink their basic understandings of their subject and the pedagogy which supports it. Knowing and understanding a subject in an academic sense is, as Dewey (1902) has shown, very different from under-standing it in a pedagogical sense. Thus the transition to pedagogical thinking (Feiman-Nemser and Buchmann, 1985) needs to start as much with the subject as it does with pedagogy. Methods courses are ideally suited to help prospective teachers examine, question and explore the nature of their subjects and where necessary to reconceptualise their knowledge so that teaching and learning can take place.

Subject method tutors also have close relationships with classrooms and schools. An essential part of the process of reconceptualising is therefore the need to engender a creative tension not only between theory and practice in a formal sense but also between what is observed in schools and the more idealised models presented in coursework. This reconceptualisation process means helping students to rethink the ways in which they believe pupils best learn their subjects. This can be done creatively by asking them to collect data by observing, shadowing and questioning learners so that their own beliefs can be tested against both the available theory and the reality of schools.

Third, student teachers need to be helped to enquire into the nature of teaching and learning. Here they should be encouraged to understand both the contextual and social constraints which influence educational achievement. Inevitably this will involve them in exploring and thinking about the personal dimensions of being a teacher. Here it is not enough for student teachers simply to be exposed to classrooms; they have to be guided to understand the complexities they encounter and to make connections between the thinking that underpins practice. As has been shown, too often student teachers use their experiences either to confirm or deny what they have seen and rarely analyse it in a meaningful sense.

Helping students make the most of their observations of skilled practitioners can also take them beyond the pupil's-eye view of teaching. Looking backstage and understanding the reasons and thinking behind the pedagogical choices of teachers is therefore vital. In method courses students need to be taught not only how to observe and analyse lessons but also how to engage practitioners in a meaningful dialogue in a nonjudgemental way. Getting at the rich complexity of teachers' planning, for instance, and being able to access their 'in-flight' (John, 1993) thinking can enlarge the horizons of new teachers while at the same time helping them put their beliefs into context.

Furthermore, allowing them the space to experiment with new and different teaching and learning styles is vital if the effects of the apprenticeship of observation are to be addressed. Higher education has a vital role to play here in that it is free from the contextual constraints of schools and provides an open, safe arena for students to explore practice.

More directly, there are numerous examples of the ways in which courses have harnessed research methodologies such as life history and biography (Clandinin et al., 1992; Troyna and Sikes, 1988) to get students to confront their implicit theories. In addition, various critical incident and dilemma frameworks (Berlak and Berlak, 1981; Tripp, 1993; Woods, 1994) provide an ideal conceptual underpinning for a number of writing strategies aimed at exploring the key events that have shaped their ideas. Here questions and issues can be framed with reference to their own beliefs and memories in a rigorous way which allows issues to be discussed and anecdotes to be examined.

Fourth, a growing body of literature on school improvement and teacher effectiveness reports the beneficial effects of collaboration (Fullan, 1991, 1993; Hargreaves and Hopkins, 1991; Nias, 1989). However, student teachers often enter teaching not only with a highly individualised conception of teaching but also with a born, not made, view of teacher development. Creating situations in which they can be encouraged to collaborate in the planning and execution of lessons, in the construction of materials and resources, and in the process of post-lesson and general reflection may help them to see teaching as a matter of creative teamwork where collaboration is not only a focus for the challenging of existing beliefs but also a process for creating new ones.

Fifth, prospective teachers can be helped to reconfigure their existing beliefs if they are presented with a variety of alternative models. Research has shown that student teachers often take an imitative stance towards teaching, a process which is accentuated by the numerous exemplars they have been exposed to during their own education. Providing them with different models could be a powerful way of challenging their pre-existing notions.

Grossman (1991) urges subject teacher educators to go further and 'overcorrect' their latent beliefs by providing 'extreme examples of innovative practices' (p. 350). Work in cognitive psychology, she suggests, shows that providing a balanced account for and against a particular perspective can lead student teachers to listen only to the evidence that supports their prior point of view. Her advice is that going to extremes in teacher education may 'ensure that when beginning teachers drift back towards the models they have observed for so long in classrooms – which they almost inevitably will – they may still retain elements of the approaches or beliefs advocated by teacher educators'.

This modelling of reasoned practice can also help student teachers make the necessary connections between goals, strategies and outcomes in their own and others' teaching; also it may help them see the intricacies of a particular teaching strategy from the perspective of the learner. Developing empathy with learners, for instance, may also enable student teachers better to understand common pupil misconceptions and difficulties within their subject area.

Finally, this direct modelling should be complemented by tutors ensuring that their own teaching styles are consistent with their espoused theories and actions. This not only will help the process of reinforcement but may also help student teachers to see the value in thinking about and reflecting on practice as they themselves experience it. Attending to both the style and substance of subject sessions is therefore of central significance (Adler, 1993).

CONCLUSIONS AND IMPLICATIONS

The research presented in this chapter shows that prospective teachers enter courses of training with a vast array of personal theories about teaching, learning and learning to teach. These are grounded in their own experiences and are constructed from their prolonged experience of compulsory classroom life. However, their views are both incomplete and oversimplified. And yet these partial understandings are likely to play a significant role in shaping their practice and may not only underwrite many of their demands for a predominantly practical training experience but also influence their already ingrained suspicion of theory in whatever form it is presented.

Critics of formal teacher preparation see this apprenticeship as an ideal precursor to school-centred competency-based training. Here the process of learning to teach is viewed as simply a matter of emulation combined with a good smattering of common sense; the students are thus seen as pre-formatted discs waiting to be programmed by the real experience of teaching. However, learning from experience alone can be miseducative and may reinforce the pervasive belief that there is little to learn about teaching. Shulman (1987), for instance, in his study of students without formal training, concluded that 'without frameworks for understanding teaching and learning, how beginning teachers without professional preparation interpret experience may prove problematic' (p. 11).

For this to be avoided we need to consider simultaneously both what students bring to courses and what they take from them. Enacting this is, however, more difficult than stating it. For it is clear that student teachers' implicit theories resemble a tangled web where each thread has been woven from the fabric of their own unique experience, with the strands relating to their own school experience proving to be particularly powerful and resilient. Helping them first to recognise and then to confront these beliefs is vital if their early conceptions of teaching are to be re-examined and the origin of those beliefs questioned. Direct encounters with teaching and learning can provide part of the answer but this has to be accompanied by a planned teacher education curriculum which sets out not simply to find common ground between students, tutors and mentors but actively explores the more problematic recesses of personal experience.

REFERENCES

Abercrombie, M. L. J. (1953) 'Emotional security as a condition for change'. *Health Education Journal*, Vol. 11 (3), pp. 112–17.

Adler, S. (1993) 'Teacher education research and reflective practice'. *Teaching and Teacher Education*, Vol. 9 (2) pp. 159–69.

Allport, G. (1954) *The Nature of Prejudice*, Reading, MA: Addison-Wesley.

Amarel, M. and Feiman-Nemser, S. (1988) 'Prospective teachers' views of teaching and learning to teach'. Paper presented at the annual meeting of the American Educational Research Association, New Orleans.

Ball, D. L. (1990) 'Becoming a mathematics teacher through college based and alternative routes'. Paper presented at the annual meeting of the American Educational Research Association, Boston, MA, April.

Ball, S. (1992) *Markets, Morality and Equity in Education*, London: Tufnel Press.

Becher, A. (1985) *Academic Tribes and Territories*, Milton Keynes: Open University Press.

Berlak, H. and Berlak, A. (1981) *Dilemmas of Schooling: Teaching and Social Change*, London: Methuen.

Bernstein, B. (1971) 'On the classification and framing of educational knowledge'. In M. F. D. Young (ed.) *Knowledge and Control: New Directions for the Sociology of Education*, London: Macmillan.

Britzman, D. (1988) 'Cultural myths in the making of a teacher: biography and social structure in teacher education'. *Harvard Educational Review*, Vol. 56 (4), pp. 442–55.

Bussis, A. M., Chittendon, F. and Amarel, M. (1976) *Beyond Surface Curriculum*, Boulder, CO: Westview Press.

Calderhead, J. (1987) 'The contribution of field experience to student primary teachers' professional learning'. *Research in Education*. Vol. 40, pp. 33–49.

Calderhead, J. (1994) 'The reform of initial teacher education and research on learning to teach: contrasting ideas'. In P. D. John and P. Lucas (eds) *Partnership and Progress*, Sheffield: University of Sheffield Papers in Education.

Clandinin, D. J., Davies, A., Hogan, P. and Kennard, B. (1992) *Learning to Teach: Teaching to Learn*, New York: Teachers College Press.

Clarke, C. M. (1989) 'Asking the right questions about teacher preparation: contributions of research on teacher thinking'. In J. Lowyck and C. Clarke (eds) *Teacher Thinking and Professional Action*, Leuven: Leuven University Press.

Dewey, J. (1902) 'The child and the curriculum'. In J. A. Boydston (ed.) *John Dewey: The Middle Works, 1899–1924*, Vol. 2, Carbondale, IL: Southern Illinois University Press.

Feiman-Nemser, S. and Buchmann, M. (1985) Pitfalls of experience in teacher preparation. *Teachers' College Record*, Vol. 87 (1), pp. 53–65.

Freeman, D. J. and Kalaian, H. A. (1989) 'Dimensionality of specific measures of teacher candidates' self-confidence and educational beliefs'. Program evaluation series no. 23, East Lansing: Michigan State University.

Fullan, M. (1991) *The New Meaning of Educational Change*, London: Cassell.

Fullan, M. (1993) *Changing Forces: Probing the Depths of Educational Reform*, London: Falmer Press.

Grossman, P. (1990) *The Making of a Teacher: Teacher Knowledge and Teacher Education*, New York: Teachers' College Press.

Grossman, P. (1991) 'Overcoming the apprenticeship of observation in teacher coursework'. *Teaching and Teacher Education*. Vol. 7 (4), pp. 345–59.

Hargreaves, D. (1988) 'Teaching quality: a sociological analysis'. *Journal of Curriculum Studies*, Vol. 20 (3), pp. 211–31.

Hargreaves, D. and Hopkins, D. (1991) *The Empowered School*, London: Cassell.

Hollingsworth, S. (1989) 'Prior beliefs and cognitive change in learning to teach'. *American Educational Research Journal*, Vol. 26 (2), pp. 160–89.

John, P. D. (1991) 'Course, curricular and classroom influences on the development of student teachers' lesson planning perspectives'. *Teaching and Teacher Education*, Vol. 7 (4), pp. 359–72.

John, P. D. (1992) 'A qualitative study of student teachers' lesson planning perspectives'. *Journal of Education for Teaching*, Vol. 17 (93), pp. 301–20.

John, P. D. (1993) *Lesson Planning for Teachers*, London: Cassell.

Knowles, J. G. (1992) 'Models for understanding pre-service and beginning teachers biographies: illustrations from case studies'. In I. Goodson (ed.) *Studying Teachers' Lives*, London: Routledge.

Lacey, C. (1977) *The Socialization of Teachers*, London: Methuen.

Lortie, D. (1975) *Schoolteacher: A Sociological Study*, Chicago: University of Chicago Press.

Miles, M. and Hubermann, M. A. (1984) *Qualitative Data Analysis: A Sourcebook of New Methods*, Beverly Hills, CA: Sage.

Nias, J. (1989) *Primary Teachers Talking: A Study of Teaching as Work*, London: Routledge.

Nisbet, R. E. and Ross, L. (1980) *Human Inference: Strategies and Shortcomings in Human Inference*, Englewood Cliffs, NJ: Prentice Hall.

Olsen, J. K. (1981) 'Teacher influence in the classroom'. *Instructional Science*, Vol. 10, pp. 259–75.

Reynolds, M. C. (1989) *Knowledge Base for the Beginning Teacher*, Oxford: Pergamon.

Ross, E. W. (1987) 'Teacher perspective development: a study of pre-service social studies teachers'. *Theory and Research in Social Education*, Vol. 15 (4), pp. 225–43.

Shulman, L. S. (1987) 'Knowledge and teaching: foundations of the new reform'. *Harvard Educational Review*, Vol. 57 (1), pp. 1–22.

Spradley, J. (1979) *The Ethnographic Interview*, New York: Holt, Rinehart and Winston.

Tripp, D. (1993) *Critical Incidents in Teaching: Developing Professional Judgement*, London: Routledge.

Troyna, B. and Sikes, P. (1988) 'True stories: a case study in the use of life history in initial teacher education'. *Educational Review*, Vol. 43 (1), pp. 3–16.

Wilson, S. M. (1990) 'The secret garden of teacher education'. *Phi Delta Kappan*, Winter, pp. 204–9.

Woods, P. (1987) 'Life histories and teacher knowledge'. In J. Smyth (ed.) *Educating Teachers: Changing the Nature of Pedagogical Knowledge*, Brighton: Falmer Press.

Woods, P. (1994) *Critical Events in Teaching and Learning*, Brighton: Falmer Press.

Zeichner, K. M., Tabachnik, B. R. and Densmore, K. (1987) 'Individual, institutional and cultural influences on the development of student teachers' craft knowledge'. In J. Calderhead (ed.) *Exploring Teachers' Thinking*, London: Cassell.

Chapter 8

PGCE student visit to The Gambia

'Learning experience of a lifetime' or 'just more savannah'?

Paul Weeden and John Hayter

The last chapter looked at the way young people absorb educational messages from their own culture. The present chapter stays with the focus on the learning of PGCE students, but examines the ways in which their implicit views of teaching and learning are brought to the fore and challenged by a brief, intense immersion in a very different national culture: a two-week field trip by a mixed-subject group of students to The Gambia. In terms of 'method', we are back with the small-scale reflective approach of Chapter 6, which not only offers insights into the views of students, but also provides food for thought for the lecturers on the trip. Do such experiences of 'culture shock' have any effect, and if so, what, and is it lasting? We might draw an analogy between this type of field trip and the commonly valued exposure of students training to be secondary teachers to life in the contrasting culture of a primary school: do we really know what the long-range effects of this are, either? The chapter provides particularly clear demonstrations of three key issues: the lack of transfer which such experiences have – echoing Mike Wallace's concerns in Chapter 2; the ways in which adults, like children, defend and withdraw when the learning that is demanded of them feels 'too much'; and the phases that learners go through, as they put it, from 'disorientation', via 'coping', to eventual 'equilibrium'.

INTRODUCTION

Young people in the UK are almost certainly more globally aware than at any time in the past. But what kind of understanding does such awareness provide when informed primarily by the media and by personal tourist journeying? What kinds of experience allow enhanced understanding; and what blockages to learning in this context are identifiable, and how might these be addressed? In particular what is the potential of a visit to an African country by a group of postgraduate students training to be teachers? Does it provide an opportunity for new and lasting insights into the education and culture of such a country together with some awareness of the role of aid? Does it inform their understanding of 'education' and give a fresh perspective on the education system in their own country? Or, as the title of this chapter suggests, is there a speedy retreat into the comfort of identifying just 'more of the same'?

The theme of this chapter is an exploration of the learning that occurred for two tutors and fifteen PGCE students during a two-week visit to The Gambia in April 1994. Though regular visits can become routinised, our concern was to observe and reflect on the process, to get beyond the excitement of the novel and to face some of the significant issues which arise during such experiences. This chapter therefore is an account of work in progress, with the findings informing the planning and execution of the next visit. It offers a piece of Schonian 'reflection on action' which focuses on the blocks and beliefs of the tutors in this situation as much as the students.

The chapter has three sections which explore the issues from differing perspectives. First, John Hayter, who has considerable experience of working in and visiting Africa, outlines the background to the visit and his thinking in developing the programme for the 1994 visit. Second, Paul Weeden reflects on his learning during his first visit to The Gambia. Third, the types of learning that occurred will be exemplified and explored through evidence gathered from the students during the visit.

THE BACKGROUND TO JOHN HAYTER'S INVOLVEMENT

John Hayter has had professional links with Africa for some thirty years. He worked for five years in the then new University of Malawi, first lecturing in mathematics and then becoming involved in teacher training. The challenging professional opportunities which were presented have had a marked effect on the rest of his career; in particular he has maintained an interest in the multiple dilemmas of education in developing countries and the possible contributions of educators from outside those countries. More recently involved in teacher education in the UK, he has been aware of the interest that many British postgraduate students have in education in developing countries. For some this interest emerges from an idealised 'needs' image. For others it reflects a personal commitment to engage immediately or at some later stage after training.

Over the last nine years he has been involved in an ODA-funded working link between the School of Education at the University of Bristol and Gambia College. The College is the major tertiary institution in The Gambia, a small West African country with a population of about 1 million people. Gambia College's School of Education was, until 1986, solely concerned with training primary teachers. The link arrangement was specifically designed to enable Bristol tutors to work with Gambia College in the development of a secondary teacher training course for junior secondary (now middle) schools. In addition to contributing to the teaching at summer schools and participating in curriculum consultations, the link has enabled a variety of other activities. One idea which emerged was the possibility of Bristol students making a study visit to The Gambia based at the College. There was immediate interest from Bristol students and ready co-operation from the College.

Since 1989, five largely self-funded visits have taken place, each one a juggling exercise with the uncertainties that surround a system that places little emphasis on advanced planning but excels in problem solving on the day! The overall aim of these visits has been to enable students to learn about education in a 'developing' country – policy, practice and issues, with particular reference to the culture and the current part played by aid. Previous visits had been enhanced by opportunities to meet Gambian student peers and to work in college and school classrooms with them. The experience of a rich and contrasting culture, the relative material poverty, the emerging and somewhat precarious educational provision, the blatant tourist traffic and the ambiguous role of the multiple aid agencies, have made an immediate and powerful impact on most Bristol students. Living and working together intensively for a two-week period has provided opportunities to reflect and work as a group on these experiences. The impact has continued well beyond the visit. For many, it seems to have been an experience that has acted as a marker for the PGCE year and, for some, appears to have been influential in decisions to work overseas or to put aside such possibilities now seen as personally inappropriate.

Experience on earlier visits had raised awareness of both the potential of such an opportunity for learning and also of some of the inhibitors which are present in that situation. Amongst the latter were:

- problems in achieving professional engagement with peers in another culture (e.g. getting beyond purely social contact; seeing the unfamiliar as a professional context for them);
- new experiences and partial knowledge leading to naive interpretation (e.g. the sun, sea and friendly people being seen as making for a desirable place to stay for ever);
- the tourist ambience providing enticing enrichment such as discos and parascending but distracting from engagement with local traditional culture.

PLANNING THE 1994 VISIT

The 1994 visit provided a challenge for the tutors to address these issues by interventions in the programme and by developing new ways of working with the group of students. Familiarity with the situation and with people in The Gambia meant that John Hayter took major responsibility for the planning of the visit. Fifteen students were selected from twenty-five applicants giving representation to all seven subject groups on the Bristol PGCE course. Some had travelled extensively before, a few in Africa; two or three had spent some childhood years with parents living in developing countries. The students had to contribute three-quarters of the cost individually and one-quarter was raised by joint activities. This then was a self-selected group that potentially was highly motivated because of the personal investment both in terms of time and money.

The intention was for the Bristol students to experience the Gambian education system by visits, meeting people, working in schools, reflecting on issues and personal responses. The programme was designed to provide a flexible structure, allowing for individual interests and initiative, that drew on the opportunities which the College link provided without 'taking advantage' of Gambian colleagues and students who were not making a reciprocal visit to the UK. The visit took place immediately after Easter overlapping with the opening of the new school and college terms in The Gambia. The College appointed a tutor as mentor and his role was vital in making arrangements and dealing with the unplanned and the unexpected as well as providing informal teaching, interpretation and insight during the visit. During the visit students were encouraged to reflect on expectations and experiences, to raise hypotheses and share insights. Diary keeping was encouraged and quickly valued by the majority. Group sessions allowed more public review and analysis.

The programme emerged over the period of the visit, in part pre-structured but responsive also to issues arising for this group and opportunities which were created or presented themselves. Activities, grouped under three heads, are listed in Figure 8.1.

LEARNING FROM CONFUSION: REFLECTIONS BY PAUL WEEDEN ON A FIRST VISIT TO THE GAMBIA

I was a new PGCE tutor, having been in post only six months when I undertook this visit to The Gambia. I had no experience of work overseas although I had travelled to Africa, North America and Europe as a tourist. As a geography teacher for twenty years with an interest in development issues I thought I was knowledgeable about the complexity of the issues relating to education and aid in Africa, but my understanding largely derived from secondary sources. The reflections which follow consider two parallel themes: my inner conflicts as a participant in a new experience that was causing confusion, and my outer persona as a tutor whom I felt had to be seen to cope with uncertainty. These tensions appeared to enable me to act as a filter for John, as someone through whose eyes he could experience The Gambia anew. The following narrative explores the dissonance that occurred for me.

I was surprised at how much I was affected by the transition, within six hours, from a wet, damp, April morning in England to a hot (34°C), dry,

Education	Culture	Aid
Lecture by Gambia College tutor on history and current system	Living in Gambia College accommodation and encounters with students	Visits to Action Aid HQ and field centre
Visits to primary, middle and high schools, teacher seminar, training college	Visits to capital, local travel and markets, tourist areas	Meet VSO teachers in schools, Gambia College and seminar
Teaching in middle school with Gambia College students following consultation with teachers	Travel 200 miles inland to stay at Georgetown, visit stone circles and village on North bank. Informal music/dancing sessions	Evidence of aid in schools and colleges
Discussions on observations in schools and on nature and role of education in The Gambia	Visit to Banjul Museum to increase knowledge of the history and culture of The Gambia	Debate with Gambia College students on the motion 'Aid creates dependency'
Planning activity with Gambia College students on the future development of the Gambian education system	Dilemmas session exploring cultural issues that face visitors to The Gambia	Dilemmas session exploring issues that face aid workers/ visitors to The Gambia
	Sharing life histories session with Gambia College students	

Resource library, informal contacts, impromptu meetings, diary keeping, group life, group tasks, group discussions

Figure 8.1 Activities undertaken during the 1994 visit

sunny afternoon in The Gambia. The culture shock of being greeted by Gambian dancers on arrival at Banjul Airport was accompanied by an unease about how to behave in this strange environment. I did not know if I could take photograph of the dancers and they felt threatening, not welcoming. The five-minute drive from the airport through the dry savannah with its red soil and large termite hills was concluded by the arrival at our accommodation at Gambia College's Yundum site, which at first sight seemed to be very basic.

My inner reaction was to retreat into a cocoon but my outer persona joined in a wide-ranging discussion with John and Momodou (our Gambian mentor) about the details of our trip and life in The Gambia. I was happy to stay in the safety of the compound and amazed at the boldness of those students who wanted to venture out to the local village to go shopping. At an intellectual level I was able to reflect on the individuality of reactions to experiences while feeling to some extent paralysed by my own emotions.

On the following day the experience of driving through the towns and villages was observed as if from a distance; everything seemed so untidy, ramshackle and different. The poverty was striking; there appeared to be people and animals everywhere and there was no recognisable order or framework to understanding. I was fascinated by what I saw but found it difficult to know how to relate to the local people. How much should you pay for a banana? How can you cope with someone who hassles you for money because you are white and rich? Who can you trust to change money? I wanted to take photographs in Banjul for use in my teaching, but if I took pictures of people should I pay them or risk offending them?

The first few days' experiences were difficult and exhausting; the movement from one event to another seemed never ending. I was living on my wits, observing, asking questions, trying to make sense of it all, eating unfamiliar food and existing in accommodation that was clean but very basic. There were some things that I recognised from previous experiences, such as the savannah landscape, but they were isolated points and weren't connecting with each other. The retreat into my room at the end of the day to swelter through another night became a partial relief. My inner confusion caused by multiple dissonances asked whether I would survive, and what was I contributing to the group? As a tutor I tried consciously to exploit this inner dissonance to stimulate discussion and was surprised that so few admitted to experiencing the same confusion. I felt at the time that this inhibited my tutor role because I was unable to initiate discussion about these issues.

After two days I made a connection with my normal life in Britain. As we drove along the main and very busy highway through Serrekunda, the largest urban settlement, with its rows of shops selling everything from car spares and fridges to meat and clothes, I suddenly realised that this road was similar to my local shopping street, a main arterial road in Bristol which also has its variety of shops and people going about their business in a seemingly random and chaotic manner. This realisation was significant in giving me a framework to understanding. Was this realisation a disinhibitor or inhibitor? Did it allow me to relax and feel more comfortable, to enable me to gain some understanding about the local economy or was it a model that froze my understanding by comparing The Gambia to Britain? By this time the tutor in me was beginning to realise that my confusion was helpful and could be used in discussions to promote questioning amongst the group.

By five days into the visit I was beginning to be accustomed to the heat, was no longer so shocked by everyday scenes and was recognising the pattern and order that existed. My knowledge of The Gambia had increased from immersion in different activities but I was still not entirely comfortable with the experience and part of me would have been happy to leave if the opportunity had arisen. I felt more able to act as tutor and help plan and execute learning experiences but was aware that John was leading and I was merely following him blindly. The long journey up country to Georgetown was tiring. At first the changing countryside was fascinating as we travelled through villages and savannah and saw people and animals engaged in their daily lives. The potholed road made travel both slow and uncomfortable and soon even the countryside became less interesting – just more savannah. On reflection now I feel that if I had felt more comfortable or knowledgeable I might have been able to exploit the geographical potential more.

Over the next few days our experiences challenged my inner self while providing many opportunities for reflection on how the experiences could be used for learning. The teaching in a school, a scorpion that was killed and our visit to a tourist camp, with its swimming pool, bar and views of the river, were a few examples of experiences raising dilemmas which we as tutors discussed and decided that we wanted to explore further with the students. The inner/outer tension came to the fore with these dilemmas. Were they just personal questions or relevant to a wider understanding? The discussions with John helped clarify my own thoughts and contributed to a sense of satisfaction that I could still function despite my continuing inner dissonance.

I was able to reflect on my changing emotions with our situation when my reaction to returning to our college base in Yundum was to join in the cheering on reaching the safety and tranquillity of our 'home', a marked contrast to my feelings on first arriving there. By the end of the two weeks my inner self was beginning to feel more at ease. I had enough understanding of life in The Gambia to get by with basic everyday living and was finding 'a place to stand'. There were some notable personal achievements: haggling with a modicum of success, using the bush taxis by myself, and even a hint of regret at having to return to England just when I was beginning to feel more comfortable. What had I learnt as a tutor? That during an intense experience like this there will always be learning but that opportunities have to be taken as they arise and outcomes cannot be predicted.

In the departure lounge at Yundum Airport I felt superior: how could these tourists know what we had experienced over the last two weeks, the range of emotions and the learning that had occurred? Arrival back in Britian was another shock; everything seemed so ordered and tidy, the signs of wealth so obvious and my reintegration into normal family life almost instantaneous. It seemed to be almost impossible to convey the discomfort of my experience to others and to explain my feelings. I rapidly gave up trying.

Why had I as a geography teacher, who had taught about developing countries for twenty years, been so shocked by experiencing the reality of life in The Gambia? It seems to me now on reflection some months after the event that my inner turmoil was largely emotional arising from dissonance between personal values, the frustration I felt in the face of poverty, the knowledge that I have a comfortable lifestyle that I am unwilling to relinquish and the difficulty in finding 'a place to stand'. What had I learnt? Was it 'the learning experience of a lifetime', affecting my life for ever, or would it fade and become an experience like many others, 'just more savannah'? Writing this chapter, preparing for another visit and discussing my learning have enabled me to begin to make more sense of the experience.

HOW DID THE PLANNED EXPERIENCES IMPINGE ON LEARNING FOR THIS GROUP?

This section considers our understanding of some aspects of the learning that occurred during and after the visit. Evidence was collected in a variety of ways before, during and after the visit. The evidence presented here comes from five sources: observations and discussions with individuals, written comments/questionnaires completed at different stages during the visit, the 'dilemmas' session on day 12, summer-term assignments arising from the visit and taped interviews with groups of students back in Bristol. After the evidence was collected four significant aspects (reflection, phases of engagement, type of engagement and transfer) that appeared to aid or inhibit learning were identified. These are discussed in some detail below and will be used to suggest lessons about learning that could be implemented during future visits.

Reflection on their learning

The uncertainties and stress created by exposure to a different culture combined with the creation of a close-knit group identity provided opportunities for reflection on and sharing of learning. Reflective opportunities encouraged were personal journals, individual and group discussions and completion of an assignment on return to Britain. This section comments on the value of two of these reflective opportunities.

First, the tutors spent many hours discussing ways that the students could be encouraged to discuss some of the issues that confronted the group. Our concern was that some complex issues were not being considered because of a lack of understanding or ability to make sense of them. Personal dilemmas had been encountered during the visit, such as how to interact with Gambian counterparts with a difference in spending power, whether to spend the equivalent of a week's pay for a Gambian primary teacher on a ten-minute parascending ride at a tourist beach, as well as professional dilemmas such as where is it most effective to place qualified VSO teachers: in primary, secondary or tertiary institutions? A workshop was organised where five dilemmas that had arisen during our trip or on previous trips were discussed and some responses to the professional dilemma about where to place a UK-trained VSO teacher are outlined below.

The majority of the students felt it was most appropriate for a VSO teacher to work in Gambia College or a high school where they could 'influence the whole system' or 'inspire future Gambian teachers'. The explicit reason for these comments seemed to be that young, relatively inexperienced, British teachers have more subject knowledge and expertise in a variety of teaching and learning styles than Gambians and would be able to pass this on. A significant minority thought the VSO teachers should work in primary or middle schools because they felt that children were being disadvantaged by the large number of unqualified teachers. Work in a school like this might 'encourage more stimulating activities than I observed. I reckon much of the under-achievement here is because pupils are put off by very authoritarian methods.'

How were they making these judgements and did they have sufficient knowledge of the education system in The Gambia to engage successfully with the issue? Certainly there seemed to be a commonly held implicit theory that knowledge and skills developed in the British education system can be transferred to The Gambian education system. Some expressed concern that they didn't feel they knew enough to make this sort of decision. This raises questions about their capacity to learn from the experiences of visiting schools but also about how much it was possible to absorb in a two-week visit.

Second, the focus provided by a reflective assignment was important. This can be illustrated by contrasting the reflection achieved by students who did an education assignment about The Gambia visit on their return to Bristol. There were two difficulties here. One was in relating their own experiences to points or issues raised by the literature about education in Africa, the second was the nature of the task. Two students chose to edit jointly the video footage taken during our stay while others chose to write individual assignments on educational issues they had observed during their visit. The concrete activity of editing and discussing their purposes required the students to make decisions about the issues they wished to cover, and they were able to engage constructively with their own experiences and reflect upon them. However, they made only limited reference to other sources of information, maybe because of time constraints. In contrast some who wrote individual assignments had difficulty in relating the literature to their own experiences and tended to write academic assignments that contained no indication of their personal learning from the visit. This is not an unusual phenomenon for PGCE students but the difficulty was perhaps magnified by the contrasting cultural context.

The dynamics of engagement

Even in a two-week stay there were identifiable phases of engagement as Paul Weeden's account suggests. A three-phase model of engagement is proposed in Figure 8.2. It is suggested that these phases may be similar to those experienced by many during major life events such as leaving home or moving job. At these times the individual has to deal with uncertainty and may be more open to learning. During the visit to The Gambia the cultural and physical differences meant there was enormous uncertainty for many which had the potential, as suggested in the title, to become a learning experience of a lifetime. It is suggested that the extent of the learning that occurred was determined by the individual's type of engagement with the experience.

No time scale is proposed for the phases because they were not investigated during our visit, but if Paul Weeden's account is used as a guide, phase 1 was two to three days; phase 2 about one week. It is suggested that there may be considerable differences between individuals in their experiences. Some may not experience phase 1 and move rapidly through phase 2 in a couple of days, others may not reach phase 3 during a two-week visit.

The first phase proposed is one of disorientation characterised by uncertainty and insecurity in the face of the unfamiliar. Such a phase is evident before departure where information is sought but is difficult to grasp or apply and continues on arrival with the impact of felt reality, with its many dimensions, and the challenge to comprehend it in the light of previous

PHASE 1	PHASE 2	PHASE 3
Disorientation *uncertainty and insecurity in the face of the unfamiliar*	Coping *constructing a framework that ties together isolated reference points*	Equilibrium *finding a 'place to stand'* a) quasi-equilibrium *a comfort zone is established where there is isolation from the environment* b) dis-equilibrium *intense discomfort and possible abandonment of the experience* c) stable equilibrium *an accommodation is achieved which incorporates both cultures*

Figure 8.2 Phases of engagement model

lifetime experience. This phase may be shorter or non-existent for some more experienced travellers.

The second phase is a coping phase, in which particular necessities of living were mastered – buying in the market, making effective use of public transport, knowing how to operate in simple social situations. Experience has suggested that the programme structure can facilitate this transition, for example by appropriate briefings, staged experiences and access to advice. Nevertheless coping has to be established as a personal experience.

The third phase is termed equilibrium. We consider it to have a variety of forms which may be end points in themselves or for some will be transition stages. The first form we call 'quasi-equilibrium' – a 'comfort zone' where personal theories and prejudices are held with minimal testing or challenge, allowing a personal sense of tranquillity. Many enjoying a package holiday in a developing country adopt such a strategy which copes with new experiences by absorption into personal theory. This form of equilibrium is adequate at some level but can be challenged by the unexpected or dramatic experience which exposure to a very different culture often brings. It could be suggested that the lifestyle of expatriate communities, in colonial days and since, bears witness to the long life expectancy of such a phase given the conditions and the will to maintain personal theories of neo-colonialism.

The second form is described as one of dis-equilibrium in which a sense of dis-ease is maintained in spite of, or perhaps because of, growing awareness. An illness, a difficult personal experience or a growing knowledge of local politics might prompt such a state. Short visits might be survived but longer stays are likely to be terminated. Within a short-term visit by a group the effect might be minimised by peer and tutor support but VSO teachers in a challenging environment with little felt support or expatriate aid workers in a politically oppressive or stressful situation may demonstrate it.

The third type of equilibrium is termed stable equilibrium, in which uncertainty is accepted, differences are acknowledged and the unexpected is expected, yet stability is not inert. Links and connections are sought both within the new situation and to the individual's existing knowledge and value system. The parts and the whole can be dealt with at some level both emotionally and intellectually. In the longer-term context, anthropologists develop the ability to take up such a position, but it is surely more challenging for the aid worker, missionary or expatriate employee.

A short-term visit by students can make only limited inroads into this third stage. Yet recognising differing reactions of peers, appreciating the complexity that lies behind the observed events and adopting a position of not understanding may be initial steps to such stability.

The costs and benefits of engagement

In this section the learning that occurred during two planned events is explored. They are categorised as low-cost and high-cost experiential events and were activities focusing on education, visiting schools and teaching in a middle school.

Low-cost experiential events: visiting schools

In the first few days several schools were visited. These visits were planned as a low-cost experiential introduction to Gambian schools and the school system but the response of the Bristol students to these visits illustrated that exposure to an experience can result in differential learning. The first school visited was closed for the holidays, there were no children, it was the end of the first full day when the group was still adjusting to being in The Gambia and most people were hot and tired. At the time few questions were asked and the experience was not followed up. Little appeared to have been learnt at the time, though the school made an impression on at least one student who referred to it in an assignment.

The second visit was planned differently. There was a short tour of the school, the observation of one lesson and a reflective session in the evening. The main points that emerged from the written reflective comments were how uncomfortable many felt because of the heat, the feeling of being on show (even as observers) and the teaching style adopted by all the teachers. There were positive and negative comments about the teachers and the school: being noisy, not differentiating work, showing patience, repeating work, the lack of resources, the good discipline, difficulties of communication in English and the contrast with the child-centred approach of British schools. Some comments were critical: 'I wondered about the relevance of the lesson (geography of Gambia . . .) and then recognised the importance, knowing where they live'; and 'As I sat there I felt myself being critical of the style of teaching I was seeing. The teacher was doing things that I would never do . . ..' But also they were looking for the positive: 'Recognised my criticism of how he was teaching, feeling uncomfortable with it'. 'I had a real sense of revelation – the children were all switched onto events and followed throughout. There was a very strong attention being paid to the teacher.'

The subsequent discussion while initially dealing with some of these feelings went on to clarify knowledge about the education system and introduced other issues such as the influence of the culture, the problem of access to education and a comparison of how parents learn from children in both Britain and The Gambia (computer skills in Britain, English in The Gambia). There was a feeling from the tutors that during this discussion the students were reluctant to criticise openly or judge Gambian education. Were there blocks that inhibited criticism? Was it too early in the visit to form strong judgements, the influence of personal discomfort (the disorientation/coping phases) or a lack of confidence of the other members of the group (this was the first real discussion session)? Certainly group dynamics appeared to be an inhibitor as the individual written comments are more openly critical than the discussion.

In conclusion the visits to schools that merely involved observation sessions appear to have been less valuable than planned. The cost was minimal to the students, some were preoccupied with coping with the heat, some did not appear to find it easy to make significant observations (had they done too much observation previously in the course or did they still not have the skills?) and were therefore relatively disengaged from the tasks in hand, and some appeared to be inhibited by the group.

High-cost experiential events: teaching in a middle school

Arrangements were made to meet several Gambia College students to have some teaching experience in a middle school some 100 miles inland. The school staff were very accommodating and teams of Bristol and Gambia College students planned a number of lessons which were given during a morning. This caused uncertainty on the part of both sets of students but once the experience was over there was a sense of satisfaction and a mutual respect of the differing qualities and teaching experience of the two groups of students. Most of the Gambia College students had taught for several years as unqualified teachers before starting their course so were more confident in handling the classes, while the Bristol students had less teaching experience but a deeper subject knowledge and a wider repertoire of teaching methods to employ.

These teaching sessions were high cost for all and some disengaged completely from the experience by opting out with varieties of ill health. However high cost had high rewards. The preparation and teaching sessions were stressful, but were later felt to be one of the most significant parts of the visit. There were contrasts in the ways that students in different subjects handled the experience. The two modern foreign language students had no Gambian counterpart to work with so had one less 'inhibitor', but they also appeared to have an advantage in that they had a lesson format to work to that fitted comfortably with the Gambian system. They were comfortable talking to the children and encouraging them to talk. Furthermore they managed to get them to participate in a game even though this is an uncommon classroom style in The Gambia.

In contrast the chemistry student felt frustrated because 'they wanted us to teach a certain thing and yet they had nothing to teach it with. Wanted us to teach a reaction of iron and sulphur or calcium and oxygen. "Have you got any iron, sulphur?" "May have" was the reply – probably thought it a strange question. I don't know how else to teach it. What a nightmare for the kids if you can't see it happening . . . awful . . . don't know how useful to teach about iron and sulphur. Seemed very western.'

Other problems were experienced by the humanities teachers because of the local nature of the subjects being taught. The Bristol students felt uncomfortable because of their lack of knowledge about topics such as 'The Gambian Democracy' or 'Minerals in West Africa' or 'Islam'.

There was, however, real engagement in this activity combined with learning and several Bristol students commented that it deepened their understanding of the constraints of the Gambian system and helped inform their decision making (both for and against) about teaching in a developing country. It exposed implicit beliefs about teaching methods and learning (by doing), professionalism and the difficulties of transferring knowledge and skills from one culture to another.

Transfer and the ability to share

Since the visit took place within the PGCE course year it is relevant to speculate on the effect of this experience on the future work of these beginning teachers. First it has to be noted that the transfer of teaching skill was not an explicit item on the agenda. Teaching some chemistry or geography without the normally expected resources was not expected to be a major focus even though it certainly turned out to be a thought-provoking challenge. Transfer seemed to occur much more at the general, personal level of 'survival' and the ability to use new perceptions and alternative frames of reference on re-entry to the familiar UK environment. Would the much-valued experience leave any mark on their future work as teachers? Clearly this is a significant question, but only tentative responses are possible at this stage.

Two extreme positions might be identified: those who, chameleon like, returned to their British hue on landing at Gatwick Airport as though they had never left the UK; and at the other extreme those whose world view had been so profoundly challenged that commitment to the needs of people in developing countries became a matter of major, even evangelistic, personal concern. In practice neither of these extremes was reached by members of the 1994 group, but a tendency in both these directions was evident in post-visit discussions. There was an intriguing tension between the affective and the cognitive – feelings were recognised, knowledge could be identified, but to what purpose? Some rationalised – the needs of pupils in difficult environments in the UK were as deserving as those seen in The Gambia. Others recognised a personal sense of purpose in the context of education in a developing country which wasn't necessarily experienced at home.

But if complete forgetting and passionate commitment were apparently absent, how did the students attempt to use the experience? The most natural channel would seem to be sharing the experience with others. However, most students expressed disappointment at their inability to do this in a way which satisfied them. Indeed many had consciously stopped trying in the wake of a few failed attempts. For those whose parents or friends had some experience of Africa, the matching and comparing of activities appeared to energise both parties, but this was a minority experience.

The experience is bound to affect their teaching in more general ways. The geographers' teaching of the savannah, or the RE specialists' account of and insight into Islamic culture will naturally be directly affected. The discussion of personal and social education issues will be enriched by the breadth of cultural difference encountered. Pupils may be touched by their teachers' personal experience, and this could well challenge a prejudice or stimulate an interest in other cultures. What this small piece of reflective 'research' suggests is that more attention needs to be given to the problems of re-entry and of sharing and using the experience, if the benefit is to be maximised; and this poses a challenge to us as tutors for the organisation of future visits.

CONCLUSIONS

The visit to The Gambia was rated highly as a learning experience by all the students. Through the study of this particular visit we feel that there are several important lessons for us as tutors.

1 It confirmed our view that such a learning experience is different in quantity and quality from that received second-hand, through books or even video-tapes, for instance. However, we are forced to question how much understanding of Gambian culture and education can be achieved in two weeks.

2 The personal and affective aspects of the visit appeared to be the dominant influences for many students. We need to make sure that there are built in to the programme ample opportunities to explore reactions and feelings, both during the visit itself and retrospectively.

3 The self-motivation of members of the group is crucial and this has implications for the selection of people participating in the visit. The beneficial effect of the trip would probably be diluted, if not actively subverted, if the party comprised conscripts as well as enthusiastic volunteers.

4 A structured visit, with its emphasis on work in schools and direct contact with a variety of Gambian peers, meant that the 'tourist attractions', while important, need not act as distractions from the main reflective purpose of the trip. It is easy (for new tutors as well as students) to get 'swamped' by the demands and impressions of a very different culture, and the provision of structure and support helps learners to stay focused on those aspects of the experience that are of most educational value.

5 Recognising that there may be different phases of engagement is important,

and constructing a programme that enables individuals to learn rapidly is vital. While in the early phases individuals may be open to the experience but have difficulty in understanding, later they may develop mind sets that inhibit learning. Clarifying the phases that students go through has helped us to develop more positive ways of supporting them. We will in future be able to recognise these phases more swiftly and accurately, and devise methods for helping students to adjust, and to extract the most valuable insights from their experience.

6 The ability to extract meaning from experience, and to become more conscious of those taken-for-granted beliefs which have been informing educational activities and attitudes, is undoubtedly enhanced by structured activities. As we noted above, these need to be started in the 'heat of the moment', and continued after the visit, if greater understanding is to be achieved. In students' spontaneous reactions to and comments on education in a very different culture, their implicit values and assumptions stand clearly revealed – clearly, that is, to an attentive observer. The challenge is to draw these responses, in a non-threatening way, to the attention of the students themselves, so that it is their powers of critical reflection which are brought to bear, and strengthened in the process.

7 Individual differences are highly significant. Prior experience, preferred learning style, inner comfort, ease of adjustment all contribute to the level of dissonance and therefore the learning for individuals. Again, our own reflections have helped us to appreciate this diversity, and hopefully to be able to respond to it in a more differentiated fashion in the future.

8 It became evident that transfer of learning to their lives, professional and otherwise, in the UK was more problematic than had been anticipated. Post-visit work to facilitate this needs development.

Chapter 9

Home thoughts from abroad

Terry Atkinson

Chapter 9 continues the examination of cultural influences on learning by looking at the experience of modern languages PGCE students undertaking teaching practice abroad, and of their continental counterparts in English schools. The experience is more extended than that of Paul Weeden and John Hayter's students in The Gambia, and therefore might be expected to have a more lasting and/or a deeper effect. Again we are in 'action research' mode, with the author's assumptions about this learning experience as much under the microscope as the students. Terry presents his data in the form of seven brief pen-portraits of the students' experiences and attitudes, and then draws them together in a general discussion. The experience of teaching and working overseas sometimes leads these students to ask awkward, but pertinent, questions about current UK orthodoxies: the belief in making lessons 'active' and 'enjoyable', for example.

INTRODUCTION

Those entering courses of initial teacher education bring with them a set of assumptions about learning of which they may be unaware. These assumptions may be inhibitive of their own learning and also of that of the children they will teach. To what extent is it appropriate to challenge these assumptions and to make the implicit explicit? One approach to providing such challenge with which I have been personally involved for a number of years is for student teachers to spend part of their training working in schools in another country, observing and undertaking teaching practice as well as attending lectures and tutorials at a local university. I have also worked with students from a number of European countries who have undertaken teaching practice placements in schools in England as well as various university courses. In this study student teachers review the ways in which this experience has developed their thinking through challenging their assumed beliefs about learning. My hypothesis is that exposure to a differently organised model of education reveals the role of local, structural or systemic features, as opposed to more universal elements of learning. This, in turn, may help the student to identify implicit beliefs and to see how they may be generated by the differing contextual features of each country in which he or she has worked.

This hypothesis had been formed by semi-formal feedback from student teachers in post-placement debriefs. An earlier account of a placement is given in Atkinson and Cummings (1992) in which John Cummings, a student teacher recently returned from a placement, begins thus:

> All students on PGCE (one year postgraduate teacher training) courses in Britain should, in my opinion, spend at least one month observing and teaching classes in another country regardless of whether or not they can speak the language, because only by examining or experiencing another country's education system can you begin to see the faults and benefits in your own.

Clearly my own beliefs about the capacity for an extended placement in schools abroad to develop the thinking of student teachers are influential on the student teachers taking part and on the research and subsequent analysis and writing. This will provide one element of the focus of the chapter. I was interested in the extent to which students would perceive differences as either superficial – simply a different way of organising and structuring learning – or fundamental, indicative of different attitudes and intentions which were created by 'systemic' differences and/or resulted from them. Ideally, I wanted students to perceive the universals of teaching and learning and to separate these out from the superficial trivia of merely systemic features. At the least, I shared the view of Woolf *et al.* (1990) that 'the wider the range of experiences, the more likely it is that students will learn and understand what strategies work'.

In their descriptions of perceived differences in learners and teachers, the professional learning of the student teachers themselves is brought into sharper focus. Of course, the students who participate in visits of this nature are a self-selecting group, and as such they may be more willing to participate in active experimentation. However, this does not guarantee the quality or the consistency of their reflection. Taken together with Weeden and Hayter's chapter, some clearer ideas on the value, purpose and effect of such visits may emerge.

DATA COLLECTION

The mode of data collection adopted was in-depth interviewing with a small group of students, effectively the cohort from one year. Interviews were conducted in the subject's mother tongue as it was felt that the quality of reflection would be enhanced. A prior structure for the interviews was devised and followed fairly closely in most cases. This does, of course, bring some constraints: some of the transcripts reveal a failure to probe some interesting replies; and it is difficult to collect uniform data because of the varying nature of the subjects' teaching and other experiences. Perhaps the biggest criticism would be the ethnocentrism of the questioning. The interviews are conducted very much from the point of view of an English teacher educator and the culture of teacher education in this country. Naturally, this was more successful with English subjects than with Spanish subjects and this theme will be considered in the conclusion.

Interviews began with a factual discussion of the precise nature of the experience with questions such as 'what did you do?' and 'what did you see?' These were followed by more probing questions such as 'how do you explain any differences?' Finally, subjects were asked to reflect upon their own personal learning and how their practice might change as a result of this experience. The data is presented in the form of seven small case studies or vignettes. Each of these collects the subject's comments under a number of headings. These headings vary somewhat between subjects because they interpreted questions differently, or had nothing to say on certain aspects, or because they introduced different areas for consideration, sometimes in response to follow-up questions. The data is reported largely in the subjects' own words with some paraphrasing and translation where necessary. Each set of data is followed by a brief analysis which identifies specific aspects of the particular subject as well as themes which are taken up in the conclusion. A social constructivist perspective is implicit in the analysis of this data.

Charlotte

Charlotte was a modern languages student teacher in England who had completed two excellent teaching practices in starkly contrasting schools – one in a highly favoured semi-rural area and the other in a poor, run-down city location. Charlotte spent three months in Porto, Portugal, where she taught English and French in a large state secondary school. She taught for eight hours per week with groups in the 15 to 18 years age range.

Students

Charlotte notes a really incredible difference in pupils' outlook in Portugal – they are much more balanced and mature towards learning, the school, the system, the teacher and teacher–pupil relationships. This she attributes to a more relaxed regime – 'no uniform, come and go as they please, holding hands & kissing in yard', and to excessive rigidity in this country leading to rebellion. When pressed, she adds that smaller group sizes, twenty maximum, helps.

Teachers

The teacher is regarded [in Portugal] as a highly intelligent, intellectual professional person with a list of degrees and people wouldn't dream of addressing a teacher like some do in this country.

Pay is extremely low but the profession is highly regarded.

They're teachers, they go in and teach and then go home and mark. They play less of the role of social worker, nanny, nursemaid and all the other things.

Teacher–student relationships

It's a lot less formal – it's not uncommon for the teacher to go out with the children, there's a lot more physical contact, touching, the children have respect for the teacher so there's a lot less conflict in the classroom. There isn't this dictatorial teacher who's going to tell you to take your coat off when you don't want to, so the roots of conflict aren't there.

Charlotte describes well-motivated, keen students answering questions well but being picked up on errors by a teacher she describes as cruel.

Pedagogy

All the lessons were teacher centred, the kids rarely got the chance to direct their own activities, they spent most of the time listening to her (the teacher).

It was strange really, as if I'd come from England with this lovely theory about what the perfect classroom is and in Portugal nothing like it pertains – windows shut, boiling hot, almost too dark to see – little attention paid to comfort or enjoyment of learners.

Subject's reflections

Interviewer points out the paradox of motivated learners and extremely dull, repetitive methods to which Charlotte replies 'I couldn't quite understand that'. She considers that students are more mature because of greater social interaction due to climate. 'Kids have more freedom, they're treated like little people and are expected to take more responsibility for themselves. For example, they are left to play in the street until they're tired.'

Charlotte notes contrasting views of ability – in the UK there is provision for special educational needs and children are divided up into sets and streams according to ability. Charlotte feels that this seems to set up different expectations with regard to achievement. In Portugal all children are expected to succeed in mixed-ability classes.

In the UK there's a lot more pressure on both teacher and pupil to behave in a certain way. It's a lot more uptight. I don't know if it's because it's taken too seriously but there's a lot more friction, a lot more stress on both sides.

Charlotte felt that she had learned a lot more from this experience than from her year as a foreign language assistant working in French schools, because of her better knowledge of teaching and schools gained from her training course and teaching practices.

Analysis of data collected from Charlotte

Charlotte was an excellent subject to interview because she had had a rich experience in Porto, she was very familiar with the practicalities of teaching and learning and her observations were perceptive. Despite this, in listening to the tapes, it is clear that her own thinking was provoked much more by the interview than by the experience itself. A number of paradoxes arose from her observations such as:

- teachers receive low pay but have high status;
- student–teacher relationships are excellent but teachers rebuke students in a fairly cruel manner;
- students are well motivated but little attention is given to their physical comfort.

Some of these she had been aware of whilst others apparently not, or not until brought to her attention during the interview. Charlotte did not seem unduly troubled by these paradoxes, a reaction which is hard to reconcile with my original hypothesis.

Anju

Anju, another modern languages student teacher at an English university, spent three months teaching and studying in Santander, on the northern coast of Spain. Previously, her teaching practices in England had been in an exclusive independent school and a multi-cultural inner-city school. She taught and observed in two Spanish secondary schools and one primary school. Teaching occupied only two hours per week but for six weeks she was in school all week, so she observed a great deal and/or acted as a support teacher. She taught English, French and Spanish. The classes she taught were mixed ability and mixed gender and spanned the 11 to 16 age range. Anju also received tuition from university tutors and schoolteachers on educational, linguistic and cultural topics.

Students

They all seemed extremely well motivated and they seemed more intelligent than pupils here. I don't think they are more intelligent, they just seemed it. It always surprised me how much concentration they've got, how they can just sit there when they're being given a lot of information, and they just sit there and take notes – in the UK that would be a recipe for destruction.

Anju attributes the perceived greater maturity of Spanish students towards learning to more serious pedagogy – 'not just one big game'. She also thinks that students come to school with a greater motivation to work: 'I read some essays they'd written and the language they use is just amazing for children of their age.'

Teachers

Anju considered that the role of the teacher is the same in each country, although there was greater resentment of the role of form tutor in Spain where it had been recently introduced as part of a series of educational reforms. Like their British counterparts, Spanish primary teachers held long meetings on assessment and reporting. Teachers in Spain seemed to have less responsibility for discipline, perhaps because there was less need of it. Anju was impressed by the sense of humour of Spanish teachers – 'they were more human in the classroom than we are'. However, 'There was one teacher who did have to verbally reprimand a child and he did it in such a way that the child was totally humiliated in front of everyone.'

> Generally, I didn't hear anybody complaining in the staffroom; in the staffroom they all seemed remarkably happy and smiley! That was something that shocked me! Everybody so laid back – nobody grumbling or moaning.

> Senior management was definitely not high profile as in the UK. I couldn't tell you now who was senior management. The teachers worked more as a team – there was less of a hierarchy of roles.

Teacher–student relationships

These were: 'Very different, more informal, laughing and joking in the classroom, it didn't seem nearly so authoritarian. Pupils come in anyway they like, no lining up outside the door.'

Pedagogy

Anju found the foreign language lessons similar to those she had watched and taught in the UK. She was surprised by mother tongue lessons:

> It's amazing what they did in the Spanish language classes. They are very traditional in their teaching methods and we're not. Their way of learning

Spanish language is to learn lots of definitions and language things and just spiel them off, children of a young age, I was amazed. You could never set a homework at my inner city practice school and get the kids to come in next day able to spiel off their definition with all the technical terms of grammar.

When pressed as to why, Anju said:

They're just not in the habit of doing that kind of thing now. We probably put too much emphasis on games, making things fun and make them lazy. But then maybe Spanish children are better communicators because they spend so much time outside on the street instead of indoors watching TV and playing Sega games and such like.

Subject's reflections

Anju would rather have been a pupil in Spain. 'Parents and teachers push you a lot more. I don't know why, I haven't got a clue, it's more a question for a sociologist.' She would also rather teach in Spain because, she feels, teachers are less defined by their job which is not so all-consuming as it is in this country.

We have too low expectations of children in this country, we worry too much about making things enjoyable. It did start me thinking about a lot of things we do here and why we do them. It sets you thinking but you never really use it in a school here. You can't change pupils.

Anju feels that school-based training keeps students in an overly narrow context, recycling existing practice. Going to Spain helped break out of this but so could more diverse experience here in, for example, Steiner schools.

Analysis of data collected from Anju

Anju articulates her observations very clearly over a range of areas. She reports a number of differences between British and Spanish schools. Equally, she feels that there are broad similarities in conditions, the role of the teacher, the intelligence of students and pedagogy. The essence of Anju's interview, which may not be properly conveyed from the extracts, is that there is much in common between the two contexts, even though her interest is naturally drawn towards the differences.

In her own reflection Anju's judgements are somewhat contradictory. She feels that Spanish students are more motivated and achieve more. This she attributes to such factors as:

- teachers and parents push children harder;
- pedagogy is more serious – in the UK it is more frivolous;

- teachers are more human in class, laughing more but also reprimanding more vitriolically;
- children have more social interaction and are, therefore, better communicators.

However, she sees this as uniquely Spanish and does not feel that she can change pupils in the UK except by raising her own expectations.

Anju appears to have gone a stage beyond Charlotte in the depth of her reflection but is not transformed by the experience and does not expect to apply very much from it. For her, the prime benefit of the visit was linguistic.

Jeremy

Jeremy was a modern languages student teacher at an English university who had recently completed teaching practice in two comprehensive schools, neither of which was located in specially favoured or deprived areas. Jeremy then spent three months teaching in a Portuguese state school in Porto. He taught for around ten hours per week but observed few lessons taught by regular teachers. Jeremy taught English to students aged between 16 and 18.

The students

They never seemed to have the no-hope attitude I found here. They don't question the education in its own right, it's an end in itself. Young people are happier in Latin countries. They have mature points of view.

Teachers

The teacher has a completely different role to here, the teacher was expected to do no more than just teach the subject and walk out of the classroom at the end of it. Once outside the classroom the teacher was just like an ordinary person, a man or woman in the street.

I don't think the teachers took it quite so seriously as they do here. They certainly don't seem to get so stressed about it, or try to carry the world on their shoulders as I've seen them do here.

They saw kids as lazy. They would victimise a child in the middle of a class – something I'd been told never to do.

Teacher–student relationships

I think that rather than confront the pupils, the teachers were more ready to contact parents than here. There was no question, ever, of children being rude to teachers. They'd be lazy or they'd be noisy, but never any confrontation at all. I don't know if I can attribute it to anything. The teachers were nicer to the pupils so the pupils were nicer to the teachers.

Pedagogy

I think teaching is more a matter of human relationships than we realise here. I think we concentrate too much on getting techniques right. I think planning was something they didn't do so much of there, it was very much 'We'll do this text with them to-day' and every day it was a different text. I think the kids got a bit bored with that, being faced with sheets all the time. They seemed amazed when I did songs and quizzes and little bits and pieces with them – they were amazed, I don't think they'd ever done anything like that before.

The French lessons I saw reminded me a bit of what I imagine lessons must have been like in England about 50 years ago, people sitting at individual desks, writing, and a few of them at the back chatting, and one or two asleep in the corner. They're expected to be passive and just take notes. I think here there's so much emphasis on getting the kids to do things – everyone gets hyped up and perhaps that makes it harder for the teacher in the long run.

Subject's reflections

In the UK the kids are not really so much against the teacher as against certain aspects of the establishment, the school as oppressor and they take that out on the teacher. It's hard to say why things are working. Perhaps it's more human, natural to react to bad behaviour more directly.

We mustn't take teaching beyond what we ought to teach – family and society should look after the rest.

Analysis of data collected from Jeremy

Jeremy provides a lot of interesting factual data but the interview tape is characterised by pauses, false starts and frequent utterances of bewilderment or incomprehension in the face of the various paradoxes revealed in this interview. In the area of teacher–pupil relationships Jeremy had reflected rather more fully, going beyond technique and speculating about the under-pinning quality of these relationships. He seems prepared to attribute a great deal to these but to have thought rather less about students and their learning. Jeremy had functioned in this way during teaching practice and could have been critiqued in similar terms to those which he now applies to teachers in Porto – an irony he does not appear to appreciate.

Seamus

Seamus, a modern languages student teacher at an English university, spent three months teaching English and German in Liège, Belgium. He taught for twelve hours per week in three different schools and also did some teaching in private companies. The experiences were arranged as a series of blocks with observation for one week followed by two weeks of teaching. The students were all aged 16 or over and their level of language was intermediate or advanced. Seamus had recently completed two teaching practices in the UK. In Belgium, Seamus received extensive feedback from teachers and regular contact from a supervising university tutor. Seamus observed a number of different teachers.

Teachers

The teacher is seen very much as a deliverer of material and a deviser of his own curriculum. There didn't seem to be much contact with other teachers. You went to your classroom and out again.

Pedagogy and didactics

There was a thorough approach to text analysis, especially at the upper end of the school. In one German lesson they were using a text-book from 1940. The main difference was that teacher autonomy lead to a great deal more variety than in UK.

Subject's reflections

Very detailed lesson planning taught me to tighten up. I really began to think about the communicative method and how to synthesise that with a more grammar based approach. As a result of sessions with the university tutor (who is heavily influenced by Kolb) I am more aware of how my own learning preferences have influenced the way I teach. Culture shock as a mode of teacher training worked for me.

Analysis of data collected from Seamus

Seamus has virtually nothing to say about the learners or teacher–student relationships despite being asked the same questions as other subjects. One reason is that he spent comparatively little time in each school before moving on to the next. Another is that he was placed in a context which tended to emphasise teaching and the role of the teacher. His reflection is entirely concerned with pedagogy, unlike the other subjects who often emphasise the social interactions of the school. Seamus has a thoughtful approach to teaching and does tend to be more concerned with pedagogy than with interaction. It was therefore unsurprising that his reflection was dominated by technical considerations, indicating, perhaps, an implicit belief in the primacy of technique over affect. Equally, the differences between student–teacher relationships in Belgium and the UK are much less striking than they are between the UK and Latin countries.

Tony

Tony, a modern languages student teacher at an English university, taught in Santander, Spain, for three months. He observed teachers of French, Italian, Spanish and English in three different schools. The main teaching element consisted of a nearly full timetable during the last month of the placement in a school where he taught classes in the 9–14 age range. He also received considerable support and tuition from university and school staff.

Students

It was striking how much they looked forward to language lessons. Motivation was higher than in comparable schools in England.

Teachers

I didn't see them doing much preparation or marking. There didn't seem to be many meetings or the kind of management structure that we have and they don't have the controlled assessment. The lack of formal structures was compensated by informal meetings – there was a good atmosphere in the staff room.

Teacher–student relationships

There were no discipline problems to the level I saw on teaching practice in England, nothing to disrupt a lesson. They were very friendly, calling me by my Christian name. I think the teacher is more of a friend but there is still a distance.

Pedagogy

The Spanish lessons were very grammatically based. It was very demanding, extremely high expectations.

Schools

A weakness in the Spanish system is a lack of classroom display. Both the secondary schools which I visited had very cold atmospheres.

Tony felt that there was a similar difference between primary and secondary schools in both countries, with primaries emphasising more student involvement and secondaries being more teacher centred and dominated by content.

Subject's reflections

> Teacher training is much more theoretical in Spain, based on the view that good practice arises out of sound theory. That works there because good pupil-teacher relationships prevail so it is much easier to teach, you can get away with teaching badly.

Tony saw some poor lessons delivered by student teachers which did not lead to the problems he would have anticipated in England.

Tony felt transformed by the experience but thinks it is not something that can be described easily:

> You can say what it's like but it doesn't really communicate how it was. The more variety of education systems you see the better, it's very easy to get strait-jacketed into a certain system. For instance, the idea of assessment, there are no exams to put pressure on the children, it does make you question the way we do things. I think that's coloured by my own slogging through the system which I didn't enjoy.

Tony sees the key difference as positive attitudes towards teachers and schools, good behaviour, little disruption. He attributes this to deeply cultural origins – 'it's engrained in them, this respect for adults and being part of school, in a way we perhaps don't have'. Tony thinks more inventive methodology is necessary in England in order to cope with more difficult classes, that the behaviour dictates the methodology, not the reverse.

Analysis of data collected from Tony

Tony is clearly very concerned about disruptive behaviour and is much impressed with the relatively relaxed climate of the classrooms he visited. He attributes this to greater social cohesiveness and family stability. Tony has a very positive attitude to the placement but finds it hard to articulate this and is unsure if it can be articulated. There is a sense almost of resentment that Spain has more orderly classrooms, that teaching is easier and that this contradicts an implicit belief in British superiority.

Mari-Juana

Mari-Juana is a student teacher from Spain who undertook twelve weeks of teaching in England as part of her initial training course, the rest of which was based in Spain. She taught in two different comprehensive schools in England, one in a semi-rural location and the other in an inner city. She taught Spanish to students in Years 8, 10 and 12. She had some limited opportunity to observe lessons. She also followed a course in second-language acquisition at university. Her main teaching subject is English.

Students

They were seen as highly motivated to learn the language and enjoyed and looked forward to Mari-Juana's lessons. She found no behaviour problems and was impressed by good standards of Spanish. Very lively younger students were also well motivated. Year 10 students were much less well motivated, had poor discipline, it was hard to keep their attention, and 'school seemed low priority for them, they had little respect for teachers'.

Teachers

Mari-Juana felt that there were more meetings and administration in English schools than in Spain.

Teachers are enthusiastic and love their work.

Teacher–student relationships

There is more control in the UK.

Mari-Juana was surprised at the detailed knowledge of their students that English teachers had. She felt that there was much more student–teacher contact because of smaller classes.

Pedagogy and didactics

I saw lots of games and activities in the inner city school – those kids wouldn't accept more formal methods, such as those which I saw in use in the other school and which reminded me of what I am used to in Spain.

There is much more variety and better quality of didactic material in the UK of all sorts including realia and authentic materials.

Games and activities very varied, with lots of suggestions in course books.

School organisation

Setting, although a good idea, is not permitted in Spain where it is seen as 'unconstitutional'.

Subject's reflections

Mari-Juana is not clear about conditions in Spain and how recent reforms have changed schools since she was a pupil. Her training course in Spain did not include teaching practice.

This was her first experience of a multi-cultural school. The experience of the placement confirmed her prior opinion that every school is different and that there is no universal method of teaching. She would prefer to have studied at the rural school here and to teach here. She attributes relatively little importance to national differences and much more to local conditions such as class size, school ethos, etc. 'You have to love teaching to stay sane.' She particularly valued the exposure to some more difficult classes.

Analysis of data collected from Mari-Juana

Interestingly, Mari-Juana is a product of the training system mentioned by Tony. She has had a sound theoretical introduction to teaching and is aware of the need to suit teaching to local conditions and the needs of students. However, she has had very little exposure to the reality of being a schoolteacher in her native country and this makes it much harder for her to reflect about differences because she is not able to perceive fully the complexity of teaching.

Lucía

Lucía is also a student teacher from Spain who undertook twelve weeks of teaching in England as part of her initial training course, the rest of which was based in Spain. Her teaching experience in England was exactly similar to that of Mari-Juana and she, too, followed a course in second-language acquisition at university and has English as her main teaching subject.

Students

Lucía found English students to be well motivated to learn Spanish and that they had a similar level of interest to that of Spanish students towards learning English. She was pleasantly surprised at the good level of their Spanish, which compared favourably to Spanish students learning English.

Teachers

Teachers in England and Spain have broadly similar workloads and range of activity.

Teacher–student relationships

She found teacher–student relationships to be 'normal', broadly similar to Spain.

Pedagogy and didactics

Pedagogy is quite different in the UK, it is much less rigid than in Spain but sometimes is too flexible.

Lucía feels that materials used in each country are broadly similar.

Subject's reflections

Lucía compares her observations of English schools to her own experience as a learner in Spain. She feels that methods in use in Spain then and in the UK now are both extreme, although in different ways. She has observed one lesson in Spain during her training from which she concluded that a move to more student-centred learning has begun! Lucía is aware of her own lack of skill in teaching. She would be comfortable teaching in the UK where she 'felt at home'.

Her views on teaching and learning did not alter radically as a result of this experience. She feels teaching is very difficult and that she has profited from overcoming her initial fear and anxiety.

Analysis of data collected from Lucía

In many ways Lucía's comments are typical of a student on first teaching practice:

- initial fear of the unknown giving way to familiarity and confidence;
- awareness of her own lack of skill and technique, that is operating at Dubin's (1962) stage of 'conscious incompetence';
- making comparisons with her own experience as a school student.

Given that Lucía is only able to make comparisons with her distant experience as a pupil she has much less to say than the British students in this study who had all had recent teaching practices. Lucía's reflection is at a much lower level owing to her more restricted experience and also to the fact that she has not been taught to reflect or encouraged in that direction by her university course. One might speculate that the very passive school education she appears to have had would not have prepared her well for critical reflection. Lucía does not refer to the theory of education that she learned before coming here and it was unfortunate that she was not asked about this. Here, the interviewer's own implicit belief in an experiential approach to teacher education is obtrusive. Given the vastly differing approaches to theory of education between the various countries it would have been interesting to question subjects on how their understanding of theory had helped or hindered them.

CONCLUSION

Research methodology

From a research perspective the timing of the interviews at the end of the placement still seems most advantageous although a follow-up interview six to eighteen months later would be of benefit in looking at longer-term effects and the outcomes of deeper processing of the experience. From the teacher educator perspective it might prove useful to encourage students to think about the experience as it unfolds, perhaps through the keeping of a reflective journal. Would this facilitate reflection or might it lead to a forced and counter-productive reflection? The latter might lead to a shallow form of reflection that merely aimed to satisfy course requirements. More seriously, it might push students into a degree of reflection that is premature and unhelpful.

Engagement/reflection

The refusal to engage can be helpful, a kind of defence mechanism, as discussed by Claxton in Chapter 1. Beginning teachers do need to hold on to preliminary understandings for long enough in order to grow. The critical time for deeper reflection may be when their growth takes them beyond the useful life-span of these preliminary understandings. At that point they reach Claxton's stage of disinhibition which enables the learner to avoid or overcome tendencies to defend or withdraw unnecessarily. Here we can identify a dynamic aspect in the process of engagement with reluctance to engage for healthy, defensive reasons gradually being disinhibited so that readiness to learn (Gagné, 1965) arrives at a critical point. While the student teacher is defending fragile and temporary insights against the full glare of public or even personal scrutiny, engagement is refused. Disinhibition occurs as confidence and competence develop. It is also probable that disinhibition occurs in some aspects of competence sooner than in others. Equally, there is a danger that the healthy defence mechanism that prevents premature engagement may exceed its useful shelf life and begin to inhibit learning.

Reluctance to reflect too deeply on these experiences may merely represent a struggle to make sense of complex factors. One might agree with Jamieson that 'left to their own devices, student teachers at least do not always embrace the dictum "I do and I understand"; very often they declare "I do and I'm even more confused!"' (Jamieson, 1994). However, a number of reasons for a reluctance to engage in reflection suggest themselves:

- it did not occur to the student teachers to undertake such reflection;
- they were unable to do so, perhaps through a limited awareness of teaching and learning or limited skills in reflection (Mari-Juana and Lucía);
- they were reluctant to do so, perhaps unwilling to challenge the fragile certainties of their relatively recent induction into educational theory within the socio-cultural context of their home country (Charlotte);
- they saw no potential gain from the foreign experience – it couldn't work here (Anju).

The foreign experience

I had hoped that students would see through the more superficial, 'systemic' differences between the different educational systems, and would be able to come to a greater sense of the more universal and hence more important aspects. However, these structural features seem to be those which strike students more forcibly. Thus, any more fundamental or universal elements do not readily emerge and often remain at an unconscious, implicit level. In rare instances these do emerge: Tony's realisation that formal assessment structures such as we have in the UK are not necessarily a given fact of life begins to get below the surface. Unfortunately, there are disappointingly few such examples to support Tony's own view, also mentioned by Anju, that experience of different systems and approaches *is* important in challenging basic assumptions.

National differences

In addition to aspects of student teacher learning, this research does raise some questions about pedagogy, motivation and the differences in ethos of schools in different countries. Do these differences arise out of genuinely different educational philosophies and policies, or are they the result of a series of historical accidents? Do we in England, for example, owe our strong tutorial/pastoral system to having evolved our school system partly from the boarding school model, where it was necessary for teachers to act *in loco parentis*? Are different approaches to teaching in different countries the result of or the cause of different approaches to learning? Such questions are beyond the scope of the present work but are of crucial importance and comparative studies in this area have much to offer.

Implicit beliefs

The degree to which students were able to bring their implicit beliefs to the fore depended on the pre-existing nature of those beliefs. For some, these are deeply buried, whilst for others they are near to awareness. Students commonly evince a preoccupation with pedagogy, discipline or subject knowledge, for example. These concerns tend to dominate their experience and their thinking, so that reflection in these areas may go further, while it is correspondingly neglected in other important areas. From this very small sample there was some evidence of variation in implicit – and explicit – beliefs according to national identity. This variation may arise in part from contrasting and quite overt theoretical differences in approaches to learning to teach. English teacher trainers have assimilated the strong critique made, primarily by Revans (1982) and Schön (1983), of the model of teacher education which predicated a movement from theory to action. They operate a model which stresses experiential learning and reflection upon experience so the English students in this study are generally willing to attempt this process – with varying degrees of success. Spanish teacher trainers expect their students first to master educational theory and then go to school and apply it. As a result, the Spanish subjects do not really expect to reflect, to have opinions. Theory is a given constant from which practice must flow.

Marilyn Osborn reports in Chapter 5 that, from her research, 'English teachers emerged as significantly more likely than their colleagues in France to adopt a reflective stance in considering the nature of their role and how to carry it out'. She notes one of the causes of these disparities is differences in initial teacher training, differences that mirror those between the training programmes now operating in the UK and Spain. Thus, an implicit belief in the value of reflection would appear to operate to a greater or lesser extent in different cultures.

Transfer of learning?

What transfer of learning occurred, or might occur, from this experience to the task of teaching upon which these interviewees are now embarking? Was the experience too 'vicarious' (Wallace, Chapter 2) for transfer to occur? There was certainly some element of difficulty in articulating the experience in order to share it. Tony states this directly and several of the subjects have difficulty at various points in the interviews in expressing what they really want to say – a finding also noted by Weeden and Hayter (Chapter 8). We might speculate that what is important for transfer to take place could be the extent to which the student teacher is personally able to 'engage' with the learning experience. This may depend on:

- the extent of first-hand knowledge and familiarity with practical teaching and learning situations, which was absent for Mari-Juana and Lucía, and for Charlotte in her year as a foreign language assistant;
- their ability to reflect on experience resulting from practice in observation, self-evaluation and reflection in action;
- their awareness of implicit beliefs or the possible existence of these, the depth of such beliefs – how near to awareness they are, and their strength – how self-defining they are (Atkinson, Chapter 15), either personally or culturally;
- their awareness of and ability to think about social structures such as schools or the education systems of different countries.

These four aspects approximate to Zimpher and Howey's (1987) idea of four kinds of competence. These are:

1 Technical competence, or effective day-to-day teaching skills.

The subjects in this study were quite able to engage in reflection upon these, confidence in their own competence tending to facilitate their reflection.

2 Clinical competence – the ability to make judgements about problematic situations and to solve problems through reflective action and enquiry.

The interviews required the participants to display this kind of competence and the varied results indicate variations in competence. They also indicate variation in implicit beliefs, not least a belief in the usefulness or otherwise of clinical competence. Evidently, these implicit beliefs also influence the degree to which clinical competence may be developed.

3 Personal competence – self-confrontation, the development of values.

These came through forcefully with several subjects articulating strong beliefs in a range of educational and social values.

4 Critical competence – the capacity to critique institutions, social structures and the norms and values or ideologies which operate within them.

The interviews were geared towards promoting this kind of analysis but subjects revealed surprisingly limited capacity for this. My implicit belief, as revealed in the introductory section of this chapter, was that mere exposure to a different model of education would result in this kind of learning. I had overlooked the degree to which participants might lack the necessary critical competence. This appeared to be more highly developed in the English students who had recent extensive teaching practice experience of a number of schools. The exception to this proved to be Seamus, whose school placements in Belgium were too short for him to learn enough about the institutions he visited.

To conclude, this form of placement provides an interesting opportunity to develop critical competence as opposed to the preoccupation of much of teacher education with technical competence and of teacher educators with personal competence. Zimpher and Howey's (1987) competences are not necessarily hierarchically linked. Implicit beliefs might be revealed differently in each area. In the domain of technical competence they could help determine the choice of techniques and their application. With regard to clinical competence, implicit beliefs could provide one way of understanding particular choices, strategies or courses of action. Concerning personal competence, implicit beliefs are likely to inhibit self-actualisation – raising another question mark over the teaching of abstract theory as in Spain today and in the UK until comparatively recently. Finally, implicit beliefs could be a barrier to the development of critical competence, the forming of objective assessments of institutions and social structures.

REFERENCES

Atkinson, T. A. and Cummings, J. (1992) 'Teacher training in Oporto'. *Vida Hispánica*, Vol. 5, pp. 15–20.

Dubin, P. (1962) *Human Relations in Administration*, Englewood Cliffs, NJ: Prentice Hall.

Gagné, R. M. (1965) *The Conditions of Learning*, London: Holt, Rinehart and Winston.

Jamieson, I. (1994) 'Experiential learning in teacher education'. In G. Harvard and P. Hodkinson (eds) *Action and Reflection in Teacher Education*, Norwood, NJ: Ablex.

Revans, R. W. (1982) *The Origins and Growth of Action Learning*, Bromley, UK: Chartwell-Bratt.

Schön, D. (1983) *The Reflective Practitioner.* London: Temple Smith.

Woolf, A., Kelson, M., and Silver, R. (1990) Learning in context: patterns of skills transfer and training implications. Sheffield: TEED, Department of Employment.

Zimpher, N. L. and Howey, K. R. (1987) 'Adapting supervisory practices to different orientations of teaching competence'. *Journal of Curriculum and Supervision*, Vol. 2(2), pp. 101–27.

Chapter 10

Overseas scholarships

Culture shock or learning opportunity?

John Hayter

In this chapter John Hayter applies the idea of implicit theories of learning to the experience of overseas students attending a Masters' course. Many of these students have previously studied in their own countries where they have imbibed a model of adult professional learning based on assumptions that in the UK are now considered to be old fashioned. The author presents data that suggests that the conflict between the underlying principles of the course and the implicit theories and expectations of the students can be resolved, provided tutors are themselves aware of the issues, and can help their students over the learning barriers that are commonly initially encountered. The question that remains for further study is the extent to which students' adaptation to new styles of teaching and learning is 'skin deep', enabling them to meet the course requirements, or actually pays off in terms of working principles and practices on the students' return to their very different cultures. Linking with Chapter 2, he suggests ways in which the transfer issue can be explicitly addressed as part of a formal course.

INTRODUCTION

New learning opportunities come in many forms. Some will be short in duration, barely disturbing the normal pattern of life. Others involve a conscious decision to suspend 'normality' and to undertake learning with a potentially direction-changing outcome. We saw in Chapter 2 how, in management training, one approach to suspending normality is to place learners in a setting and to give them tasks which are, by design, far removed from their workaday world. Two issues arise from learning so divorced from the context of its use. First, learning may not easily be transferred back into the home/work situation unless there is further support within that situation to help the learning become re-embedded. And second, participants may find that their habitual approach to learning is at odds with the principles underpinning the new learning programme, and therefore be inhibited from making the most of it – unless they are able to learn how to learn in a new way.

The experience of overseas educators participating in professional studies at higher education level in the UK entails a disjunction in learning styles, contexts and demands which raise exactly the same issues. For 'home' students, learning occurs in a familiar physical and cultural setting, whereas for those from very different countries and societies, there is much dislocation. Moreover, when they return home they will be expected to transfer back with them new course-based learning, and to be able immediately to translate it into their working practice. Such radical shifts in learning context, coupled with novel learning tasks, could either constrain, or potentially liberate, them as learners.

Students from developing countries, given the opportunity to study for advanced degrees in education in the UK, represent a particular, critical, case of such maximally displaced students. For some, their situation involves an opportunity presented through no active desire on their part. For others, the awarded scholarship will be the culmination of years of diligent effort and careful planning to achieve a desired career-enhancing break. In a series of studies about adult learning for professional educators, the experience of such international students seems particularly worthy of consideration, and may throw light on the central role that culture and context play in learning.

This chapter examines the experience of overseas students who participated in Masters' level studies in mathematics education at Bristol. First, aspects of the context of their study situation are considered, and, in particular, the evolution of mathematics education and the particular programme of study which they followed. The experience of a cohort of students is examined in detail, exploring their perceptions of themselves, the content and delivery of the course and the outcomes which were seen as significant for them. The data is used to identify the putative implicit theories of learning which they brought with them to the course. Such implicit theories, it appears, were substantially at odds with the principles which underpinned the content and pedagogy of the course. A question is raised over how the directors of such courses should best cater for this disparity, and what kinds of support are most effective in helping students to comprehend these principles, and to begin to incorporate them into their own practice both as learners and, eventually, as educators when they return home.

THE CONTEXT

Since recognition of its capacity for change in the 1960s, mathematics education has been in a continuous state of flux. Changes in curricula and in approaches to teaching have begotten new problems, novel insights and urgent incentives to yet more change. Problems have emerged more readily than stable solutions; indeed a continuously evolving system is now seen to be inevitable in the UK. As a country, we now have not only ways of teaching the subject of mathematics but also a rapidly expanding library of knowledge and expertise on the phenomenon of 'mathematics education'. Meanwhile, though physically an island, we exist in a historical context that includes the exporting and imposing of our ideas on mathematics teaching to many parts of the world. These have been an integral part of shaping whole education systems which existed at the time of independence, when aspirations to emulate the Western world (including former colonial masters) led to the rapid adoption of new waves of curriculum reform. 'Modern' mathematics was not to be denied to anyone – it was seen to exist and was being embraced in a variety of forms by the USA, UK and elsewhere in Europe; it had to be incorporated.

Mathematical missionaries were soon winging their way to all corners of Africa and elsewhere by invitation of new governments and funded by the taxpayers of First World countries. But modern mathematics often fared no better than the ill-fated post-war ground nuts scheme in Tanzania. Clearly, other peoples' texts and materials did not transplant easily into the environment of a newly independent country. In the wake of these developments, Howson (1979) has identified the stages of *adoption* and of *adaptation*, and looked forward to *appraisal* as a third and more desirable approach to the development of appropriate curricula in developing countries. In practice, there is evidence of all three strands still co-existing but the move to enabling mathematics educators, amongst others, to study and to experience UK practice has been a major part of the educational aid strategy. The complexity of the learning processes involved in such study has too often been oversimplified or has simply not been considered.

A specialist MEd programme relating to mathematics education has existed for a number of years in the School of Education at the University of Bristol. Designed to appeal to both local teachers and overseas educators, its elements and structure reflect a number of assumptions about study at this level for experienced professionals. It assumes that a working group which has some continuity over the year can create confidence and a consequent ability to share ideas with both other students and the tutors. Consequently a core programme provides introductions to broad themes in the fields of teaching, learning, assessment and curriculum in mathematics education. Other units are optional, catering for those with particular interests, for example in primary education or in teacher education. Two more specialised courses are provided by the units 'Subject updating' and 'Children learning mathematics in school'. The first acts as a marker for the belief that being active in widening one's experience and knowledge of mathematics is desirable practice for a mathematics educator. The second course provides contact with British mathematics classrooms while carrying out a student-selected small-scale research study in the school.

COMING TO MED STUDIES FROM A DEVELOPING COUNTRY

The present investigation took place as the members of a small group of MEd students from five African countries were completing twelve months of study. As part of the data collection students participated in a semi-structured interview with the author who had worked with them throughout the year on several course units. At other times the discussion draws on more general experiences over time working with the students.

One limitation of the study should be noted. A year's experience is substantial and complex, making recall of early feelings, reactions and problems difficult. The experience was cumulative and its development would take some unscrambling. Further, the crucial stage for participants of returning to their families and their professional bases still lay ahead, making the validity and permanence of their learning a matter of speculation.

Certain characteristics of students from such countries are worth identifying since they provide part of the context. They contrast in nearly every case with the characteristics of home students, and may be grouped under three headings: perceptions of their own competence; beliefs on where answers to problems of mathematics teaching may be found; and conviction about the relevance of their learning for the situation at home.

Their own competence

The professionals taking the course have been locally successful, and this has brought them to the notice of those who make personnel decisions and control funds for professional learning. As life histories of those involved in the education systems of developing countries show (John and Hayter, 1995), surviving in the system is a matter of considerable determination and good fortune as well as ability. People emerge with relatively high degrees of confidence in themselves. Further they have been selected in a competitive situation for the award of a scholarship; others also have faith in their potential. Interestingly, this positive self-image seems to be transportable: the majority face the prospect of functioning effectively in a totally new environment with marked confidence. The colonial and post-independence links give a sense of access to and ability to cope with this other world. Successful past experience as learners in formal settings predisposes them, initially at least, to perceive the course as a learning *opportunity*, despite the unfamiliarity of the setting.

The source of answers

The perceived universality of mathematics suggests that knowledge gained in one place is applicable elsewhere. Such a view seems to incorporate not only the subject matter but also the related pedagogy. Educational knowledge and in particular that relating to mathematics has come from the UK throughout the history of formal education in many countries. Seeking current up-to-date knowledge from institutions in that country seems natural. Not only has it been regarded as the source but also it is manifest that the mechanisms for dispensing knowledge through taught courses exist and the availability of abundant resources, particularly books and journals, provides scope for substantial study. Beyond the acquisition of knowledge there will also be the recognition to be achieved by certification in internationally renowned institutions. Valued knowledge is seen to have an external and high-status source, one such being a higher education institution in the UK. The credibility of the institution as a source of knowledge also predisposes overseas students to adopt a positive attitude towards their learning in a strange environment.

Relevance to their own situation

The studies take place in an educational setting very different from that experienced in their own country. Every student's situation may not be as challenging as that faced by a recently qualified Gambian teacher sent to study engineering in Russia, but there are still important questions about the transfer of learning approaches between cultures. There are the twin dangers of failing to see transfer when it exists, and of assuming the transcultural relevance of learning when in fact there is none. Beyond the learning experience is the return to a different culture and the need, perhaps only then, to explore in reality the implementation of ideas nurtured in very different, partially controlled conditions. On leaving the academic hothouse for the cooler reality of life in a punishing educational environment, it is always possible that the seedlings of learning will fail to thrive.

EXPLORING STUDENT EXPERIENCE AND THINKING

The responses of students interviewed as they completed dissertations and were preparing to leave the UK can usefully be examined under three major headings: engaging with the unknown; contextual factors; and learning achievements.

Engaging with the unknown

Initial feelings and expectations

News of the award of a scholarship was generally warmly welcomed. For some it was thought to be a well-earned reward; others saw it primarily as the gateway to professional advancement and to the further development of their own understanding. Expectations varied from a 'blank' to partially understood images established from the information conveyed by those who had been before. But accurately anticipating the quantity and the demands of the work was all but impossible. However, having never failed any exam before boosted the confidence of one student as he prepared to travel. For some, there were uncertainties about the nature of the material to be studied. Conceptions of the subject matter inevitably reflected the students' experience in their own country. In some cases specific needs and interests springing from their current work articulated uncertainly with what the course would offer.

The subject of study.

'Mathematics education' was for many a hybrid phrase which conveyed little. Training and experience had brought them into contact with the terms mathematics and education. The former was often regarded in largely algorithmic terms – methods for solving certain types of question were learned and then practised. Methodology was largely didactic though some scholarship holders had already started to move away from this. The willingness to make a shift in their learning may well have been a feature in their selection. For some of the students, ideas which they had met in theory (through articles read or sessions given by advisers) suddenly came to have meaning in this new context with more time to read, discuss and observe.

'Education' on the other hand was associated with that part of initial teacher education which was theory associated with the traditional 'foundation disciplines' of education – psychology, sociology, philosophy and history – which was often regarded as having no direct bearing on mathematics teaching. So the concept of mathematics education as a subject for study was one which had to emerge. Its existence was demonstrated by the books and journals which were quickly encountered. Its theoretical nature, and the direct links to psychology, philosophy and sociology, had come as a shock – but not necessarily an unwelcome one – to those whose mental image had been shaped by more practical in-service courses at home. Here, then, was a growing body of knowledge, as well as methods of thinking, distilling experience and drawing on research, which had the potential to illuminate issues in the teaching and learning of mathematics. Willingness to embrace the notion of mathematics education had enabled the students to replace old assumptions with a revised basis for thinking about their subject.

The experiences provided

In attending at least eight taught units students encountered a variety of teaching styles. Most were tolerant of this variety, one expressing it in the form 'Not fully accepting – tend to be content with what is given (as if offered by a friend)'. But formal lectures had been the expectation of most. To some, the idea of working from direct experience, through reflection, towards theory was disturbing – surely at this level lecturers would simply 'tell'. Yet the majority quite quickly came to appreciate a style of working where questions were addressed and considered by the group. 'I am so happy that we do most of the thinking. The course tutor does the polishing up, gives time to think and listens to us rather than it all flowing from one end . . . there are contributions from others too.' The opportunity to focus on questions, considered by members of a group of professionals, seemed both a revelation and a powerful and empowering stimulus. The prevalent attitude of tolerance towards unfamiliar teaching styles and tasks had helped participants to reap the benefit of these new experiences.

The tasks set and requirements of the course

Appreciating the role of class sessions in relation to personal study and written work was for many an immediate challenge. Assignments provided a valued focus in a large field of knowledge but could absorb a disproportionate amount of attention. Mathematicians often express particular worries about their ability to write essays. The perceived enormity of a dissertation is daunting, particularly initially when determining a topic and making a start with the writing. Self-perceived weaknesses in writing may possibly have been a contributory reason for their specialising in mathematics in the first place, but even if this was not the case, mathematics teachers may not have written extensive essays for many years. Students therefore needed encouragement to define purpose and establish confidence in their writing.

Providing a sense of audience had helped, for example through suggesting a specific target for their argument – perhaps a principal to whom they were expressing a concise argument for developing information technology, or a group of professional peers with whom they were sharing the significance of discussion in the mathematics classroom. Sharing their writing with other members of the group could also reinforce the notion that writing can benefit others, and that some degree of self-help was possible. Strategies of this kind had assisted in breaking the assumption that essays are for assessment and for the appeasement of lecturers. The assignments could be split into several parts, giving opportunity for shorter tasks, shared risks and different kinds of writing.

Informal feedback was also useful in this period of coming to terms with written work, though even here communication might be prone to difficulties where recipients were expecting a clear evaluation of worth rather than a discussion of issues and identification of particular strengths and weaknesses. A mark out of ten would have been the most readily valued response in these initial stages it seems. Nevertheless as the year progressed students reported a growing confidence, together with an increasing awareness of whether they were expressing arguments well in written form. Other tasks, such as joint presentations, were novel for those who had seen learning only in terms of individual performance. Yet the students had rapidly come to terms with the assumptions about the nature of mathematics education and adult professional learning which underpinned these tasks.

Finding and meeting the standards

Acceptance for a course often carries an expectation of successful completion, at least at the tertiary level of education. In practice few fail. But entering an unfamiliar system poses a challenge of recognising standards which are not yet personally understood or accepted. The move to a unified Advanced Diploma/MEd programme at Bristol threw this into sharp relief. One student who had only a teaching diploma but substantial teaching experience found himself anxiously assessing his performance against other students in the oral contributions to discussion. For another student who had the expected entry requirements for the MEd course, the possibility of 'only' getting a diploma had been a major worry. There is a strong case for using students' skills as the basis for deciding their level of entry and aspiration, within the formal educational system, rather than the qualifications they have managed to accumulate – in the way that better high-jumpers are allowed to miss out the early rounds and enter the competition at the point where their abilities start to be stretched.

Contextual factors

Learning takes place in a context whose elements are, in large measure, not self-selected. Yet there is always some scope for individual choice. Students may choose to work at their hall of residence or flat or in the library. They may prefer to work late into the night and seldom in the early morning, despite the early rising habits of a lifetime. But certain crucial aspects are determined by their place of study – the location itself, the resources, the other students and the tutors. Each of these seems worth examining for the perceived impact on the learning experience.

Location

As a way of raising the value of studying overseas, in a different context, students were asked during the interviews to justify coming to the UK to a friend in their home country who suggests that studying appropriate books sent to their country would provide an adequate alternative. While one student commented that more students could benefit from such an arrangement, none considered that they would have gained so much by this means alone. For some the separation from home and its demands, both domestic and professional, created the space to study in a focused way. Others considered that it was the distance, the being outside their own 'world', that enabled a new appreciation of the situation and its problems.

Indeed the cultural issues relating to mathematics education may only have emerged through the distancing from the familiar and the immersion in the unfamiliar. One commented: 'We tend to blame pupils but it is not their fault – nor the teacher, its the system. e.g. If I don't know about gender as an issue then I may blame the pupils. When you stand away from the system you are able to look at it.' The location brings together people – tutors, other students and the wider population – together with resources and access to experience in schools, conferences and other encounters. The unfamiliar setting, and its divorce from their everyday world of work, could help to remove learning barriers such as the distractions arising from being close to home and the workplace, and to facilitate in-depth reflection. It is a common experience that, out of one's normal context of roles, responsibilities and habits of conceptualisation and action, one is freed to think in new ways, even to experiment with being a different person.

Resources

The wealth of resources in the UK education system was a consistent source of wonder to newly arrived students. Like the coming of the rains in a drought-stricken area, there was the delight of just wallowing in so much easily available written material. Finding strategies to make effective use of it all took longer but the quantity and relevance of much hitherto unknown material, going well beyond mathematics education, was a valued part of learning, part of the mental (and sometimes physical) baggage to be taken home. Technology was a major factor, with most students professing no expertise and sometimes no knowledge of computers. The potential of word processors was quickly appreciated, and skill in their use had steadily grown. The efficiency of usage varied, but nevertheless the acquisition of the skill gave a sense of being where the technological 'action' is and led to enhanced aspirations and expectations on their return to their own country.

Other students

Each student had contact with other students in a number of contexts, but the core mathematics group was regarded as most significant. 'One of the biggest components of this study has been meeting people from other areas and getting their experiences also.' Fellow students had, for the most part, experience in economic circumstances similar to their own. Yet education systems differed, and relating to that other experience gave access to a kind of knowledge that was particularly valued. This fascination with others' experience, though tending to be somewhat uncritical early on in the course, developed into more analytical and reflective discussions as the course unfolded.

Tutors

Experienced teachers who were returning to the student life had their own professional practice, and a wealth of experience of being taught, on which to draw. How did they come to terms with the practice of new tutors on the course? They quickly learned to work by the clock, appearing at lectures and tutorials with a promptness that is a model for many UK students. The timekeeping and reliability of the system was much appreciated by the majority of students.

Use of first names between tutor and student opens up a whole area of cultural expectation and social interaction – some persisted in using 'Sir' in spite of discouragement, while others moved happily onto first–name terms. All contrasted the tutor–student relationship with that experienced at home. In part, this reflected a mode of study which offered more personal contact than they were used to, arising from smaller classes and individual super-vision for the dissertation. Yet it is something which was quickly noted and with which each student needed to come to terms if it was to be used. 'Friendly, quite relaxed, more like colleagues. Don't know whether it's a matter of culture but it's not like home.' Others recognised a style they would like to adopt – 'teachers here are able to encourage students to talk . . . they seem to be very free . . . but [at home] this could be interpreted as a loose teacher', 'teachers should be authoritative'. The expectation was of little interaction with contact only in the lecture room. 'Not time to sit and talk freely about issues, where here this is the case. Wouldn't look forward to a tutorial at home – more judgemental, less developmental [than here] . . . but this took time to realise.' Learning is clearly involved, in part in finding how to make use of the system, but also in the more subtle matters of respect and recognition of the student's professional worth, and in seeing criticism as aimed at development and encouragement to improve.

The learning achieved

Although the experience of overseas students is a complex one it is possible to consider the learning in three areas: knowledge, skills and attitudes. The knowledge gained was not defined by a tight syllabus. Rather it consisted of an awareness of processes, methods, ideas and outcomes of research. Expert knowledge was encountered both directly (in the university, in schools and at mathematics teachers conferences) and through publication and reputation. Through lectures, seminars and assignments, knowledge of mathematics education research was enhanced, and this knowledge was of both practical and academic interest. 'The assignments were valuable; all of them had something which I intend to implement.'

Skills of at least three kinds were evident: those required for the prepara-tion of assignments – reading, summarising, writing and producing the required work; those of self-organisation of enquiry and action; and those latent skills of teaching and implementation which were as yet untried – as yet only mind experiments – and awaited the return home for full development. As one expressed it, 'it is difficult to know until one is in the situation to share knowledge, whether it will be accepted or rejected'. The first set of skills involved a greater sense of direction and efficiency in using sources, extracting and organising information, and establishing an argument. But as long as all this effort was a response to tasks set by a tutor then the long-term value could be limited. Self-direction grew through the year and for many culminated in a dissertation rooted in their own interest and strongly grounded in their own professional situation.

But for many it was an attitudinal change, a change in their approach to the nature of mathematics and the purposes of teaching it, that comprised the most significant learning. For some, mathematics came to be seen as not just a classroom phenomenon but evident in the environment and deeply rooted in culture. A vagueness about the nature of the mathematics behind the teaching methods was partially overcome and there was renewed confidence in 'why I want people to learn it'. One student reflected somewhat ruefully on some of the best students to pass through his hands when a mathematics teacher and who are now engineers and doctors, 'smart, intelligent people, but do they understand [the mathematics]?' According to Wallace's model of learning and learning support (Chapter 2), the course had been quite successful in promoting critical understanding, providing practical information, and inculcating certain skills. Yet the crucial element of integration of what had been learned in England into practice in students' home countries, remained still to be tackled.

IMPLICATIONS FOR STUDENTS' FUTURE

It is appropriate to consider, first, what were the implications for their work on returning home, and, second, what this experience of study implied for their approach to studying in their future. Anticipating what will be applied in a year's time poses a major challenge in separating complex and interrelated learning experiences, and is an unreliable exercise in imagination. Nevertheless, students were actively contemplating the future and the strongest impression they gave was one of a new vision and new approaches which they were impatient to apply in familiar contexts at home.

What I wasn't able to do previously I can put right: for example, teaching approaches, relationship with students. There are things I want to try out in the classroom. The department has developed critical thinking which was not developed in my three college experiences – I was not even aware that it's an important skill in life. Difficult to learn instrumentally but efforts to query there [in previous educational contexts] were blocked. At

University of X there was a difference in what I put on paper . . . drawing on my own experience when making arguments would be very unusual to them – might get low marks. Will pass this on [creating a supportive group to substantiate the validity of such an approach in a different setting].

The dual intentions of personal implementation and of influencing other professional colleagues came through strongly. The zeal of the convert, suggesting that the benefit achieved was of value to others, fits perfectly with the Nyerere emphasis on the responsibility borne by those going to another place for education.

Fatigued at the end of a twelve-month course and ready to return to the familiar place of family, friends and work, all students expressed the hope of engaging in further study. The majority emphasised their valuing of the learning opportunity provided by the MEd over the instrumental aim of simply gaining a further degree. 'I've not had a tenth of what I would like to study'. 'I want to go deeper into teacher education'.

While some had a PhD in mind, others saw more beneficial routes to extending their professional knowledge through updating work and specialist studies. The means to achieve this was less evident. A further period of higher-level study in their own country was not an option, yet many felt reluctant to spend long periods abroad again. The pleasing prospect of returning home was tinged with pessimism with respect to continued study in an environment so notably short of resources and sometimes of people who could provide support and guidance. These aspirations to study might well fade unless enabling mechanisms emerge. The potential of self-help strategies seems promising, and it would be important to know, in a year's time, whether the course experience had made a significant contribution to such thinking.

CONCLUSION: MEDIATING BETWEEN THEORIES OF LEARNING

The findings reported in this chapter indicate that, for many overseas students on the MEd course, the principles informing the learning opportunities presented to them contrasted markedly with their initial expectations. This fracture arose, we might suppose, from these students' previous socialisation into a professional culture that had probably been imported from the UK, or other Western countries, years before. Such assumptions have been largely superseded in institutions of higher education in the UK by principles that give higher status and autonomy to the learner, acknowledge a wide range of experience as valuable bases for learning, and reflect a less absolutist view of mathematical and pedagogical knowledge. Ironically perhaps, this represents an attempt to export new assumptions about learning, the current orthodoxy, to replace the 'bad old views' which were enthusiastically promoted by our educational predecessors.

Table 10.1 summarises the putative implicit theories of these overseas students, set against the principles embodied in the course. While there was evidence that many students rapidly overcame any culture shock and embraced the new learning opportunities, it is less certain that their initial implicit theories of learning had been replaced, as opposed to supplemented, or even simply put in abeyance, for the duration of the course. 'Good students' are, after all, used to a chameleon-like adoption of the colour of the particular pedagogical leaf on which they happen to be sitting, without necessarily undergoing any deep or lasting personal conversion. Proof of the pudding would only be found in an abiding shift in the students' teaching and learning habits once they had returned home. It is perfectly possible that they might revert to behaviour consistent with their original implicit theories.

Table 10.1 A comparison of students' implicit theories and the learning principles embedded in the course

Perceived implicit theories of the students	Learning principles embodied in course
Authority determines what should be learned – i.e. the curriculum	Students determine what they will learn by selection of material and by filtering
The teacher determines what is learned	Learning arises from a variety of courses, experiential and reflective as well as the input of peers and tutors
Learning is by accumulation of knowledge	Learning involves changing attitudes and beliefs; knowledge fits into a web of understanding
Learning is for transmission /application	Learning which has been self-selected has uniqueness and value in itself; it cannot be simply transferred to another
Knowledge is an absolute	Knowledge is determined to some extent by the knower, his or her present state of knowledge and ability to perceive
Learning is culture free	Learning and knowledge have cultural dimensions

If transfer is to occur, and to last, it is likely that some 'by the elbow' support and guidance, back home in the everyday working context, would be necessary. To try out activities reflecting the new principles unaided would run the risk of experiencing a form of 'reverse culture shock', as their students and colleagues reacted to unfamiliar learning tasks and methods. Without support, and a very firm personal, experiential grasp of what they are trying to achieve, these reactions could well inhibit the returning educators from pursuing the additional learning that transfer into the home context would require.

Ideally such support should be offered actually within the normal working environment. But it is also possible that higher education providers might be able to facilitate this kind of learning from afar, perhaps through some form of re-entry counselling and/or action planning sessions towards the end of the course. Students could be encouraged to develop strategies that would be feasible within their own cultural context, and given the level of resourcing that they can realistically expect. For an advanced education course to be truly liberating, as it crosses national and cultural boundaries, it seems that explicit and enduring efforts must be made to mediate between the principles which the course both espouses and, more importantly, genuinely embodies, and the assumptions that learners bring with them, and which will still be prevalent within the culture to which they will be returning.

In working with students' beliefs, it will be important to take into account the stage they are at in the course. Too early, and they may be too dazed by the culture shock, or too defensive – as reported by Weeden and Hayter in Chapter 8 – to be able to stand back and adopt a reflective stance. Too late, and they may already have taken on the protective colouration of the 'successful student', and be unwilling to have their strategy called into question. It may be useful in this context to develop Howson's (1979) stages of learning a little. First comes the stage of *encountering* examples, either implicitly or explicitly, of alternative principles and theories. If change is to occur, this then has to develop into *recognising* that these conflict with one's own implicit beliefs. This recognition inevitably has an affective component, and support may be needed to allow it to 'sink in'. Three differing degrees of adjustment may then follow. The difference may simply be *absorbed*: it is noted and accepted rather unquestioningly. Or it may be *synthesised* or assimilated at the level of what is espoused, but fail to penetrate to the level of what actually guides and informs spontaneous practice. Or there may be the effort to resolve the tension and to *choose* one of the alternatives, old or new, from a position of conscious appraisal. What happens in the final stage, that of *application*, depends on what kind of resolution has been achieved. We might speculate that it is only if the new approach has been deliberately chosen that it will carry through into practice – and even then there may be much trial and error before it is fully embodied in one's *modus operandi*.

REFERENCES

Howson, A. G. (1979) 'A critical analysis of curriculum development in mathematics education'. In *New Trends in Mathematics Teaching, Vol. 4*, Paris: UNESCO.

John, P. and Hayter, J. (1995) 'Students' writing on their own education in The Gambia'. In *Linked to Good Effect: The Gambia College – Bristol University Schools of Education Link, 1986–93*, University of Bristol.

Part III

The facilitation of learning

This part of the book describes a number of studies that aim to facilitate learning in professional development contexts, by paying attention, in a variety of ways, to the assumptions about learning that are embedded either in the learning context, or in the learners' minds. Each chapter aims to contribute to our practical understanding of learning blocks, and to ways of circumventing or overcoming them. The first two chapters focus on the difficulties encountered by highly experienced teachers and managers as they become learners again in contrasting ways. In Chapter 11, Valerie Hall continues the 'higher-degree' theme from Chapter 10, but this time looks at the 'culture shock' experienced by senior professionals in education as they embark on a novel doctorate programme, the Bristol EdD. Agnes McMahon, in Chapter 12, explores some of the strategies adopted by new headteachers to facilitate their mastery of the unfamiliar demands of the job, and describes a peer mentoring scheme for new headteachers.

The next pair of chapters look in detail at the effects of collaboration and conversation on learning in in-service contexts. In Chapter 13 Jan Winter describes the effect of an extended INSET programme on teachers' views of themselves as learners, again highlighting the value of peer relationships in this process, while in Chapter 14 Laurinda Brown and Alan Dobson discuss the value of 'dissonance' both for individuals and in groups in challenging and modifying implicit theories. In the final pair of chapters in this part, the focus shifts back to mentoring in initial teacher education. In Chapter 15 Terry Atkinson investigates the way in which experienced teachers' views of teaching and learning are transmitted to student teachers through their role as mentors. And in Chapter 16, Peter John teases out the conceptions about learning that are being negotiated by mentors and students during the discussion of observed lessons.

Chapter 11

When the going gets tough

Learning through a taught doctorate programme

Valerie Hall

In this chapter Valerie Hall draws on her experience as tutor to the taught doctoral programme in education at the Bristol School of Education, the first such 'EdD' to be offered in the UK, to investigate the particular conflict and difficulties experienced by senior professionals as they embark upon, and engage with, intellectual study at the highest level. Interestingly, she contrasts the experience of the programme's participants with that of its tutors who are, in their own way, also seasoned teachers cast in the role of learners, as they attempt to adjust their teaching styles and expectations to new formats, levels and clients. Valerie explores the concept of 'resilience', the quality that enables an adult learner to 'bounce back' from frustration or disappointment, and shows both how this is spontaneously manifested by learners at this level, and how its development can best be supported. The chapter exemplifies particularly well the book's concern to bring together sociological and psychological perspectives.

INTRODUCTION

This chapter is concerned with the concept of 'resilience' in adult learning, in the context of tutors' and learners' experiences of learning on a taught doctoral programme in education (EdD). It draws on interviews with a small group of tutors and students to explore empirically the claims for an integrated learning theory that Guy Claxton outlines in Chapters 1 and 4. A small-scale study like this can only begin to scratch the surface of 'implicit theories'. It can, however, show the strategies used by some adult learners on a taught doctorate programme to manage their learning experiences in a novel and potentially threatening situation. The tutors provide some of that context for adult learning, basing their assumptions in part on their own implicit and explicit theories of learning. The dynamic of the learning situation is thus the outcome of what each group brings to the learning experience. Studying resilient learners and teachers provides a way of understanding resilience in adult education which takes account of both its social and cognitive dimensions.

The chapter argues that people who elect to join and are accepted on a taught doctoral programme are likely to be competent learners whose approaches to learning demonstrate characteristics associated with resilience. By resilience I mean the ability to stick with or come back to the task when the going gets tough. I anticipated that resilient learners on this kind of programme, as well as their tutors, would demonstrate a range of characteristics and strategies to cope with difficult and unfamiliar situations. These would relate to their capacity for and experience of self-direction. Being resilient is not the same as being competent which relates to just one of its components: ability. Being resilient also involves judging oneself as 'ready' (to take on a challenge) and 'willing' (to do whatever is necessary to achieve the goal). Resilient learners encounter the same kinds of difficulties as others, but have ways to bounce back from their frustrations and anxieties, and these strategies, over the years, are transformed into a valuable learning resource. Resilience is about recovering from blockage or upset, and maintaining equilibrium, focus and commitment to learning.

Mainly in their late thirties and forties, participants on the EdD programme are mid-career professional educators who have, by applying for the course, declared themselves 'ready' to undertake study at this level. Their readiness is complemented by their motivation, or 'willingness', and by a belief in their ability to work for a doctorate, combined with an assessment of the appropriateness of what the programme has to offer for their preferred approach to learning. Looking at the strategies used by such learners to deal with the challenges and the difficulties of learning in this way at this level provided an opportunity to explore resilience as a relevant concept for understanding adult learning. A parallel concern was with the concept of the 'resilient tutor', since the features that make the programme challenging for participants also constitute a challenge for those responsible for teaching it. For both groups the focus of the interviews was on their concerns, their self-doubts, their vulnerability and the strategies they used to surmount these.

The EdD differs from conventional PhD programmes in a number of ways. Aimed at practitioners, it rejects the 'apprenticeship' model in favour of an approach that seeks to develop 'scholarly professionals' rather than 'professional scholars' (Gregory, 1995). Its purpose is similar to the PhD in so far as they both seek to develop intellectual leaders who are highly skilled in objective critical enquiry and dedicated to its importance (Kerlinger, 1965). At the same time it encourages learning that develops from making links between the work context, theory and research. Most significantly, it requires participants to attend twelve taught modules and complete a written assignment for each. They also have to write a research-based dissertation of about 30,000 words. The focus of this chapter and the interviews it reports is on the learning experience embodied in the programme's *taught* component, as perceived by tutors and students.

The decision to embark on doctoral studies is often accompanied by fears of intellectual incompetence, social isolation and difficulties in sustaining motivation. These are particularly heightened for adults who are already established in their careers and, in most cases, in positions of considerable management responsibility. In choosing to follow a taught doctoral programme, participants were balancing an academic or career decision (Would it be as good as a conventional PhD?) with a pragmatic decision (It provides the kind of support I know I need.). Similarly experienced university tutors, used to more homogeneous student groups, are potentially destabilised by the diversity, seniority and high academic expectations of this particular learner group. The high expectations derive in part from the programme's relatively high cost but also from the critical awareness of quality in teaching and learning that participants bring from their own professional experience in education.

An attractive characteristic of a taught programme for people embarking on a doctorate is that it is mapped out as a series of small steps (involving intense three-day group study periods), rather than one mammoth journey; a network of footpaths rather than one featureless mountain slope. Willingness or motivation is thus enhanced by the type of journey and clear markers at each stage. Both participants and tutors are highly skilled, generally confident but, in this context, vulnerable. Each, potentially, feels intimidated by the other. Their resilience then becomes an important factor in their survival.

The degree to which that resilience is sustained by participants once the journey has begun depends on the accuracy of their initial self-assessment, the nature of the learning obstacles en route and the types of support they can draw on to overcome them. This personal act of engagement leads them to take on the learning opportunity provided by the programme, and carries them over hurdles as they occur. Similarly tutors survive by drawing on the repertoire of teaching skills and beliefs about how people learn that they have been constructing throughout their own learning and teaching careers.

MAPPING THE TERRITORY: CONTEXT AND SETTING

The programme described here is novel in that it requires doctoral students to learn, in part, through formal 'teaching' as well as writing a dissertation; and programme tutors to 'teach' their subject at a level at which their subject has not previously been taught. Being the first in the field in Europe, Bristol University's EdD programme has had to explore and trial a range of approaches to teaching and learning at a level that has previously been experienced and assessed solely through research. Its taught component can be seen as a preparation for the mainly 'self-directed' dissertation but it is also conceived as a way of supporting the autonomy and learner control that is advocated as appropriate for all adult learners and particularly for senior professionals combining academic learning with demanding careers. In his discussion of the scope and meaning of self-directed learning Candy (1991) suggests:

> that self-direction can never, and should never, replace the position of the teacher in every learning situation and that attempts to induce people to be more self-directed must be based on a deeper and more comprehensive understanding of the nature of learning, of knowledge and of society than has prevailed up to the present.

Unlike supervisors of conventional doctorates, tutors on a taught doctoral programme have a unique role in supporting learning at this level through their teaching.

The willingness of many institutions to support staff on the taught doctorate by providing financial help and time to study demonstrates the value placed on the kind of continuing professional development the programme represents: an opportunity to develop, through advanced knowledge and understanding, the competencies and skills to deal with the multiplicity of changes facing higher and further education, schools, Local Educational Authorities and the Health Service. It attracts ambitious, mid-career professionals in challenging jobs, seeking more knowledge, skills and understanding through the acquisition of a 'doctoral' identity.

The setting for the programme described here has significance too. It takes place in a School of Education in a traditional university, in which research and scholarship are valued more than teaching and in which university-defined standards constitute the required levels of achievement. Some manipulation of language has taken place, in recognition of what some perceive as a different 'teacher–learner' relationship at doctoral level. 'Students' are called 'participants'; 'supervisors' have become 'advisers'; but tutors are still tutors. In this way the taught doctorate represents a changing culture for adult learning but one that continues to be situated in a traditional 'academic' environment, albeit one which is mainly concerned with formal professional development. Whether Claxton's characterisation of some taught knowledge as pre-packaged 'supermarket meat' is applicable to university teaching at this level is debatable, but it is evident that teachers away from their own familiar teaching contexts do readily fall back into the comfortable ways of teaching and attitudes to learning that characterised their own school and college days. Even the EdD participants, many of whom work in 'state-of-the art' educational settings, welcome the familiarity and other-worldliness of the School of Education's academic setting: 'It's just like being at home, somewhere I go every day. I feel entirely comfortable here'. Another says:

> As a learner on the taught doctorate which focuses on education management, I'm perfectly capable of providing professional input and context.

What I want is not about those things. What I want is the context of the theoretical background. I want the interaction of professionals from other sectors. I want the input of people who have been immersed in education – the fact that they haven't stepped inside a school for 20 years matters not a jot. What I'm looking for is what I can glean and gain from their experience and research. I want to know the gloss they put on their research. I can go and read their papers, but what do they say about what they have written? It's about getting inside, finding out about people's approaches, how they approach their own learning, what are their relationships within their own college. That's what I was looking for.

The participants' willing acceptance of the more ivory tower features of the programme's setting derived in no small part from their keenness to become part of the academic elite that a doctorate in Britain still represents. Their concern with the symbols of having doctoral status (the shape of the bonnet, the colour of the gown) can appear at times almost as great as their concern with the substance. In this respect, symbols become strong motivators.

On the other hand, the same setting of a School of Education which is reassuring to students can create anxieties for tutors about teaching adults at this new level. From their point of view, the tutors have little to gain and much to lose. I interviewed four tutors (two men and two women) who were 'survivors'. They had come through a variety of educational and career experiences that had contributed to their self-concepts as teachers. For these mid- to late-career professionals, the programme challenged teaching approaches which had been honed in different contexts for different audiences. Deemed academically successful, by virtue of their qualifications, publications and status as university lecturers, the tutors had survived the demands of university teaching at other levels. Now they were subject to the scrutiny of 'students' who, in many cases, were senior and/or more expert than they considered themselves to be. This created some tensions, differently resolved. One tutor, Mavis, said:

> what I'm conscious of with a lot of them is that they are peers . . . I'm conscious that it's a delicate relationship particularly because I'm sometimes making judgements about their work which are not favourable. They are the kind of judgements they probably haven't had made in years and who am I to say, quite frankly, I wouldn't have done it this way. I think for many of them it's high risk. There's a lot they might lose and I hope I'm sensitive to that.

In contrast to Mavis whose behaviour tried to take account of how the students felt about their relative status to tutors, another tutor, Robert, remained more detached:

> I feel sometimes they feel this sense of status inconsistency between themselves adopting the role of the learner in an institution, sometimes

being taught or even taught at by people who they might consider are of less social standing within their discipline than they are themselves. I believe some people find the contradiction between their job status and themselves as learners quite difficult to cope with. I don't feel either equipped or disposed to help them with that. I think that's their problem.

THE ENQUIRY

The interviews were designed to explore how this particular group of learners and tutors go about learning and teaching and the contribution of the resulting learning environment to learner resilience. The focus was on the social/contextual and personal/cognitive factors that facilitate or impede learning and which constitute students' and tutors' preferred teaching and learning style while on the programme. Two men and two women participants were chosen (as well as the four tutors) who had completed the taught component and were well advanced with their dissertations. They were chosen, too, as coming from very different professional backgrounds and for having demonstrated different approaches to learning on the programme. They thus had much in common with each other but appeared also to differ in how they managed the EdD experience.

The enquiry was intended to raise issues as a basis for a research agenda for a larger-scale study of resilience in adult learning in the future. A 'learning history' interview schedule was used, drawing on the strengths of life history interviews in exploring individuals' thoughts and practices (Woods, 1993). The students' learning paths were traced from their early school days to their involvement in the EdD programme. A similar tracking process was followed with the tutors, to identify the origins and development of their teaching styles and the implicit learning theories underpinning them. The novelty of the EdD programme meant that both were faced with similar challenges: managing individual performance on a programme that is partly self-directed, partly other-directed; dealing with the potential dis-equilibrium of being senior professionals (usually in control and demonstrating competence) in an unfamiliar teaching/learning situation where loss of face was possible; drawing on and modifying maps from other learning journeys to help them through uncharted territory.

As 'survivors' the students had come through the peaks and troughs of their professional and personal learning experiences in a way that left them wanting more and being prepared to take risks to acquire it. They manifested the 'mastery-oriented' characteristics that Dweck (1986) identifies with the 'go-for-it' attitude of learners who are not discouraged by difficulties. Bill, for example, had 'failed' repeatedly and unexpectedly at secondary school, in spite of doing well at 11+. At each failure the next educational step was always a reaction to doing what had come to be expected of him as a failure. The turnaround, when it came in the sixth form, from failing to succeeding, was accompanied by a sense of responsibility for his own actions, a diminution of dependency on what teachers were teaching and increasing confidence in his autonomy as learner. For Pat, the determination to succeed academically survived lack of family support, early school leaving, and unstimulating work. In both cases, their sense of self-efficacy as learners helped them transcend others' expectations and developed them into self-directed learners. Following Candy (1991), self-direction in this case can be seen as both process (a method for learning) and product (a goal of learning). I was interested in the ways that their characteristics as self-directed learners meshed with tutors' approaches to teaching on the EdD programme, with positive or negative outcomes for learning.

READY, WILLING AND ABLE

Each of the characteristics of readiness, willingness and ability has a social and cognitive dimension. A high level of readiness to learn must reflect a high level of both the social and the cognitive dimensions. For example, there are points in someone's career when he or she is ready to learn, the circumstances are right but the motivation is not there: the programme may be unattractive or the incentive inadequate for the effort required. The person may be ready and willing but doubt his or her capacity to perform at the required standard. Readiness to take on a new learning opportunity like the taught doctorate reflects a self-assessment that includes being in a position to engage, wanting to engage and feeling competent to engage with learning. The confluence of these at a particular point in time may propel someone into the learning experience.

At that point a judgement has been made of being in a position socially and cognitively to take on its demands. Social factors may include domestic circumstances that make time out for study feasible, financial security that makes expenditure on a learning programme possible, and a job that includes a doctorate as an explicit or implicit requirement. Cognitively, it means being ready to be a student again, to be exposed as a learner.

Willingness is the continuing source of motivation that carries the participant over hurdles and through difficulties. It involves those factors to do with wanting to engage in the particular learning activity. It may include others' expectations for next career or academic steps and characteristics of the programme design that appear supportive. These combine with a cognitive disposition towards wanting to achieve long-held instrumental learning goals, such as receiving the academic title of 'doctor' or intellectual goals such as 'pushing back the frontiers of knowledge'. Feeling able to take on a new learning experience means judging that you have the capacity physically, emotionally and intellectually to meet its demands.

The idea of being 'ready, willing and able' is equally applicable to tutors responsible for a new programme, though the manifestations of these characteristics may be different. Being ready socially may mean having reached a status and expertise level that publicly acknowledge a tutor's appropriateness for teaching on the programme; cognitively it may mean being ready to have one's expertise exposed and challenged. A tutor's willingness to engage in this kind of novel teaching experience may rest in how the engagement is valued by the organisation and the kinds of rewards anticipated from working with adult learners in this way. Gibbs (1994) argues for promotion on the basis of teaching excellence as the only sure way of improving the quality of teaching. In a university intent on securing rewards for research excellence, this particular carrot is neither evident nor, from the tutors' perspectives, relevant to their own strategies for providing quality teaching. The rewards are intrinsic and closely related to the type of learning situation that is the outcome of both students' and tutors' construction of the learning events.

GETTING ENGAGED TO LEARNING

How far did the participants interviewed judge themselves as ready, willing and able at the point of starting the EdD? How far were tutors ready, willing and able to undertake teaching at this level? For each participant, the EdD represented the pinnacle of their learning activities to date. All had briefly considered studying for doctorates at earlier stages of their careers, but the time had not been right; they were not 'ready'. Their sense of unreadiness was influenced by wanting to do other things (get a job, marry, train as a teacher) and unsureness about their ability to tackle the level of learning involved. Their descriptions of their decisions to embark on the EdD demonstrated a combination of their conscious, rational appraisal of its potential value and the culmination of an inner personal, emotional and vocational journey that, in their estimation, had equipped them to meet the challenge. Bill said:

> There is undoubtedly elitism, a cachet about the title of doctor, particularly in the occupation I now find myself. And that has to be a motivation, even though in higher education it was something I had as my life plan, something I wanted to return to. But the title's not more important than the learning. If that were the case, I would have done it a long time ago. What was critical about the EdD for me, bearing in mind that my formal education was 20 years ago, was the opportunity through its modular approach to breach that gap of 20 years, that's crucial . . . and the prospect of coming to terms with all that individually without the support of taught modules was something I wouldn't have managed, as a professional working in a stressful, time-consuming job.

Having made the decision to do the taught doctorate, Bill's experience on his first module provided the 'Road to Damascus' experience he needed, to assure him he had made the right choice. His assignment arising from the unit's topic led to a publication:

> It was significant because it impressed on me that even without the background knowledge for that module (even though I'd done the reading, and I'd found the concepts quite difficult), being able to make a contribution that was valued, and seeing how the theory related in such a clear way to one's professional practice, I knew that this doctorate was within my grasp. It became much more than the aspiration of having the title. It actually meant that one could achieve the highest degree of study.

Ben's sense of 'readiness' also came from an assessment of his personal circumstances, professional needs and relative ability:

> The children were grown up. I could make time. I could take it at my own pace. I wondered about whether I'd be able to achieve it intellectually over the intervening years, but what reassured me was that I knew a lot of people who had doctorates, some of whom were very able people, but there were some who were not particularly.

Janet provided a *post hoc* rationalisation that encapsulated her delight at the successful outcome for once in her life of the synchronicity of readiness, willingness and ability:

> When I look back over my career, I realise the pattern all the way through was always to make decisions which subsequently have clearly shown to be wrong, but something else has quickly opened up, and I wouldn't have done it if I hadn't made the wrong decision in the first place. Virtually everything I've done in my adult life was wrong, but I've always felt I must get on with it. Doing this EdD programme is the only good decision I've ever made.

All the participants interviewed resembled what Candy (1991) describes as self-directed individuals, 'that is people who exhibit the qualities of moral, emotional and intellectual autonomy'. Although Bill was overjoyed when the rightness of his decision was confirmed, he was already secure in his belief in his ability to undertake study at this level because of what he had learned about himself in earlier learning experiences. While judging she was ready for the programme, Pat had initial concerns about whether it was right for her or she for it:

> Some of the modules I've been very, very enthused about. As the material has been explored, laid out in front of us, I've been able to see the relevance of the module to my work situation. When I first started, not being sure of the level or the expectations, there were some very vibrant people on that module who seemed to know it all, and I thought oh dear, have I made the right choice? It's the first time I'd felt like that. So that was a very critical

moment. It was when I was sitting up in the classroom on the very first day, so it was a new experience for me. I wondered, will I succeed?

She survived and went on, as a result of making the links she needed between theory and her area of professional practice that had always constituted the keystone of her learning style and ambitions. In another module where she found the tutor's approach not conducive to making these links, failure on the written assignment seemed imminent until she reviewed it again:

> For a week I couldn't look at it, couldn't handle it. I felt extremely disappointed. Eventually, looking at the tutor's comments, looking at the work, trying to make connections, make sense of it, make it relevant to my work situation, I rewrote it. I read back through my work from time to time, and I looked at the first submission and thought what a load of rubbish. As the course progressed, I could see the development in my work, and the difference in the quality between the earlier and later submissions. Every situation is a learning situation, that's why I read back through my work, to try to gauge my own progress.

She survived the difficult moment by realising that making the links and achieving the quality was *her* responsibility and something she must do, as in the past, for herself.

Although tutors also saw their reputations on the line, in teaching on this kind of programme, they had less at stake since the teaching was part of their contractual responsibilities and they were mainly accountable to themselves for their teaching quality. In this respect they were self-directed teachers. They deemed themselves ready to teach by virtue of their subject expertise and long careers in teaching adults. This experience had confirmed for them the rewards to be gained from working with adults who are highly motivated to learn. At the same time, they ensured they were ready and able to present the sessions, by preparing thoroughly and rehearsing in detail the script or script outline they intended to deliver. Describing how she prepared her module, Jill said:

> I revamp it thoroughly every year, I pretty well rewrite the whole thing. I'm not sure why I do that except the whole module for me has to hang together, so I have to think it through completely each time. In doing that it seems to come out differently each time, so it creates a lot of work for me. Then, having got all the materials together, I transform my thinking into handouts, transparencies, which act as triggers for me and allow me to be more flexible. I couldn't write it out as lecture notes. I feel that would tie me down and I'm not sure how I would present it. It would spoil the possibility of dialogue. I've got a tension between being extremely structured and wanting to be extremely flexible and that creates a lot of anxiety for me. I'm very committed to getting it right. That is an important

aspect of my style. I always do a needs analysis beforehand and try and shape the module to how I think they are as a group.

This tutor was drawing on past experience of a teaching approach which satisfied both her own personal style and student expectations. For her the risk was in being flexible and with it the danger of not being able to respond appropriately.

Jack valued structure more than flexibility and waited for the students to respond to him rather than vice versa:

> I've always aimed to be inspirational. Lectures serve to raise ideas and a consciousness and make people think but I don't see myself as transmitting a body of knowledge. I aim to inspire. I'm not aiming to stand up at the front and say things but I am drawing on my personality, that's where it comes from. Perhaps I'm a failed actor or performer, it's not something that I've chosen to do, it's just how I find it easiest to do. I've always been very conscious of what I was doing, I've always reflected a lot on my lecturing. I think the real impact of my teaching comes later and after. I prepare by rehearsing in my mind what I'm going to say, it's to psyche me up. All the lectures I do are typed up beforehand and always retyped every year. I do that because I need to rehearse it in my mind and that's a way of going over it so even though there are hardly any differences I need to have it freshly done and I even visualise myself saying what I say. The typed lecture notes are a prop for me, I don't give them to the students.

All the tutors had anxieties, not always very different from those expressed by participants. Did they know enough, would they be put on the spot by the group, could they fit in the necessary preparation, could they deliver the goods participants had paid for? Overcoming their anxieties meant drawing on their own experiences of teaching and learning in the past; what had worked for them earlier could work for them now. Their responses to obstacles to learning faced by participants were enmeshed with the strategies they used to overcome their own anxieties as tutors as well as their perceptions of participants' learning needs.

WHEN THE GOING GETS TOUGH

If, as has been suggested, participants on the EdD programme have made a judgement about their readiness, willingness and ability at the point of entry, what are the pressures they are likely to encounter on the programme that will require resilience and how do they deal with them? In many ways these pressures are the other side of the coin to the social and cognitive factors that brought them into the programme in the first place. Seeking public recognition through a doctorate could entail loss of face with colleagues, family and friends if success is not achieved. Judging personal circumstances to be propitious for study may be undermined by minor or radical changes in these circumstances, such as bereavement, illness, divorce. A personal learning style developed through the years may turn out to fit badly with teaching styles on the programme. Confidence in expertise as a practitioner may be challenged by a realisation of relative ignorance of the theoretical dimension. A reliance on linking new knowledge to professional experience as a way of arriving at understanding may collapse in the face of programme content that appears irrelevant to the workplace.

Tutors' expectations of coping with the programme are also likely to be undermined by a number of factors. These include realisation of inadequate knowledge, demands for pastoral support that are not included in their teaching repertoire, personal and work pressures that make it difficult to prepare the work adequately, participant learning style preferences that are out of tune with the tutors' own, ignorance of participants' work contexts leading to difficulties in making the material relevant.

For both tutors and participants, these factors combine to create physical, emotional and intellectual obstacles to continuing the learning journey. When these obstacles become too much, the temptation is to abandon the journey and go back home to more comfortable territory. Tutors' resilience in the face of obstacles was buttressed by their contractual obligations as well as their willingness to adjust their style in the light of negative feedback.

Participants, on the other hand, were there from choice. When they described these points at which they felt ready to give up, they also revealed some of the characteristics of resilience that kept them going. When the learning got hard then, in their view, it was an opportunity still to learn, not to demonstrate inadequacy. Challenges to their self-concept as 'able' drew from them what Dweck (1986) described as the 'go-for-it' attitude, in which an incremental view of ability is a spur to action when blocks to learning occur.

Janet described her experience of such a moment:

On one occasion I said something stupid in a session and the tutor responded making it very clear that I'd said something stupid. I thought that was a bit unkind. It had been stupid because I hadn't understood what he'd been talking about. As a teacher, I'd say perhaps you haven't understood. As it was I felt I should keep my mouth shut for the rest of the session. I asked one of the others why what I'd said was stupid and it was to do with a philosophical concept, rationality I think, and I always come in with the sociological point of view. At work I'd usually ask, 'Have I said something stupid?' and someone would answer, 'Yes, because . . . ,' and that would be fine. I think I'm quite open, I don't mind . . . we all say stupid things. I didn't feel angry with the tutor but he did go down in my estimation because I felt it an unnecessary reaction, but that's because I have a particular view of teaching. I know you can undermine people's confidence by doing that sort of thing so I try to avoid doing it.

Her ability to withstand this potential blow to her self-esteem as a learner came from being able to draw on the strength of her own values as a teacher, which confirmed for her the inappropriateness of the tutor's response. Later, when the same tutor gave her minimal feedback on a draft written assignment, she fell back again on her rejection of the relative value of his judgements by thinking, 'Sod it, I'll do it my own way'. In both instances, the negative responses could have confirmed her lifelong lack of confidence in her ability, in spite of evidence to the contrary. What triumphed, however, was the strength of the self-motivation and love of learning that had carried her through negative learning experiences at school, college and work:

> No-one had any expectations of me, but I didn't expect to fail in this programme. I was determined to do it. I was prepared to do whatever it took not to [fail]. Whenever I would submit a paper, every time I put it in the post my heart sank when it was gone because I knew I couldn't do anything about it. It was like being 11 again, putting yourself out for others' judgement, no confidence that it would be passed. When I got back to the university everyone was always very keen to know how I was getting on. I had a lot of support. It's a working context where I, along with everyone else, am having to transform themselves from being a teacher into a teacher and researcher. So in many ways I'm modelling to the others that I work with and I'm driving myself to put myself on the line.

On other occasions, participants' ability to withstand hard knocks was buttressed by what felt good about the programme and appeared to be taking them towards their goal. Pat's learning goals were reflected in her ambition 'to go beyond the hills' of the rural valley village where she was born. Most of her academic journey had been self-funded. Now, on the EdD programme she was engaged in a learning effort that someone else had agreed to pay for. When things were difficult, 'How could I go back and say, excuse me, you've just paid £300 and I'm giving up at the beginning?' This extrinsic incentive, combined with the satisfaction she had nurtured over the years in being intellectually stretched, carried her through stressful moments, when a subject remained incomprehensible and links to work experience elusive.

For Bill, the highlight came at the Christmas lunch, when the tutor praised the paper he had written and suggested a joint publication:

> That was an immensely positive experience in terms of not only feedback on the assignment itself, but that one had made a contribution in the assignment that might actually be publishable. That one was achieving what the EdD sets out to do, which is to produce people who are capable of producing work at that level.

A wonderful learning moment for Janet came when the group were struggling with analysing data:

The tutor was explaining how it was important when keying data in that it all went in the right columns, and Miriam said 'I know just what you mean. It's just like when you're doing your cardigan up and you've got one button left.' She was making a spot-on comment, but everyone fell about, it was just lovely. This is the way primary teachers come to understand these things. You can trust a group like that not to say, 'Isn't she stupid', but to laugh and say that's a really good example.

These identified 'good' moments bring to the surface what contributes to successful learning for this group of learners. The factors are different for each individual but are important to him or her, as part of his or her learning repertoire. As self-motivated, independent learners, all four participants had learned to make use of the different resources available at different stages of their learning careers. Experience of the positive effects of collaborative working had not been a strong feature for any; negative experiences had, to the extent that their primary determination was to go it alone, when necessary. However, for the three who joined at the beginning of the programme, the experience of a warm, supportive, close group was immediately available and provided an unexpected cushion against their initial vulnerability. Janet said:

Everyone was wanting to be there and at the same time enjoy it. Lots of jokes, and the tutor very good at facilitating a good learning experience. It's always been very important, who's in the group. We traded on people's expertise, saying 'Ben, you know about this, I don't understand what the issue is, you explain it'. If the tutor didn't give you what you wanted you got it from each other.

This support usually existed between participants on a module and, while not crucial for the few participants interviewed, they saw it as making a positive contribution to the quality of their learning experience. They could survive without it but preferred it to be there. Even Pat, who perceived the apparent cohesion of the group initially as a threat, came to appreciate its value. Sharing learning with others provided a 'buzz' and stimulation that work and independent study could not do. This sharing with others was something which later, as they moved to the relative isolation of writing the dissertation, they missed, but it had strengthened them to take this next step.

TEACHING FOR LEARNING

The tutors had clear ideas about what they were trying to achieve in their sessions and the strategies they identified as most appropriate for their goals. The interviews revealed that, in each case, their teaching style had changed little from the one that characterised their early years in teaching. How a teacher teaches is based on assumptions about how people learn. These assumptions are drawn from a combination of deeply held values about other people and education, as well as memories of their own learning experiences at the hands of other formal and informal educators (see, for example, Chapter 7). These, combined with professional development experiences, constituted the tutors' implicit learning theories. Resilience was demonstrated through the tutors' willingness to 'test the bedsprings' of their own teaching style and respond appropriately. Some preferred a hard bed that remained rock solid however hard it was bounced on. Others preferred beds that gave on impact but bounced back and moulded to their shape.

In terms of Fox's (1983) model of four personal theories of teaching (shown in Figure 11.1), the tutors' preference for the 'travelling' mode was uppermost with different emphases on the delivery vehicles used. However,

---

TRANSFER THEORY

Student	=	container to be filled
Teacher	=	pump attendant, barmaid
Subject	=	commodity to be transferred
Preferred methods	=	lectures, reading lists, duplicated notes
Explanations for failure	=	leaky vessel, small container

SHAPING THEORY

Student	=	inert materials (clay, wood)
Teacher	=	skilled craftsperson working on material
Subject	=	blue-print, pattern
Preferred methods	=	laboratory, workshop, recipes
Explanations for failure	=	flawed material

TRAVELLING THEORY

Student	=	explorer
Teacher	=	expert travel companion/guide
Subject	=	terrain to be explored, vantage points
Preferred methods	=	simulations, projects, discussions, independent learning
Explanations for failure	=	blinkered, no stamina, unadventurous

GROWING THEORY

Student	=	developing personally, growing plant
Teacher	=	resource provider, gardener
Subject	=	experience to be incorporated into developing personality
Preferred methods	=	experiential methods, more spontaneous
Explanations for failure	=	poor start, inadequately prepared, no will to develop

---

Figure 11.1 Personal theories of teaching
Source: based on Fox (1983).

within that category (in which subject takes priority over person) there were tensions about the relative weightings of attention to content and process. Tutors' abilities to overcome these tensions, when they came to the surface, depended on the degree of confidence they had in their preferred mode of teaching.

Both Jill and Jack, for example, were aiming to help students arrive at the same destination, but the routes they took were very different. Jill's approach tried to combine leading the way with encouraging others to take over where possible. Her commitment to dialogue, based on what had worked in the past for her as both learner and tutor, sometimes sat uneasily with her belief in the need to demonstrate expertise to meet others' expectations. What carried her through the sticky moments was her conviction that active participation in a learning dialogue was more effective for learning and more democratic than passive transfer of knowledge. She said:

> I'm aiming to get them to examine in a systematic way the terrain of the subject I'm dealing with. They have lots of aids from me so they have enough knowledge at the end of the unit to be able to examine their own chosen field with some academic rigour. I try to make the material relevant and I draw continuously on their experiences to help them make sense of it. I always start off a session by leading but I would say within five or ten minutes it starts developing into a discussion until I pull it back to the structure that I've got beforehand. In a way I have synthesised the knowledge and I present them with my synthesis of it but I am also open to challenge so whatever I'm saying I'm throwing back to them and saying 'what do you think?'. It doesn't always work but it is a very backwards and forwards kind of session. It aims to be a dialogue. When they go into groups I keep away from them in the hope that they will develop the dialogue without my help. When I am there I'm aware of being a kind of walking stick for them to cross this terrain and then you remove the stick and hope they will walk on their own. I provide them with a whole lot of resources about the topic and model a way of thinking about it, and then I hope they will go off and use those resources and critically analyse the modelling I've been doing and arrive at their own individual ideas.

Jack was similarly concerned with subject expertise but used his status, personality and years of successful university teaching to structure a teaching style which, if there were sticky patches, would continue regardless:

> I'm concerned on the programme to improve their understanding . . . No way am I concerned with training or improving performance. I hope that it does but I can't make that assumption. What I'm basically aiming at is to get them to think about what they're doing. I hope they take the view that although my language is a social science language with concepts that aren't everyday concepts, when I describe things I illustrate the concepts

often out of my own direct experience or by bringing in an example from outside education. I remember things, my mind is a storehouse of bits and pieces which I can call on. I remember quotations easily so I call those up when it's appropriate. I can see them coming from the back sometimes before they come out.

When he saw puzzlement, he gave examples and went on giving examples until the light dawned. He used humour frequently and deliberately to help students relax, in the same way as he would in any social situation:

People relax when you're joking and think, thank Christ, it can't be as bad as all that.

It was important to him that the learning was going well and he judged this by participants' faces:

They're attentive, agog, mouth open, nodding because what I'm doing is for them the shock of recognition that by and large I'm saying what they know but didn't know they knew, and they don't know it until then because they didn't have the concept in which to capture it. I conceptualise it for them and they learn from how it's been conceptualised to then conceptualise for themselves. They can then look at their own situation in different ways and try to conceptualise it in a way that enables them to describe it.

On the other hand, his own resilience depended on years of practice, reflection and continual rehearsal of what he wanted to say. Like an actor on-stage, he was aware of his audience's response but the faces were blurred. His own apprenticeship to learning and subsequent learning experiences had been in response to strong personalities and 'great minds'. This was the model he took for his own approach.

In contrast the two women tutors placed considerable emphasis on the importance of knowing participants individually as part of their teaching strategy. Far from being blurred, every face in the audience was viewed by these tutors distinctly and sensitively, adjusting their teaching performance in response to participants' anticipated or actual responses. Jill's starting point was her perception, based on earlier teaching experiences in other adult learning contexts, that individual participants were likely to feel threatened at different times.

In many ways I see them as putting their identities on the line by doing this programme because it's supposed to be on a very high level. They are highly experienced professionals, most have considerable status in their own institutions and yet intellectually they are probably just as vulnerable as any of the other people I have taught in the past who didn't appear to have so much to lose. I try to be extremely supportive, for example I support anything people say during the session, I draw it in and make all the right noises. I keep an eye on anyone trying to come in but having difficulties and just occasionally I actually pinpoint people and ask, 'What do you think?' I try to ensure that everyone, even the quieter people, have a chance to speak and I would never make anyone feel that what they have said is less than useful.

The priority for Mavis was establishing rapport with the group, knowing people as individuals, being aware of and meeting individual needs. This approach had characterised her teaching style since she began some twenty years earlier teaching in a secondary school. In spite of exposure to different groups of learners and a range of professional development experiences, her commitment to a style which gave priority to individual needs had never wavered. It was reflected too in all her professional activities outside the classroom. In the context of the EdD, this approach was not without its tensions:

> I spend quite a bit of the time in my head thinking X hasn't said anything, Y is hogging the conversation, Z is irritating everybody including me, how am I going to handle that? And then you think 'shall I ask X a direct question, like how do they feel about this in their context?' a bit pointed, so there's that level about how you involve people, the extent to which you can make your content matter relevant to their situation. One of the other things I begin to struggle with in my head, and this has always been a strand, is if I get side-tracked onto the process issue here, am I being sufficiently rigorous on the academic side? After all, aren't they adults, shouldn't they get on with it?

The tension for both the women tutors was in balancing participants' individual needs with what the tutors saw as the academic task to be achieved. Both perceived feeling threatened, bored or uncomfortable as detrimental to learning and adjusted their teaching styles to try and minimise the likelihood of these effects. In this respect their teaching style put attention to process above attention to task. In contrast, Jack and Robert were more assertive in their prioritisation of task over process, less anxious about 'telling' the group and expecting people to stand on their own two feet. Mavis described her inability to use this approach:

> I've never been the sort of person who writes on the board or dictates notes. I suppose it's because of the way that I manage and interact with the group but I'm not the 'knowledge to be dispersed' sort of person, the 'I know what the score is and I'm going to lecture you' approach is not me. It's not my personal style and I'm not confident I've got enough knowledge anyway.

Both Mavis and Jill were aware as teachers of drawing on their own recent experiences as adult learners in the very different contexts of learning practical skills such as playing an instrument and swimming. Their own resilience as adult learners in situations where it was easy to feel foolish and a failure, and in which motivation to succeed had to be sustained, was bolstered by sensitive teaching and a balance between being given support and being encouraged to be independent. They transferred this personal learning about what it feels like to be a learner to the EdD where the nature and level of teaching was a less important determinant of their teaching style than their respect for the quality of each individual's learning experience.

In contrast Jack and Robert preferred to separate the learner from the person, paying more attention to the intellectual rather than affective dimensions of the interaction. Providing maximum support for student learning was a priority for all the tutors but, as we have seen, they interpreted this in very different ways, depending on their own earlier learning experiences. The different attitude of tutors towards giving support was reflected too in how they felt able to receive it, when the going got tough in their own teaching. Knowing how they relied on sensitive tutor support for their own learning, Mavis and Jill were bolstered in their own teaching by 'high points' that involved tutor and participants learning together. Similarly 'low points' would be confronted and addressed jointly with the students. Robert's self-esteem as a tutor, on the other hand, included taking sole responsibility for putting things right when they went wrong:

> I didn't feel it was the students' job to help me organise the course. I thought it was down to me, it was my responsibility. Even if it was suggested to me that I should discuss it with the students, I couldn't picture what kind of outcome that could lead to that I could cope with. If it were to happen again I couldn't imagine saying half-way through the second day, 'well boys and girls this is not going at all well for me. I don't know how it's going for you, what can we do about it?' I couldn't do that because it would be a terrible loss of self-esteem. It would be a frank admittance that I hadn't got it together as far as I was concerned. I think it would be totally unfair to put on to the students that they should in some way help me salvage this. It's my fault, therefore it's for me to put right.

His own subsequent career of mainly self-directed learning (compared with the other tutors who had followed more conventional academic career paths) was a strong influence on his conception of EdD participants as independent learners and himself as an independent teacher.

These differences in the tutors' strategies for supporting adult learners in this context were united by each tutor's commitment first to the 'travelling' theory of teaching described in Figure 11.1 and second to the goal of liberating and empowering the learner. What, however, emerged from their accounts as the most appropriate teaching approach for the learning styles of participants on the programme? All the tutors interviewed had a clear idea of how they expected learners to be on a programme at this level and in this subject area, based on an approach that was prepared to take in new ideas and play around with them. The ways in which tutors viewed their own sources of resilience, and the extent to which they saw participants as resilient, influenced the teaching strategies they adopted. On the one hand there were tutors who defined these students as academically 'grown' and therefore not in need of nurturing. Any potential brakes to an individual's learning were, from this perspective, outside the tutor's control and would not be helped by a change in teacher. Indeed such a change might even threaten the tutor's own self-worth and resilience which remained private and not open to scrutiny.

The alternative approach, which emphasised flexible responses to individual learner needs, required tutor resilience which thrived on openness and sharing. The parallels between participants and tutors were close. All were competent professionals in a new terrain with a lot to lose. All were having their resilience tested in one way or another. For both groups a bad moment was when something to do with their self-worth was at stake: their reputation, understanding, ability. Good moments came with breakthroughs in learning, as with the cardigan buttons story earlier, or, where tutors were concerned, learning was shared or a light was switched on. In Jill's view, the justification for her emphasis on trying to ensure that learning was enjoyable was the possibility that enjoyment might be a necessary stimulus to creativity:

> If in the way you conduct a module you don't turn any switches on, people will go away feeling dull and uncreative. If they've been bored they aren't going to go and do something interesting. If on the other hand feedback tells us they have enjoyed the three days, then maybe enjoyment is important, like turning on the lights.

Other tutors considered participant enjoyment a low priority. Even the participants interviewed suggested that both men and women were primarily task focused and relatively unconcerned about the extent to which they were responded to personally. They appreciated praise, structure and respect for their opinions but were able to draw on their own resources if any of these were missing. The gender difference between the men and women tutors in their emphasis on process or task was not reflected in differences between the men and women students. It would be interesting to explore further with a larger sample ways in which men and women learners differ, if at all, in their need for different kinds of support for learning.

The participants' responses might be seen to imply that 'task'-focused teaching approaches were more appropriate than process approaches particularly if any residual learning difficulties could be picked up by a separate pastoral programme. Where tutors were the source of these difficulties (as opposed to the learner's own situation), it was often as a result of their use of a 'transfer' theory of teaching (see Figure 11.1) in which students figure as empty vessels to be filled. Participants on this programme were, as we have seen, potentially resilient and resilience does not sit easily with the passivity that 'transfer' theories attribute to students.

However, it is important at this level of teaching to distinguish between 'transfer' teaching and didactic approaches, such as that used by Jack, which were interactive, by virtue of teaching conditionally rather than absolutely, and inviting engagement. The participants are at a stage of intellectual development when they recognise the conditional nature of knowledge; they are ready for it and want to take it on and use it to formulate their own ideas. The positive dynamic created by this mutual recognition by teacher and learner of the conditionality of knowledge could be marred by a tutor's insistence on his or her version of the truth or, through his or her response, the learner's inadequacy in understanding what has been presented.

We saw earlier how participants considered the company of their peers as a desirable feature of their journey across new territory. The tutors also agreed that this made the journey potentially easier but were less certain about the precise form the collegial approach to travelling should take. In Robert's view, the weaker travellers were clearly supported by the presence of stronger, more experienced colleagues. Having tried initially to be the sole guide, he felt much happier when he devised a programme in which participants spent more time in small-group work rather than listening to him talking:

> I felt really happy about that. I felt that by the members of the group working together I was able to exploit the fact that some knew a lot about research and others knew nothing, and those who knew a lot were not frustrated by having to listen to someone telling them something they already knew and the ones that knew less were able to relate more easily.

The other tutors were less confident about a learning groups' ability to find its own way since, without the tutor's presence, it was more common for independent groups to stop and have a rest or wander off in directions that were not even on the module map.

Overall, both students and tutors described relatively few learning disappointments during the sessions involving face-to-face teaching which had been the focus of the interviews. When they did occur (such as disappointing intellectual level of discussion in class, minimum outcomes from group work and restricted, conservative thinking in written assignments) they were seen by both groups as challenges, opportunities to extend teaching and learning repertoires; in other words, to be resilient. Even the 'ivory tower' features of a fairly traditional School of Education were seen as supportive and appropriate for the intellectual learning which was at the heart of this doctorate programme.

SUMMARY AND CONCLUSIONS

It would appear from these learning histories that the most resilient learners will tend to achieve their goals, whatever the type and quality of the teaching approach. Inappropriate teaching methods and lack of support will make the learning experience harder for them, but their self-directedness will help them surmount difficulties. By the time they reach a programme like the Doctor of Education most have learned to use their own resources to deal with any negative aspects of learning situations. The less resilient will drop out or need support of a different order from that provided in the teaching situation.

The profiles of both participants and tutors have highlighted the usefulness of resilience as a concept for understanding some aspects of the success and failure of adult learning. Resilience in learning is closely bound up with adult needs to be self-directing whether as learners or teachers, but within a framework of providing mutual support on a shared journey. It is a quality which is present in people in varying degrees. Both tutors and students demonstrated a need to get from the journey what they individually wanted and needed, particularly in terms of self-esteem. The learning repertoires on which both drew for orientation on this journey into unfamiliar territory reflected common characteristics, developed since childhood. They included:

- making their own decisions;
- choosing to do what they want rather than should;
- loving knowledge for its own sake;
- preferring collaboration to competition;
- being ambitious intellectually as well as vocationally;
- reflecting on their own learning and teaching;
- respecting and wanting others' expertise;
- relating knowledge to practice;
- being determined not to fail.

This checklist might well act as a self-assessment profile of resilience, to be completed by anyone considering joining this kind of doctoral programme, whether as student or tutor. It does not include all the qualities necessary to succeed in this particular learning situation but indicates some of these without which the mountain top might never be reached. Representing the apex of academic achievement, the final stages of the long, slow path up the steep academic mountain slope involve learning to negotiate flatter territory near the top where paths have disappeared, there are no good maps, and bogs and boulders lie in the way. Or, to change the metaphor, if a key function of the teaching that provides a route to the top is its ability to illuminate the territory, then the challenge to tutors is in finding the precise location of the learning switches. Depending on their prior learning experiences, individuals will differ in what they perceive these to be. While enjoyment, interest and interaction may not be crucial for the more resilient learner, they may make a difference to the less resilient. More important than disagreement on their location was the agreement which all shared on teaching and learning being about switching lights on, not off.

REFERENCES

Candy, P. C. (1991) *Self-Direction for Lifelong Learning: A Comprehensive Guide to Theory and Practice*, San Francisco: Jossey-Bass.

Dweck, C. S. (1986) 'Motivational processes affecting learning'. *American Psychologist*, Vol. 41, pp. 1040–8.

Fox, D. (1983) 'Personal theories of teaching'. *Studies in Higher Education*, Vol. 8, No. 2, pp. 151–63.

Gibbs, G. (1994) 'Promoting excellent teachers at Oxford Brookes University: from profiles to peer review in 10 years'. Paper presented at Conference at Goldsmith's College on the contribution of the individual academic to university teaching: building up the picture.

Gregory, M. (1995) 'Implications of the introduction of the Doctor of Education degree in British universities: can the EdD reach parts the PhD cannot?'. *The Vocational Aspects of Education*, Vol. 47, No. 2, pp. 177–88.

Kerlinger, N. (1965) 'The EdD and the PhD'. *Teachers College Record*, Vol. 66, pp. 435–9.

Woods P. (1993) *Critical Events in Teaching and Learning*, London: Falmer Press.

Chapter 12

Learning to become a headteacher

The role of the mentor

Agnes McMahon

This chapter offers an interesting contrast to the previous one. The central concern, with the particular anxieties and coping strategies of senior professionals re-entering a phase of learning, remains the same. But Agnes McMahon's study differs in certain crucial respects. First, in addressing the learning needs of new headteachers, she is focusing on learning 'on the job', which is both more directly practical, and more openly visible to colleagues, than that of the EdD. In so far as headteachers are expected – and expect themselves – to be instantly and perpetually competent and knowledgeable, their learning has to be conducted 'invisibly'. Yet there is also pressure, for those who espouse the notion of schools as learning communities, to model 'being a learner'. Agnes explore these tensions in the context of an experimental peer mentoring programme, which paired experienced and new headteachers.

INTRODUCTION

It is extremely rare to hear a newly appointed headteacher say that he or she is 'learning to become a headteacher'. While such statements are perfectly acceptable from a deputy headteacher or a more junior teacher, there is a widely held view that someone appointed to headship, like those appointed as surgeons and football managers, is fully competent. The reality can be very different. Research has shown (e.g. Weindling and Earley, 1987) that newly appointed headteachers may have to handle very difficult situations, be unsure about what action to take and yet feel inhibited from sharing their concerns with their colleagues in the school. There are things that they must learn if they are to survive and, in the majority of cases, this learning is about how to behave in a new role rather than acquiring technical knowledge. This chapter is concerned with the issue of how men and women learn to become headteachers and the factors that can inhibit their learning. It will focus specifically on the ways in which a headteacher mentoring programme can aid the transition into headship and will draw upon data collected during the national evaluation of the headteacher mentoring pilot schemes (Bolam *et al.*, 1993a).

FEATURES OF HEADSHIP

Although teachers are generally not held in such high regard in society now as they were a few generations ago, gaining a position as headteacher is still a mark of considerable achievement. It means that the particular individual holds one of the most senior and responsible posts in school teaching; one which is of higher status and which is paid at a higher level than other teachers in the same school; and is a post which carries a great deal of power and responsibility. The model of school organisation which applies in practically all British schools emphasises the superior position of the headteacher in relation to the other staff: the headteacher, with the governors, is ultimately responsible for the school. Headship is a challenging and demanding job which requires long hours of work and can frequently be very lonely and very stressful. A 1994 survey of teachers' workloads (School Teachers' Review Body) indicated that on average, primary headteachers worked 55.4 hours a week and secondary heads 61.1 hours. Expectations of the headteacher are high; numerous studies have indicated that the type and quality of leadership provided by the headteacher is a key contributory factor for school effectiveness (e.g. HMI, 1979; Mortimore *et al.*, 1988; Alexander, 1992).

A quantity of Government legislation, particularly since 1988, has devolved increased powers to headteachers and school governors (e.g. for the budget, staff appointments). The introduction of the open enrolment policy has given parents greater choice about which school their children should attend and 'league tables' of school examination results are now published on a regular basis; these changes have compelled headteachers, particularly in secondary schools, to compete for pupils in an educational marketplace. In some instances the desire to hold a competitive edge in the market has precluded headteachers from talking openly about school matters to their peers in the locality. School governors now have the power to introduce an element of performance-related pay into headteacher salaries. All these factors are potential sources of pressure for a new headteacher. The vast majority of them will be coming into a new school context, probably with a clear agenda for change, conscious that others will be expecting a great deal from them in a relatively short period of time and will be faced with immediate practical tasks that can occupy the whole of their week. Moreover, they may regard their fellow heads as market competitors and, as such, not to be fully trusted.

WHAT HAS TO BE LEARNED?

There is no precise job description for headship. A key clause in the conditions of service for headteachers (DFE, 1994) states that the headteacher 'shall be responsible for the internal organisation, management and control of the school'. The scale and quantity of the head's tasks can be daunting. A recent statement by the Teacher Training Agency (TTA) defined them as being:

> to determine the overall purpose of the school; to determine planning, resource allocation and strategic management; to develop, implement, monitor and evaluate the curriculum, quality and standards and pupil support; to manage personnel; be responsible for administration, financial management and the premises; to develop relations with the community and to be accountable to the governing body.
>
> (TTA, 1994)

The core competences that the TTA considered necessary if these tasks were to be accomplished were leadership; the ability to communicate and build relations with others; problem analysis; adaptability; personal organisation and motivation; the ability to extend and update one's knowledge base (TTA, 1994). Recent research on effective schools and effective school management (e.g. Scheerens, 1992; Fullan, 1992; Bolam et al., 1993b) has emphasised the importance of the staff being in broad agreement about the school goals, values, mission and policy; staff involvement in decision making; teachers working together as a team; a collaborative professional subculture; norms of continuous improvement for staff and students; and strong, purposive leadership by the headteacher and senior staff which encourages these features. Seashore-Louis (1994), writing about the school as a learning organisation, commented:

> The leadership task in a learning organisation is both subtle and unstable. On the one hand one must empower and delegate; but on the other one must also become a raconteur who leads through building value consensus and vision, and an intellectual who provides the stimulus for others to seek and interact with new information.

The educational environment is turbulent and seems likely to remain so; coping with multiple change will be an on-going task for every headteacher. The headteachers' specific individual learning needs are likely to vary widely; some will find that they need to acquire particular knowledge or a specific skill (e.g. knowledge of employment legislation or how to present a report to governors) but, perhaps more often, their main need will be to find a way of establishing themselves in a leadership role in their schools, something which involves a more intangible form of learning. They need to be able to act both as inspirational leaders and as efficient managers of their schools. How can they learn to do this?

Claxton suggested in Chapter 1 that, to be a good learner, one must be ready, willing and able to learn, be ready to seize upon and exploit any learning opportunities that are presented and be free from internal blocks and barriers that might inhibit learning. How many new headteachers fit this description? The difficulties that many of them face are, first, that they have been appointed on the basis of their existing expertise to undertake a particular job and feel that they need to demonstrate competence rather than be open about their learning needs; second, they may not be aware of what they need to learn. They are not usually in a position where they can make a prior decision about whether or not they want to engage in learning; typically they will be taking actions, some of which will achieve what they intended while others will not. A central question is: what is required from them and from others if these varied experiences are to be interpreted and used as learning opportunities?

WHO ARE THE LEARNERS?

Every year some 2,000 people are appointed to their first headship in an English school. The majority of these people will be male and the largest group will be taking up headship in primary schools. They will all be highly qualified and experienced professionals, probably in the age range 35–45; most of them will hold a first degree, some will have postgraduate qualifications; they are likely to be good classroom teachers and will almost certainly have had some previous experience of school management, as a middle manager or deputy headteacher. It can be assumed that, since they chose to apply for a particular post as headteacher, they want the job and feel that they have the capacity to do it well. Like the *resilient learners* on the EdD programme, whom Hall discusses in Chapter 11, they feel ready for the task ahead. The very fact that they have been appointed to such a senior post demonstrates that they have been successful learners throughout their career. Although there is no hard evidence on which to draw, it is unlikely that many new headteachers take up their appointment feeling that they have a great deal to learn before they will be able to handle the job. However, even when they have identified that they have some development needs, meeting these needs may be difficult. Whereas selecting a training course or a textbook that will help you master a new computer program may be relatively straightforward, learning how to lead a group of teachers, some of whom may have applied for your job and resent your appointment, will be much more problematic. It is in the latter case that the support of a mentor may be a valuable aid to learning.

WHAT PROBLEMS DO NEW HEADTEACHERS EXPERIENCE?

A questionnaire issued to the new headteachers who participated in the pilot mentoring schemes (Bolam *et al.*, 1993a) included items asking them to indicate the problems that they had experienced and why they decided to participate in the voluntary mentoring scheme. Questionnaires were returned by 239 (66 per cent) of the sample of new heads. A wide range of problems was reported which can be roughly categorised into three broad groups. First, there were issues about the substantive work of the school: 63 per cent of the sample said that improving the standards of teaching and learning in the school was a very or moderately serious problem; creating/maintaining a good public image for the school was reported as a problem by 54.5 per cent; dealing with LMS and finance was perceived as a problem by 63.5 per cent of the sample; and producing and implementing the school development plan was problematic for 56 per cent. None of these issues can be resolved quickly; all require strategic thought and they cannot be solved by the head acting alone. Yet, it was problems with the management of people that formed the second set of issues. For 56 per cent of the sample the existing staffing structure of the school was a problem. Other concerns that they reported were: getting the staff to accept new ideas (47.2 per cent) and to work as a team (45.8 per cent); dealing with a weak member of the senior management team (43 per cent); improving consultation and communication procedures (53.6 per cent). The third set of issues was more personal: 67.2 per cent of the sample reported that they had difficulty managing time and deciding upon priorities.

In summary, the three main learning areas that were highlighted concerned the strategic management of change, the management of people and respondents' own self-management. Typically, new headteachers are not short of ideas about what to do but deciding how to do it is usually much harder. Unfortunately for them, new heads cannot begin with a clean slate but have to work with the existing situation: for example, 64 per cent said that the practice and style of the previous head had been a source of difficulty for them. An extreme example of this was provided by one new headteacher who said that she had been given a brief by the governors to turn the school around. She had been deputy head at her previous school and a member of a strong senior management team whose members trusted and respected each other. She found herself in a situation where the two deputy headteachers, both of whom had applied for her job, had effectively run the school for years taking decisions on an *ad hoc* basis. There was no trust between staff and 'passive and active resistance to me and to each other'; her first six months in post had been 'the most stressful of my life'. Another headteacher reported that, though the technical problems that she faced in the school had been solved easily, and that she had clear ideas about what she wanted to do, her relationship with the governors had proved to be the stumbling block.

> I knew from my experience in other schools how I wanted this one to work, but that was relatively easy. People were looking for leadership here, it wasn't difficult to find a vision for the school. I've had difficulties with the governors on everything, they want to make all the decisions.

Her school was in a university town and, in her opinion, part of the problem was due to the fact that the governors were so well qualified.

Most of my governors are university lecturers and they are experts in everything – I've got three accountants on my finance sub-committee. It's very difficult to be good at anything here because everyone is much better than you to start with.

Experiences such as this are unlikely to boost one's confidence.

BARRIERS TO LEARNING

The decision to learn is essentially a personal one; other chapters in this book have illustrated how an individual's approach to learning can be influenced by previous experience and the timing and context of the learning opportunity. New headteachers are no different in this respect; they will have individual barriers to overcome. However, their descriptions of the first months of headship also highlighted a number of common factors which can inhibit learning. First, there were their implicit theories of headship and in particular the feeling that they always had to project an image of competence. As one new headteacher commented:

One of the things I found very difficult in the first term was that you were always expected to be the oracle. There was no time when you could switch off. You couldn't switch off in meetings and have a bit of a day dream because someone was going to ask you for an opinion, for a decision, and it had to be the right answer. I found that very difficult to come to terms with.

A second new head said that, although he had thought that the experience of being a deputy prepared one for headship, he now doubted whether it could:

[Headship] is a different role and people's perceptions of you are different, people want you to come up with the right answers all the time, you cannot say, 'I don't know'.

A third head who had been promoted to headship after several years as deputy in the same school reported a similar experience. Even though he knew the organisation very well he still had to make a transition into this new position:

I was the main mechanic, the nuts and bolts man – if you wanted to know anything about the school then I was the guy you went to. That's not my role any more. Now I'm driving the train, not shovelling the coal – that was the big step I had to make. There is no doubt in my mind that I am the head of this school, but to start with I found this odd – me as the head was alien.

A second inhibiting factor was that they felt that they could not admit to having any learning needs for fear that this would be perceived as weakness. This was compounded by the fact that often they needed to learn how to handle their staff and felt that to share this concern would be unprofessional:

By the nature of the job, a head is alone and is unlikely to divulge 'failures' to colleagues.

As a new head one feels quite alone and there are very few people with whom it is appropriate to discuss your problems to do with school. Because of inexperience, a new head needs advice.

I found the job extremely difficult, especially during the second term . . . I needed some confidant and/or friendly critic to discuss possible strategies.

Stress and overwork can also prove to be barriers to learning. If the pressure is sustained individuals are less likely to be open to learning; less likely to find opportunities to stand back and reflect about what they are doing, to share experiences with others or to experiment with new strategies. Many of the new headteachers reported feeling pressured. They found it difficult to manage their own time and, faced with innumerable tasks, struggled to identify priorities. Sometimes it was easier to try to do everything themselves rather than tackle the broader management issues:

As I am the head of a small school and have a large teaching commitment, plus the role of caretaker, and I have no deputy head, I have very little time to talk to anyone – it is easier for me just to get on with the job.

There are so many pressures on me . . . that it's sometimes very difficult to know if I am getting the balance right.

I have learned so much this year, I need to do some reflecting – but I haven't had time to reflect.

Several reported that their confidence had suffered since they had taken up their appointment; they felt isolated and longed for someone to tell them that they were doing the right thing. Offered the opportunity to join what was a voluntary mentoring scheme the majority of new headteachers jumped at the chance since it would enable them to discuss their concerns, in confidence, with an experienced headteacher. As one of them said:

I had a feeling of part of my burden being unloaded [to the mentor].

THE HEADTEACHER MENTORING SCHEME

The main strategy that has been used in recent years to support headteachers in the early months of their appointment has been the headteacher mentoring scheme. Mentoring is a common practice in industry but occurs much less frequently in educational organisations. The heart of the mentoring process is a relationship between two people working in the same business, one experienced, the other a noviciate; it may even have the flavour of apprentice and master. The purpose of the relationship is to induct the newcomer into the organisation and to provide support during his or her first year or so in post. In industry mentoring is often perceived as a form of career development for young professionals and as something that can also offer benefits for the mentor and the organisation, particularly because it provides a means of inducting a newcomer into company policy and norms.

Mentoring in industry has often been conducted on an informal basis, and many companies are now establishing formal mentoring partnerships because they recognise their value (Clutterbuck, 1991). In January 1992, a government-funded pilot scheme for headteacher mentoring was launched by the School Management Task Force (SMTF). The scheme was based upon a system of peer support: new headteachers were partnered with an experienced headteacher mentor from a different school, usually, though not necessarily, one from the same phase. The scheme was organised on a regional basis and funding was provided for up to five days training for mentors and new headteachers and up to seven days for the mentoring process itself. Written guidance about the conduct of the scheme was provided by the SMTF.

It was clear from the outset that models of mentoring used in industry could not be simply applied to education; neither would it be appropriate to utilise the model of mentoring that was being developed in initial teacher education (see Chapters 15 and 16). Unlike the relationship between a mentor and a beginning teacher, the headteacher mentor has no tutorial or assessment role. The new headteacher is assumed to be competent for the post and remains responsible with the governors for the management of the school. In the majority of cases, the mentor will not be familiar with the headteacher's school so cannot induct her or him into the norms of the school and offer insider information, even if this were considered appropriate. The key decision taken at the outset was that mentoring was to be based on a peer relationship which started from the recognition that new headteachers were senior professionals who would have had to demonstrate competence and skill in order to gain their appointment. The mentors were to be experienced headteachers, ideally not so experienced that they had forgotten the difficulties of the early months in the job. The mentor's task was to support the new headteacher but the relationship was to be based on negotiation and mutual agreement; there were no particular activities that had to take place. Indeed the guidelines for mentoring produced by the School Management Task Force (1991) stated:

> Although a familiar concept, its application varies greatly and definition as to what is meant by mentoring is equally varied. There is a sense in which mentoring is whatever the two people regard as appropriate.

The guidelines emphasised that the mentoring process should be both non-evaluative and non-prescriptive and should concentrate on encouraging new headteachers to take responsibility for solving their own problems. A more precise definition of headteacher mentoring was contained in the guidelines produced by the Welsh Steering Group (1993). Mentoring was described as a support process which was intended to help the development of the new headteacher and it was suggested that its central purpose was 'to help newly appointed headteachers manage the transition into headship'. This phrase reflects the challenge of the headteacher mentoring relationship which is that the mentor has to provide support for the new headteacher and encourage his or her professional development without being directive. The definition of mentoring used by the East Midlands scheme made a similar point: the task of mentoring was seen as being:

> To encourage and support the new head in taking up the role of head, by exploring their experiences of the school to understand how they can take authority to act for the benefit of the school as a whole.

In all the schemes mentors were actively discouraged from offering solutions to the headteachers' problems or being judgemental and were warned not to let the headteachers become dependent upon their support.

WHAT WERE THE COMPONENTS OF THE MENTORING PROGRAMMES?

The relationship between new headteacher and mentor normally lasted for a year and typically involved the following components:

- An initial meeting, possibly at a neutral venue, between the new head-teacher and the mentor, the main purpose of which was to clarify their understanding of the mentoring process, to establish rapport and to agree some ground rules (e.g. confidentiality).
- A meeting, often held at the new headteacher's school, where the partners exchanged information about each other's schools and during which the new headteacher was encouraged to discuss the challenges of his or her new role. The new headteacher and mentor would then begin to build an agenda for subsequent meetings.
- A regular pattern of visits, typically one every half term. These usually took place at the new headteacher's school but occasionally at the mentor's school. The discussion that took place on these occasions normally focused upon issues and problems raised by the new headteacher, and general reflection upon and discussion about aspects of management and leadership.
- A period of working towards closure nearing the end of the twelve months.

Several of the preparatory programmes for mentors had provided training in and an opportunity to practise relevant skills such as active listening, observing/shadowing and reflective interviewing. A rather different approach was adopted in one region where mentoring was conceptualised as the process by which newly appointed headteachers 'find, make and take the role of head' and the mentor's task was seen as being to provide support to enable the newcomer to determine and take authority for what he or she wished to do in the school. The training programme for mentors in this region concentrated on clarifying what was the mentor's role and placed less emphasis on skill acquisition. As it happened, the national evaluation data subsequently revealed that very few of the mentoring partnerships used observation or work shadowing: one-to-one discussion was the main strategy adopted.

VIEWS ABOUT THE MENTORING PROCESS

The majority of those who had been involved in the mentoring schemes thought that they were valuable and should be continued (and indeed they have been): 82.5 per cent of new headteachers and 89.7 per cent of mentors said that the schemes were worth the time and money involved. New headteachers said that mentoring had helped to break their isolation and in many cases was the only form of support available to them. What did they gain from their mentors? Where the partnership worked well, the new headteachers were helped to reflect upon their practice and to talk through and clarify the actions they were proposing to take. They clearly found this beneficial. One new headteacher, speaking about her mentor, said:

> She brings her experience, confidence and empathy. She's an excellent listener – listens and makes connections. She asks excellent questions . . . she has helped me to prioritise, advising me to start with those things that I have to do by law . . . she helped me to draw on my past experience as head of a dreadful department which I'd turned around . . . advised that I apply what I'd done there to my present situation. She helped me put things in perspective.

Another said of her mentor:

> She gave me confidence. She advised me not to let them [the governors] ride roughshod over me, that I should take a stand. So, at the end of last term I said "no" to one of the governors and it worked! He said, 'Thank you for putting me in my place – you need to show that you are in control'.

Mentors enabled headteachers to clarify their strategies:

> To share your ideas, to reflect on your ideas, to be challenged . . . I came away with a whole series of thoughts which had been more sharply focused.

They could help new headteachers to reveal their feelings and could provide an outlet for their frustrations. Comments from two new headteachers illustrate this:

> It's knowing that I have somewhere I can escape to . . . to vent feelings or whatever . . . you spend so much time in here being supportive or directive that it's nice to go somewhere where you can have some personal support.
> I feel that I have to do the job to the best of my ability, but being only human, it does get on top of you a bit if you have an anxiety hanging over

you and also a fear. It's having the confidence – I really needed to feel that people believed in me, and I got that from my mentor.

Acting as a mentor isn't an easy role: 68 per cent (303) of the mentors who responded to the evaluation questionnaire reported that the roles that they adopted most frequently were assisting their partner in problem solving and acting as a catalyst/sounding board. They tried hard not to be directive and not to give solutions to problems, though this was sometimes a source of tension. Many of the mentors had a very clear view about what they were trying to achieve:

> It's using focused questions to get the new headteacher to say why he's done what he's done . . . it's making the individual articulate the whys of decision making – which we don't often do.
>
> You start from the assumption that you are both good. There's also the assumption that the other person could end up even better . . . you support and encourage, but at the same time you challenge and you push. This is much more than being good pals . . . it's centred on children's learning and taking the school forward.
>
> I asked a lot of questions about his teaching workload. 'Why are you teaching the amount you do? What purposes does this serve? How is the school benefiting? What benefits are you getting from it? Is this at a cost? How does it influence other work that you do?' I wanted to get at the basis of his decision making; for example, what were the implications for other aspects of his role as a head . . . could he have attained the same ends by different means?

The following features of the mentoring process were regarded as being particularly helpful by both new headteachers and mentors:

- Establishing mutual trust and confidence.
- Recognising and respecting each other's style of management and preferred learning style.
- Drawing up a loose 'contract' at the outset, which spelled out the confidentiality of the exchanges; the aims and function of the mentoring process; what the mentor felt able and willing to offer; what the new headteacher hoped to gain from the process.
- Visiting and being given a guided tour of their partner's school.
- Working to an agenda on which the lead was taken by the new headteacher, though jointly negotiated.
- Engaging in open-ended discussion.

At best, mentors helped their new headteacher partners to become more effective problem solvers and more reflective practitioners. They also played an important role in boosting the new headteachers' confidence and reducing their feelings of isolation.

WHAT WERE THE FEATURES OF THE MENTORING PROGRAMME THAT MADE IT A POWERFUL AID TO LEARNING?

Engaging in frank and open discussion about one's problems and concerns with a second person is not something that most of us do lightly. Though they usually worked in the same Local Education Authority, the majority of the mentors and new headteachers did not know each other at the start of the process, and there was little time for the relationship to develop. In this situation the personality and skills of the mentor become paramount. The mentor and the new headteacher had to establish a rapport and build a relationship based on mutual trust. The mentoring process was a potential learning opportunity for both of them but they had to be prepared to commit themselves to it, and the new headteachers in particular had to be prepared to be open about their experience of headship. The majority of new head-teachers and mentors were agreed that the most important characteristics required of mentors were that they were good listeners; demonstrated open and warm behaviour; had experience of headship; and were able to give the new headteachers feedback without being judgemental. New headteachers said that they valued working with mentors who had high professional credibility and were known to be good managers in their own schools but who nevertheless were open about the fact that they had encountered problems in headship. The following comments indicate the qualities that they hoped to find in a mentor:

> They should be good listeners . . . have a clear idea of strategies to suggest to the new head that enable without destroying or undermining confidence. Be perceptive so that they can identify strengths in the new head on which to build.
>
> The ability to create friendly relationships. The ability to give advice in a non-threatening way. Provide examples of own experience; be a good listener. Be prepared to share with the new head any mistakes that the mentor feels he/she has made.

They wanted someone who they could respect, who was perceptive and questioning but who could also admit to having made mistakes. Someone who appeared to be too competent could cause anxiety.

The selection of experienced headteachers as mentors is a crucially important task as is the task of matching mentor to new headteacher. The successful mentors were clear about their role and generous with their time, often suggesting that the headteacher should contact them by telephone if he or she felt the need to discuss something between formal meetings. It was notable that, where the mentoring partnership had not worked well, the main difficulty that was identified was finding sufficient time for the process. Particular individuals also had difficulties with funding, the distance that had to be travelled for meetings and in a minority of cases personal incompatibility.

Gender differences between mentor and new headteacher were not generally regarded as a significant issue. None of the male headteachers who had a female mentor identified this as a problem but responses from a few of the women who had a male mentor indicated that they had found this a barrier:

> The different genders made the relationship slightly uncomfortable at times.

Another woman, a secondary headteacher, said that her male mentor was a high-profile headteacher in the LEA and that she had felt inhibited from speaking openly about her concerns for fear that this would demonstrate that women could not cope with headship. Her views were coloured by the experience of being one of the few women in the predominantly male group of secondary headteachers in the authority.

Organisers of the mentoring schemes spent a great deal of time discussing whether new headteachers should be allowed to choose their mentor and what information they would need if they were to make an informed choice. The conclusion that was often reached was that the logistics of doing this fairly were too complex. Nevertheless, when a new headteacher would prefer to have a mentor of the same gender, it would seem sensible for those organising the scheme to respond to this preference. The partnership is unlikely to work if the new headteacher feels that he or she cannot relate to his or her mentor.

The mentoring process focuses directly on the real problems that headteachers face in their schools; the meetings with the mentor usually take place in the new headteacher's school and the agenda is largely determined by his or her immediate, practical concerns. This is a further reason why mentoring can be such a powerful aid to learning. Wallace has argued in Chapter 2 that experiential learning strategies based on vicarious experience can only achieve a limited amount. He has suggested that on the job support must be provided if the aim is to produce improved performance in the job. Regular meetings with a mentor provide such opportunities for new headteachers. They can discuss the action they plan to take in advance and the mentor can later help them to reflect upon and analyse what actually happened. The learning potential of the meetings could be enhanced if the mentor undertook some systematic observation of the new headteacher at work and provided feedback on this experience. But the evaluation showed that the headteachers and mentors were reluctant to do this. Perhaps observation was considered too threatening an activity in the early months of headship when the new headteachers were striving to become familiar with their new schools and cope with the challenges that faced them. If the process had continued into a second year, when they felt more ready to focus on wider issues concerned with school leadership, this initial reluctance might have dissipated.

CONCLUSION

Can participation in a mentoring programme help a new headteacher to make the transition into headship? Can it help the headteacher to learn how to behave in this new role? The evidence collected in the evaluation of the pilot mentoring schemes would strongly suggest that it can, although this needs qualifying. Earlier in this chapter reference was made to the fact that headteachers need to be both leaders and managers. No one style of leadership will be appropriate for each situation. Rather, leadership is contingent upon the situation in which one finds oneself. No mentors, however skilful and experienced, can transform other individuals. They cannot easily make them more creative, improve their interpersonal skills, change their habitual patterns of behaviour or improve their skills of financial management. However, they can help them develop the confidence to realise that they have things to learn and that there is nothing shameful about this.

Many researchers now argue that schools must become 'learning organisations' if they are to cope with the pace of change. For Senge (1990) the learning organisation is one which has 'discovered how to tap people's commitment and capacity to learn at all levels in the organisation'. Fullan (1992) sees it as one which is 'expert at dealing with change as a normal part of its work, not just in relation to the latest policy but as a way of life'. Leaders in learning organisations need to show that they see themselves as learners; they need to be flexible and have the ability and confidence to empower their staff. The difficulty is that the organisation and staffing structure in many schools makes it unlikely that new learning patterns can emerge. Van Hoewijk (1993) has argued that school leaders:

> are socialised into a leadership model that prescribes knowing the answers instead of searching for the answers. If these leaders want the organisation to grow into a learning organisation, then they themselves must unlearn the knowing leadership model and learn how to think, feel and behave in a searching leadership model.

If new headteachers have no opportunities to share their feelings of anxiety and isolation, if they lack the confidence to admit that they do not know all the answers, then it is possible that they may block themselves off from learning opportunities. By working with a mentor in a non-threatening, non-judgemental partnership a new headteacher can be prompted into a more reflective and questioning pattern of behaviour and so become a more effective learner. However, if the ultimate aim is to turn the school into a learning organisation then some deeper structural changes may also be required. Given the challenging but essentially supportive and non-judgemental nature of the mentoring programme and its limited duration it is unlikely that the new headteachers will be pushed hard to reconsider their fundamental assumptions about the nature of headship.

REFERENCES

Alexander, R. (1992) *Policy and Practice in Primary Education*, London: Routledge.
Bolam, R., McMahon, A., Pocklington, K. and Weindling, D. (1993a) *National Evaluation of the Headteacher Mentoring Pilot Schemes*, London: Department for Education.
Bolam, R., McMahon, A., Pocklington, K. and Weindling, D. (1993b) *Effective Management in Schools*, London: HMSO.
CBAC/WJEC (1993) *The Mentoring of New Heads in Wales: The Process*, Cardiff: Wales Education Management.
Clutterbuck, D. (1991) *Everyone Needs a Mentor*, 2nd edition, London: Institute of Personnel Management.
Department for Education (1994) *Conditions of Service for Teachers*, London: DFE.
East Midlands Nine Headteachers Mentoring Scheme (1992) Handbook for Mentors (mimeo).
Fullan, M. (1993) *Change Forces*, London: Falmer Press.
HMI (1979) *Ten Good Schools*, London: HMSO.
Mortimore, P. *et al.* (1988) *School Matters: The Junior Years*, Salisbury: Open Books.
Scheerens, J. (1992) *Effective Schooling: Research, Theory and Practice*, London: Cassell.
School Management Task Force (1991) *Mentor Scheme for New Headteachers: Notes of Guidance for Regional Executive Groups*, London: DES.
School Teachers' Review Body (1994) First Report on 1994 Teachers' Workloads Survey, London: Office of Manpower Economics (mimeo).
Seashore-Louis, K. (1994) 'Beyond "managed change": rethinking how schools improve'. *School Effectiveness and School Improvement*, Vol. 5, pp. 2–24.
Senge, P. M. (1990) *The Fifth Discipline*, London: Century Business.
Teacher Training Agency (1994) Headteachers Leadership and Management Programme – Consultation, London: TTA (mimeo).
Van Hoewijk, R. (1993) 'Integrated management development, does that solve the problem?'. In R. Bolam and F. Van Wieringen (eds) *Educational Management Across Europe*, De Lier: Academisch Boeken Centrum.
Weindling, D. and Earley, P. (1987) *Secondary Headship: The First Years*, Windsor: NFER/Nelson.

Chapter 13

Development through collaborative working

A case study of mathematics INSET

Jan Winter

In this chapter we are back with a small-scale, illustrative piece of action research, this time by a lecturer in mathematics education who had been, until very recently, an advisory teacher in the county of Avon. Jan's concern was to evaluate the long-term effects of an in-service course she had run, over four years, in the hope of identifying some of the 'active ingredients' within the model on which the course had been designed. The course consisted of three elements: sessions in the teachers' centre, led by the advisory teachers; regular visits by an advisory teacher to each participant's school; and visits by participants to each others' schools. Somewhat to her surprise, the follow-up interviews clearly identified the peer visits and peer discussions as having been of most value. Here we have a clear example of a professional educator putting her implicit theory of learning to the reflective test, and finding it wanting. Collaborative learning, as Marilyn Osborn discovered in Chapter 5, turns out to be more powerful and more preferred than the gentle supportive advice of an adviser. The chapter casts light on Mike Wallace's contention, in Chapter 2, that it is reflective work on the job that counts: it is, but peers seem to be of more value than advisers, perhaps because the presence of the latter in a classroom, however friendly, still raises performance anxiety, and fears of being judged, in ways that the peers do not.

INTRODUCTION – 'DEVELOPING YOUR MATHS TEACHING'

This chapter presents a case study which illustrates some of the features of adult learning described elsewhere in the book. In Chapter 1 Guy Claxton describes some central ideas about adult learning and this chapter looks at an in-service – INSET – course offered to teachers which attempted, through its structure, to create an environment in which the 'cost-benefit analysis' would be such that teachers would be prepared to engage actively. It also aimed to address the idea that learning is not a homogeneous activity and provide situations in which learners could choose how best to tackle their development needs in their own ways. For me, as a facilitator, it felt like a powerful way of working which was strongly focused on teachers' own agendas. In this case study I returned to participants to attempt to assess the value they felt the course had for them.

The course in question was an INSET course for secondary mathematics teachers which I ran with two other advisory teacher colleagues during the period 1989–93. At this time, Avon Mathematics Advisory Teachers (ATs) organised and ran a course called 'Developing Your Maths Teaching'. Avon employed a team of three secondary maths ATs, of whom I was one, and we all worked on the course. Its intentions can be appreciated through its title. Our aim was for the teachers who came on the course to be able to *develop* their teaching. We wished to provide opportunities for teachers to consider different teaching methods and to choose what was appropriate for them. It was important that the issues worked on in the course were those which the teachers themselves had chosen: hence 'your'. The focus was the teaching of maths and it was development of this aspect of the teachers' professional work which was central to the course. At all times the focus was on the *teaching* of maths and the effectiveness of that teaching for pupils.

The course developed over the four years as we, the tutors, became clearer about what was effective in promoting this kind of learning. An early description of the course, by another of the ATs involved, Greg Morris (1990), noted:

> during the time the course was running all the school-based work of the Advisory Teachers would be with the individuals who were on the course . . .. From the point of view of the Advisory Teacher the new way of working appears to have provided a coherence which the job has lacked previously . . .. The Advisory Teachers have found it more comfortable to get to know the group of teachers over quite a long period of time and to begin to work with them in their classes rather than to arrive cold in a school and spend a block of, say, three weeks with the department.

One of the principal ways in which our thinking developed considerably over the four years involved altering the focus from *our* work to that of the teachers. The benefits of working as we did seemed to address many criticisms often levelled at INSET provision:

> Teachers . . . tended to comment on the lack of detail about the course content and to criticise the fact that there was often a lack of differentiation, continuity and depth in the INSET they had received under the centralised model.
>
> (Harland and Kinder, 1994)

STRUCTURE OF THE COURSE

Each time the course ran it consisted of three main components, spread over a period of between a term and a term and a half. These components were as follows.

Centre-based sessions

These sessions introduced teachers to ideas they could work on to develop their own mathematical thinking or could use in their classrooms. They also, and just as importantly, provided an opportunity for the group of teachers on the course to get to know one another and to work together. The sessions gave them access to a wider range of resources than they would have in school and the time to experiment with them and discuss their possible uses. Each session had a major allocation of time, usually first thing in the morning, for discussion of classroom work done since the last meeting. This was to allow teachers to share the work they had done with a small group of teachers they got to know well. It enabled the group to discuss classroom practice from a basis of shared experience.

Each cohort of participant teachers was divided into smaller groups to work directly with one of the ATs. A cohort normally consisted of about eighteen teachers, divided into three smaller groups. Some of the work on the centre-based days was done with the whole group, but discussion sessions were always in the three small groups of six with one AT. These discussions were a crucial part of the course and, since they were being led by three different people, no doubt varied. We intended to use these times to open up for discussion work which teachers had done, either with the AT or with another teacher, between sessions. The AT initiated the discussions while trying to encourage the participating teachers to decide on what experiences to follow up. The different experiences teachers had in these groups were also reflected in the different ways the ATs worked with them in other parts of the course. Some of these differences will be apparent in the interview extracts.

The number of centre-based days was reduced as money for funding the course reduced and this made the development of relationships between the participants more difficult. All components of the course were reduced as funding diminished, in an attempt to keep the balance of the contrasting aspects of the course similar. We felt that this was the most appropriate way of dealing with reduced funding.

Work with an AT in school

While it was running, this course formed a major part of the ATs' work, as each AT worked regularly with participant teachers in their schools for the duration of the course. We would normally visit each teacher about once a week for some time in lessons and some time discussing the work being done.

This structure allowed teachers to develop their own foci for their work and to have a supporting teacher working with them in the classroom for advice and discussion. It was an important part of the structure that time in school was always spent discussing work done and making future plans about how work would progress.

Visits between participant teachers

Each small group of teachers took part in a number of visits to one another's classrooms during the course. Time was spent on the centre-based days preparing for these visits in terms of how the teachers would work together in the classroom, what the visitor's role would be, what topic would be covered or what style of teaching would be used, as well as other practical issues concerned with having a visitor to the classroom. These visits were supply covered as part of funding for the course and one of the changes, as conditions changed throughout the time the course was running, was that this money was reduced, thus reducing the number of visits which could be made.

BACKGROUND TO THIS RESEARCH

Having described the structure of the course I will describe why I felt it would be valuable to go back to the participating teachers and talk to them about their experiences. At the time I felt that the model was a powerful way of working with teachers and supporting their own personal professional development. They controlled a large part of the agenda for development and had the support of professional colleagues in exploring the issues of interest to them. They were able to explore, in a supportive environment, their own issues in a reflective way and I now wanted to see what had stayed with them of that way of working, and whether it had affected either their practice of teaching or their preferred way of working on their own learning. I wanted to find out which parts of the course now seem to them to have been most significant and compare their views now with some expressed in evaluations completed immediately after the course.

In looking at the effects the course had on those teachers who took part, my own role as a learner during the period is relevant. I was undertaking research as part of an MEd degree at the time and was therefore interested in examining and improving my own practice in working with teachers. Part of my research involved an action research project to look at the effectiveness of my role as facilitator of discussion groups, based on discussions which took place as part of this course. I found that the discussion sessions were very important in developing the teachers' own views of themselves as learners. I looked at my own role in those discussions and tried to improve my effectiveness by careful consideration of inputs I made. That is a lesson I am still working on! The role of 'critical friend' in supporting another person's thinking is a subtle and delicate one. Some of the responses teachers made to questions about aspects of the course they valued shed light on my colleagues' and my success in undertaking this role.

In order to address these questions I approached a sample of participants from each of the four cohorts of the course. I wrote to twenty participants asking them if they would agree to be interviewed. I selected the sample across the small groups who had worked with each of the three ATs. Twelve of those I approached agreed to be interviewed. They had all worked with me as an AT in recent years and so knew me, so I recognised that their responses might be affected by that. Of the twelve, six had been teachers who had worked with me on the course so I recognised that their responses in particular might be affected by what they thought I 'wanted to hear'. (The whole area of the use of interviews as a research tool has been explored by Pope and Denicolo (1986), who consider the implications of its interactive nature and what this means for the results obtained. Lengthy transcripts are not presented here as they would make the chapter unwieldy.) Other limitations to the study include the fact that the course changed in nature during the four years it ran and therefore interviewees were not necessarily reflecting on the same experiences; and finally that I had access to the immediate post-course evaluations of only two of the four cohorts, the second and fourth. Since direct comparison of the views of teachers immediately after the course and later was not being attempted, this last point is not a major problem.

The interviews lasted about half an hour. I began by asking the participants what they remembered from the course and then I described the components. I asked if anything still happens in their classrooms as a result of work done on the course. I then asked what their 'ideal' INSET would be and their 'ideal' way of working with pupils. I asked these questions to try to find out if there was a correspondence between what they said they valued at the time and what they said they would like ideally. I also wanted to find out if their views of learning transferred between themselves and their pupils; that is, if they wanted the same kind of learning opportunities for themselves as they wanted to provide for their pupils. I then asked about whether they felt their development needs had changed during their careers and whether they had any current aims or goals for their own development. Finally, I asked what they felt were the kinds of experiences which helped them learn.

My intention in asking the above questions was to elicit comments in different contexts, so that I could see whether their views were consistent and how they related to the experiences they had on the course. By asking them to recall the components of the course before talking myself about it I hoped to elicit what mattered to them rather than following my cues of what I was suggesting had been important. By outlining the course components I was aware that I may be affecting the comments they later made about 'ideal' provision. I developed the questions in discussion with a colleague with the aim of providing 'starting points' which teachers could develop into stories about particular aspects of the course which were important to them and which might provide insight into their views of learning, both for themselves and for their pupils.

RESULTS OF THE INTERVIEWS

In considering the interview responses by some of these teachers I will look at whether the longer-term effects they identify are similar to those they thought important at the time and what parts of the course they now think contributed to these effects. I will refer to comments made in the written evaluations where they relate to the same area as the response to the question. In describing the results of the interviews I will be trying to identify factors which were important for them in terms of their own learning and what made that learning possible. I will identify each participant by a letter from A to M so that cross-reference can more easily be made between related answers to different questions.

Valued aspects of the course

My first question, concerning what they remembered from the course, elicited some, for me, surprising answers. My subconscious hypothesis had been that they would value the work they did with the advisory teacher most highly but that was not the case for the majority of participants:

K: The best thing I remember about it is going to other people's lessons, other people's schools. I remember that, it was fascinating because very often in your own school you don't do that.

C: The main thing was having the opportunity to spend time with other maths teachers and visit their schools.

G: I was feeling rather unsure and vulnerable. At [School X] it was quite a difficult group – it was nice to be in the classroom and seeing someone cope with that sort of group.

The collaborative work and time spent with other teachers was a strong memory for the participants and one which they greatly valued. This may be partly because it is a rare opportunity, particularly outside their own school and with the purpose solely of their professional development. These peer visits were the first recollection of eight of the teachers. Three spoke first of the centre-based activities, and only one mentioned the AT work first.

When asked about what they had found useful the responses were quite wide ranging. All aspects of the course were mentioned and the emphasis shifted slightly away from the visits towards the work with an AT and the discussion with others about their teaching. Visits to other teachers' class-rooms were one of the most highly valued components: seven teachers valued the visits between schools most highly, and seven mentioned the value of the shared discussions between peers. Five referred to the work with the AT; three mentioned the activities and resources; and one each referred to time to work on their own teaching, and to the value of all parts of the course as a whole. The range of these responses covers all the main parts of the course and shows how teachers were able to work in their own way on the course by taking from it whatever suited them best.

Those who mentioned work with the AT did so by describing pieces of work which they had particularly valued:

L: The most useful thing was actually having you in the class and then sitting down and talking about it afterwards. . . . I felt you were actually working with me to create something.

J: Discussions with [an AT] were important. She helped to organise my thoughts by asking questions back.

J: Having a non-threatening and supportive observer coming in and watching what was going on was obviously crucial. She had the skills to observe and pick up discussion points.

These comments match what was identified in the written evaluations as being 'good or useful to their work'. The most commonly mentioned points were talking to other teachers, exchanging ideas and support in planning work. This supports the finding described by Marilyn Osborn in Chapter 5 of an increasing emphasis on collaboration between teachers in their work. This course was taking place in the early days of the implementation of the National Curriculum in Mathematics and the collaboration which this course encouraged was recognised by participants as being very valuable. This links, too, with what was identified by seven other teachers as important – the shared discussion of work done:

A: People discussed how they used it [an activity] and I found that valuable. In a way I think you valued it in the same way as you valued the person as you got to know them over the weeks.

K: We talked about teacher intervention and that was very interesting . . . I'd never thought about it before.

M: When you have an idea and tell others it motivates you to do something with it – there's more commitment. I got a lot of things done or tried that I wouldn't have done if I hadn't made those commitments to other people.

These comments reflect some of the things we were trying to achieve in the course. These teachers were reflecting on particular parts of their own practice and developing them in collaboration with colleagues. Sometimes the ideas were sparked off by the group discussions and sometimes they were things the teachers had been waiting for an opportunity to work on – either way the structure of the course provided the individual support which enabled it to happen.

TEACHERS' VIEWS OF THEIR LEARNING

Many of the comments about what teachers valued (or in some cases did not!) reflected on their attitudes to their own learning:

- *M*: It was having a mirror. Being able to look at what you thought about maths teaching which the course at that time provided for me. You were getting support and encouragement. Your ideas were important and valued.
- *A*: [The visits] were valuable because it's not always necessary to see something working well to get some positive feedback from it.
- *C*: The other sessions gave me confidence to try things in the classroom but I think at my sort of age, just sitting and listening all the time and not actually doing doesn't get you very far. You take it in but you need some sort of boost to actually get up and do it.
- *J*: We made pop-up birthday cards and I couldn't do it and felt inadequate. It gave me an opportunity to experience failing.
- *H*: I can remember frustrating sessions where you wouldn't give us any ideas! . . . I can remember feeling quite threatened initially – thinking [the AT] was coming in to watch.
- *F*: Work with other teachers was very good – having to actually, in the context, become quite close to that person, for there to be that trust that would enable them to visit your classroom and you to visit theirs. That made the activities memorable.

While the teachers displayed a wide range of attitudes to their own learning there were certain recurrent themes which came through: wanting to have some control of their development but at the same time checking against the expectations of others that they were 'in line'; wanting to observe other teachers' practice both for reassurance about their own work, and to extend; sometimes wanting to be 'told' things; and recognising the responsibility which a commitment to others imposed and the motivation this provided.

The ways in which we worked with teachers had to resolve some of the tensions which are implicit in these attitudes. Our aim of encouraging autonomy had to be balanced against teachers' wishes to be 'told' and their resentment when we were not prepared to accept the role of 'expert' which they wished us to take. These tensions are the same as those faced by teachers if they wish to develop their pupils' responsibility for their own learning.

IDEAL PROFESSIONAL DEVELOPMENT

These attitudes sometimes conflicted with the answers to my next question, about their 'ideal' professional development. I asked what kind of course they would find most helpful, and what sort of activities they would like it to include. Some teachers, perhaps still thinking about the course we had discussed, described the components of that course which they had most valued, but a number stated that they wanted information about parts of the curriculum in which they feel weak:

A: I am quite happy using the computer. It's that I don't actually know what's available on software and also how the programs are structured and I think that is the type of information I would need. And possibly techniques on how to integrate using that into a normal lesson.

When asked what sort of activities would help her work on this she did mention observation of other teachers:

A: I would like to see how other teachers who are good at integrating IT into maths lessons are working.

C: I think something on sixth form teaching . . . I think there ought to be some courses on the new modular type A levels.

E: I think if I could spend some time it would be with calculators and computers. Medium length courses that would enable me to sit in front of a computer and go through all the things I'd like to try and then give me a chance to try those things with a class.

K: I think it would still be the issue I looked at then – the conflict of having to get through the syllabus but wanting to do interesting things.

M: I'd want to start looking at school design. What I want to do is limited by school organisation. I'd want to look at schools designed for practical activities.

When I probed beyond the content into methods of working, the majority identified observation of other teachers and shared working on issues as desirable ways to work, but there remained a strong undercurrent of the need for 'content input'. Perhaps a 'quick fix' is an immediately attractive option and it is only on deeper reflection that the value of more 'process-based' development becomes apparent. The need to be actively involved in practical activity is also apparent in these answers.

Those who identified similar activities to those on 'Developing Your Maths Teaching' may have been reflecting on what I had said to them or may have continued to find the methods valuable:

F: My 'ideal' course would have to be practical in the sense of visiting other people or people visiting me. A part of it would have to be discussion, I suppose. There would have to be something worthwhile fed back from those activities.

G: Finding time to do more of the same [as on the course]. To see what other people are doing and talk to them and find out ways that they're finding of coping with difficult kids.

Mike Wallace's discussion of experiential learning in Chapter 2 seems to resonate with these ideas. In this course the learning was truly experiential.

It took place to a large extent in their own or other teachers' classrooms and was firmly rooted in their own practice. The work by Joyce and Showers (1988), quoted in Chapter 2, has clear links with the structure of the course being considered here. In an informal way the features of theory, demonstration, practice feedback and coaching were all present in the teachers' work.

TEACHERS' LEARNING AND CHILDREN'S LEARNING

When comparing their views of their own learning with the ways they teach, teachers in most cases recognise some parallels or some similarity of approach:

G: I don't like to be working on the board too much. I think the kids find it boring. How much they're actually learning when you're talking to them I doubt. You get comments like, if you've been talking half the lesson, 'Can we get down to some work now?' It's going in one ear and out the other.

G: The main way I learn is by learning by my mistakes I suppose. I can't seem to do it any other way.

M: [I like to teach] by thinking of them as mathematicians as well. By taking ideas from them and giving them opportunities to make discoveries – like no-one has ever heard of Pythagoras before. You've got to be enjoying maths. There's a tingle factor when a kid knows they're discovering something.

L: I prefer working with individuals or small groups. I always went to sleep when the teacher stood up in front of the board when I was at school. It was an automatic switch off.

J: I am aiming for reflective mathematicians. I am interested in them writing about what they're doing.

J: The main components [of ideal development] would be working with other teachers coupled with time to think about what you're doing yourself.

H: I teach by tackling some skills in a routine way but as far as possible through seeing applications, doing things through problem solving rather than doing it because we're doing it.

For the most part, teachers considered the learning needs of their pupils to be very similar to their own. They were thinking about what worked for them and expecting it would also work for their pupils.

LASTING EFFECTS?

In trying to identify what had stayed with them from working on the course it was often not clear where changes had originated from. Some teachers, however, could specifically identify aspects of their practice which they could track back to work on the course. These varied in nature. Some were related to particular pieces of content and ways of teaching them; some were to do with how they thought about their teaching and their pupils' learning; and, in a very few cases, they were related to their awareness of themselves as learners:

C: Looking back on it, because I could share things and try things with other people then I had the confidence to try things out in the classroom . . . I have changed quite a lot in the way that I do things.

B: I think what I took away from the course at that particular time is the way of working with other colleagues. . . . I think I went away from that course feeling more able to communicate with fellow colleagues.

D: [In my teaching] I try to be a bit more vague! With investigations I think I tended to be a bit too leading.

E: I still rely quite heavily on the work I did [on Logo].

H: This department works very much that way [using open-ended tasks] and I think I used my experience on the course and built on that in my time here [having moved to another school].

J: Feeling activities are worthwhile even if they don't produce what you expected.

K: Intervention – I'd never thought about it before. When I felt like saying something I'd say it. Now I'm very reluctant to interrupt them. I use the word interruption rather than intervention because I think very often you say too much.

K: One of the most useful things – I've used it again literally every year since – you said write down a few targets for yourself and we'll post them on to you in six months' time. That was extremely useful. I do it every year with the pupils, setting themselves targets. Each time I've done it with a group I've done it myself.

M: Loads of things! Ropes, I still use ropes a lot. [To make co-ordinate axes so the children can be points on a graph] I try to scale up the experience of maths. I try to get the problem big enough for the children to work on the inside.

M: The notion that things are best learned and understood by discovery and best enjoyed too.

SUMMARY OF FINDINGS

To return to the main question of this chapter, I feel that there is good evidence in these interviews of the effectiveness of this type of in-service provision. From many of the participants there was evidence that they felt there were lasting effects on their teaching as a result of taking part in the course. Some identified the course as having provided them with a foundation on which to build throughout their teaching careers. Some identified particular ways of working with pupils which they still find useful now. In terms of their own learning, many are still using similar ways of working on their teaching: they look for other situations in which they can work collaboratively and share practice. Some commented, for example, on taking opportunities to work collaboratively when they could, and some deliberately engineered such opportunities in their departments.

On the effectiveness of various components of the course, I think the teacher who identified the whole process as being interlinked pinpointed the essential feature of the structure, in that the relationships which teachers built up in order to work together depended on the experiences of working together on centre-based days, working with someone in their classroom and spending time discussing their work together in a group. It is not clear that any one part was less important than any other, nor that the close working relationships could have been developed with less time input from the course organisers, the advisory teachers. However, if such courses are to use facilitators' time effectively, it is important that the main benefits of this work are recognised explicitly; that is, the benefit of collaboration amongst a varied group of teachers who have extended opportunities to develop close working relationships with one another. The focus has to be the work of the participating teachers and facilitators have to be responsive to that.

> L: I think ultimately the end is to have somebody helping you with what you actually want to do in the classroom and not telling you how they'd have done it differently but saying 'Did you notice this?' – that sort of working.

For me, at the time, the collaborative nature of the course was at three levels: first in the planning of the course with two colleagues; second in working to develop teachers' practice with them in their classrooms and in the group; and third in collaborating with other teachers through the action research project in which I examined and worked on my own role in these teachers' development. Now, the outcomes of these interviews have reinforced my belief that lasting change can come about from this kind of collaborative work if it is firmly rooted in practice. Participants were able to collaborate on issues of their own choosing, both with classroom teacher colleagues and with advisory teachers. This enabled these teachers not only to work on their own teaching but also to develop their learning skills in ways which they are still using to develop their practice now.

REFERENCES

Harland, J. and Kinder, K. (1994) 'Patterns of LEA INSET organisation'. *British Journal of INSET*, Vol. 20, No. 1.

Joyce, B. and Showers, B. (1988) *Student Achievement through Staff Development*, London: Jossey-Bass.

Morris, G. (1990) 'Combining INSET and school based work of advisory teachers'. *British Journal of INSET,* Vol. 16, No. 1.

Pope, M. and Denicolo, P. (1986) 'Intuitive theories – a researcher's dilemma'. *British Educational Research Journal,* Vol. 12, No. 2.

Chapter 14

Using dissonance

Finding the grit in the oyster

Laurinda Brown (with Alan Dobson)

With this chapter we continue the theme of working with experienced teachers on improving their classroom practice. Again the theme of collaboration emerges as of vital importance; but Laurinda Brown takes us on an interesting journey into the micro-structure of these interactions, and explores, through two case studies, the valuable role that 'dissonance' can play in helping people first to become aware of the foundations of their existing practice, and then to formulate new directions. Laurinda is particularly keen to develop, through these examples, a model of how the facilitator of professional learning in this context can be of most value. She illustrates very nicely how guided reflection on the small details of classroom behaviour can develop this sense of 'grit', like becoming aware of a pebble in your shoe, that, once noticed, provides the irritant stimulus to cause deeper and deeper insight into one's implicit theories of teaching and learning. And she demonstrates clearly how the activity of trying to help another adult learn is itself an excellent opportunity for the 'teacher' also to learn. Teaching is, at least potentially, as much a 'learning' role as 'learning' is.

I have two childhood memories concerning wet hair. First, I can clearly remember being told by my parents that I must not go out with wet hair or I would catch a cold. And second, I equally clearly recall what a pleasurable experience it was to dry my hair, in winter, by a coal fire in a house with no central heating. My family lived by the sea and I can remember going down to the beach in late autumn and early winter in very cold conditions with a rough sea and playing in the waves. With wet hair and feelings of elation we would return home. So on the one hand, getting my hair wet was judged to be a 'bad' thing, while on the other, it was associated with positive experiences. These two conflicting strands of experience from my childhood saved me from getting stuck with a set attitude to 'wet hair outside'. The dissonance between them led me, I suspect, to have a rather more open mind on the subject than some of my contemporaries. It *is* important not to go out with wet hair under some circumstances. I once went out on a freezing cold morning with wet hair and the ends of my hair froze. As my head turned, the ends of the hair sliced across my face and cut it. I didn't catch a cold, but I won't do this again. I have learnt to adapt and extend my theory of going out with wet hair.

Some of my adult acquaintances, however, still seem to carry behaviour patterns about wet hair left over from such early admonitions: for example, those who do not like to get their hair wet when swimming. A common comment on seeing me arrive at work with wet hair on a cold morning is 'Don't catch cold' or in the North, more dramatically, 'You'll catch your death!'. The thesis of this chapter is that such taken-for-granted attitudes can inhibit learning, and that, in such cases, change in attitude is liberating for the learner. This change is not like throwing away an old suit of clothes. Personal theories develop over time and the original roots may never be lost. It should be remembered that the only person who can do the changing is the person undergoing change; and that it is important that the idea of change, in a particular domain, is not felt to involve any kind of catastrophic change to either behaviour or personality.

In the language of Festinger's theory of cognitive dissonance (1957) any two cognitive elements (beliefs or bits of knowledge) may be consonant, dissonant or irrelevant to one another. Dissonance occurs when one element follows psychologically from the contrary of the other. Although, as Bannister and Fransella (1974) point out, cognitive dissonance is more a 'notion' than a theory it has, nevertheless, proved useful for me in practice. In the case of my example, the two strands of experience from my childhood were dissonant and therefore, I believe, allowed for a continued exploration of the 'wet hair' domain, so that I could continue to learn about the pros and cons of going out with wet hair, and what to do in different circumstances.

Allport (1935) (quoted in Kulm, 1980) defines an 'attitude' as 'a mental and neural state of readiness, organised through experience, exerting a directive or dynamic influence upon the individual's response to all objects and situations with which it is related' (for a discusion of alternative definitions of attitude see Jahoda and Warren (1966)). Here there is the feeling of fixed behaviours in relation to particular events which have become automatic, and possibly tied up with images of self, so that it can be difficult to bring the attitude into question. This chapter explores practical uses of 'resonance' (my preferred term for 'consonance') and dissonance which may allow the learner the possibility of uncovering such fixed attitudes and altering consequent behaviours. (I will not consider the case when cognitive elements are irrelevant since then there is no grit in the oyster.) The argument will be explored with reference to two practical examples: a way of working in a single session of an MEd course; and an account of working more intensively with an individual over a longer period.

The first example concerns a group of overseas mathematics educators meeting for an MEd session on a course entitled 'Professional and Social Issues in Mathematics Education'. Most of the group had not worked with me before. The topic we were due to cover concerned attitudes to the subject (mathematics), and ways in which we might work to influence the negative attitudes to the subject experienced internationally by pupils and adults. The way I planned to work in the session was by progressing from a consideration of *experiences*, via the formulation of *issues*, to the delineation of possible *actions*. This methodology is adapted from Jaworski (1991) and it is one I had used in many varied situations before.

After introductions and some discussions centred on the meaning of the word 'attitude' we were ready to work. I began by asking what experiences the students had had of their own attitudes to mathematics changing, or of being involved with teachers and teacher educators whose attitudes were undergoing shifts. Had they worked in situations where they were concerned with attitude change in others? I asked the individuals in the group to reflect back and try to bring vividly to mind a time when they were aware of their attitudes to mathematics or to their work as mathematics educators changing or, if the story came more easily to mind, a time when they themselves had influenced the attitudes of others.

Having given time for the stories to be identified, I then asked the students to be ready to tell their story briefly to the rest of the group. We would hear one story at a time and, initially, responses might take the form of questions for clarification, or the telling of a related story (not necessarily the one prepared) which was sparked off either through resonance ('that reminds me of . . .', 'that's similar to . . .') or dissonance, a strong feeling of difference. The group would then work to try to identify any general strands or themes underpinning the stories – the 'issues' – which might be tentatively stated as hypotheses about change in attitude.

Finally, we considered possible actions to take, in the light of these formulations. In an overseas MEd group extended actions must often wait until the participants return home; but there can be feedback as to what ideas have been generated, and what the students will take away with them to work on. In a part-time home MEd group of practising teachers, participants may take actions back into the classroom with them to see if they will have any effect on a perceived area of concern.

I have found that this structure often generates a quality of attention in listening to each other's stories which, in some cases, sparks off another member of the group to share a related story. Students are invited initially to stay with the factual details of the story. But it soon becomes possible for individuals to explore underpinning attitudes within themselves through resonance and dissonance with others. Underlying assumptions and fixed attitudes can be brought into question within the group and can form the basis of further exploration for individual participants either in the session or outside. With resonance, possibly because, by definition, it tends to signal a confirmation of or concordance with 'self', it often seems possible for the individual, alone, to probe the issues behind the story. With dissonance the speaker may be unable to make such a move alone, yet in my experience it is dissonance that seems to bring with it the greater 'energy charge', and which provokes the stronger engagement with self which I describe as 'the grit in the oyster'. Students are engaged by the disparity between stories, and quite possibly irritated by them, but are unable single-handedly to probe behind the surface details and discover the implicit theories that may have underlain the way they experienced the event.

Hence the way the students work together in a collaborative group is crucial in supporting the working through of the dissonance by the individual. The strategy of initially only allowing responses to the detail of the story, through clarificatory questions and related stories, first allows all the stories to be heard with no pressure on the individual to articulate, for the moment, more than that which comes easily. The group then works at what the issues underpinning the set of stories might be and individuals are left with possibilities for development in their ideas. Provoked articulation through the use of dissonance is a powerful tool for uncovering implicit theories and beliefs (Claxton, 1984, 1989), and thereby creating the platform from which the individual can move to a new position of conscious decision making.

To illustrate the move from 'experiences' to 'issues', let me quote from a piece of writing by one member of the group, written in response to the invitation to students to describe their story and related issues:

It was in 1972, during the last year of my secondary school education, when I was taught by a very sarcastic mathematics teacher (sarcasm – one of the long-term destroyers of trust). My performance in mathematics was like that of a pupil who had no aptitude in the subject. I believe that the major factors constituting the problem were a) I could not ask questions in class when I wanted to, with the fear that I would be given sarcastic responses as was done to other members of class; and b) I did not feel motivated to learn the subject because of the type of teacher I had.

Later on, in the course of the year, we were joined by a different teacher. Unlike the former, the latter encouraged a lot of questioning in his class. He used different techniques to encourage this to happen eg he treated pupils as individuals, he also showed great concern in helping pupils to overcome problems encountered during the process of learning. Clearly he created a conducive environment for learning.

I suddenly felt a great change in me. I started asking questions in class. My performance in mathematics improved and I developed a very strong liking for the subject. Since that time the liking for the subject has stayed with me regardless of the type of mathematics teacher I had.

Issues: a) attitude may change as a result of a change in environment;

b) resistance may be used as a strong tool to discourage the change of attitude that could be as a result of the change in the environment.

(Eunice Kolitsoe Moru, Lesotho)

The session concluded with a consideration of more general issues developed from the process which are then explored in terms of potential hypotheses for action. These are not meant to be taken as universal truths, but as having some tentative validity within the group, grounded in the first-hand experience of the group. Seemingly contradictory statements can be explored through discussion to map their validity under particular circumstances. The dissonance between these contradictory statements can generate the energy for other metacognitive shifts of attention (Mason and Davis, 1990). This way of working provides a vehicle for comparing one's own attitudes and beliefs with those of others, through the questioning and identification of individuals' implicit theories. The way that the seminar is organised is also a possible model for how the students could work with groups in their own countries.

Just 'reflecting' has never seemed enough to me. There is often also the need for challenge or tension really to confront people with difference so that they feel uncomfortable, and are impelled to resolve those feelings. According to Festinger (1957), decisions are supposed to be followed by residual dissonance between awareness of the decision and awareness of the reasons supporting the alternative course of action that was rejected. (This also, he suggests, applies to feelings after compliance to a distasteful request.) One way of resolving the dissonance would be to undergo a change in private attitude. In a classroom, say, if teachers are able to make decisions in the moment, they will also be able to make the subtle developments in their behaviour as they continually reappraise their 'cost–benefit analysis' (Claxton, Chapter 1), before making a similar decision. This sort of work is often carried out on 'automatic pilot', and yet the ability to act and be aware of acting allows also the possibility of learning new behaviours. As Claxton says in Chapter 1, it is often the fact that these considerations weigh in the learning balance unreflectively that leads to self-defeating learning choices being made.

As a contrast to the first example, the second focuses on the learning of a single member, also studying for an MEd, of a small group working in this way. The course title was 'Professional Development through Collaborative Working in a Group on an Issue in Mathematics Education'. Since I wanted the agenda for the group to be set by the concerns of the individual participants, each member of the group decided on his or her own issue. My focus as tutor, however, was on looking for evidence of any changes in attitude or behaviour of the students as they carried out their work. These changes can emerge in various guises not necessarily related to the students' initial thinking on their identified issue. The course has been designed therefore to facilitate learning rather than to deliver a predetermined content. When the group met, once a fortnight, each student could ask for time to present his or her current experiences and observations to the rest of us for comment, clarification and shared resonance and dissonance, to explore embedded issues and help consideration of future actions. The sessions could also involve a discussion of a piece of the research literature which one member of the group or the tutor suggested, or of research techniques such as interviewing or diary keeping based on the course reader (Altrichter *et al.*, 1993).

The student I want to focus on, Alan Dobson, is a home part-time student who is also the head of a mathematics department in a secondary school. The material I want to discuss is taken from Alan's research diaries, final assignment, profiles of pupils, transcripts of his interviews with pupils, and an extended interview between the two of us. I hope we shall demonstrate that it is when the dissonance 'bites', provided it is accepted as a challenge, that personal growth, learning and a change in attitude become possible. (Since so much of the evidence in this section is his, the chapter should from this point on be seen as a joint effort, reflecting his input. In addition, I am most grateful for his comments on and amendments to earlier drafts of this chapter.)

To illustrate the two complementary levels of learning that are going on – the student working on his issue, and the tutor working on her role as facilitator – the discussion that follows is in three parts. The first is 'the voice of the student', which draws on a report Alan wrote on the issue of 'Teacher versus researcher' as part of the assignment for the course. Alan's specific issue concerned 'blockages': what was really going on for a group of low achievers in mathematics? This study had led him to do some interviewing of some of his pupils in an attempt to find out what they knew and what they did not know. The second part is 'the voice of the tutor': three vignettes (Miles, 1990) are offered to illustrate the tutor's deepening understanding of a perceived implicit theory, to do with Alan's central concern with 'rightness'. And the third part, which we might call 'teaching strategies and purposes', considers a possible model for supporting the student after the identification of an inhibiting implicit theory.

THE VOICE OF THE STUDENT (BY ALAN DOBSON)

This issue, 'teacher versus researcher', took on a great significance throughout the time I spent interviewing the pupils. The main purpose of my talking to them on an individual basis was to try to establish the points at which their knowledge of mathematics was breaking down, and it was obvious, from the first interview, that to be in 'teacher mode' was not the most efficient way of doing this! As a teacher, I am encountering 'blockages' every working day of my life. When a child raises his or her hand and says, 'Sir, I'm stuck', my assistance is required to clear up an obstruction. As a teacher, I go to that child, and try to move him or her forward, as efficiently as I can. As a researcher, however, with a focus on trying to delve deeper into students' understanding, I wish to move the child 'backwards', to find the root causes of the blockage. This tension between the two roles proved to be both stimulating and frustrating!

As a teacher trying to be a researcher, listening to the tapes of my first interviews was in many ways a disconcerting experience. Lacking in foresight, I had simply sat down with a child, a tape recorder, a set of questions and a misguided hope that I was going to discover the root of all problems. In fact I did learn a lot about the mathematics the youngsters were doing, but, equally, I realised the need for changes in my behaviour in this situation, to encourage the interviewees to release more information about themselves as mathematicians.

What, then, was I doing 'wrong'? First, and probably most importantly, I was not really listening. On reflection, I was only hearing the answers I wanted to hear – as teachers, is this not what we do all of the time? Consequently, I was not really probing incorrect responses thoroughly enough, and when the correct answer arrived, I was not challenging it, but moving straight on to the 'next one'. Also, on listening to the recordings, there were many occasions when the pupils came out with more or less 'throw-away' lines, which, with the hindsight the technology offers, were certainly missed opportunities to explore sources of difficulty. Because I seemed to have this fixed idea of where the conversation should be heading, at the time, I was just not 'hearing' these comments.

Second, and this cannot be totally disconnected from the first point, I was having a seemingly insatiable tendency to lead the students, and not allow them truly to make up their own mind. Again, I guess, I was really wanting them to do my mathematics, and not their own. I was also being very conscious of silence. There were pauses on the tapes, but they were invariably ended by me trying to move the students forward – again, this is the sort of behaviour we, as teachers, exhibit every day in the classroom.

Third, there were occasions when I really did struggle to find the vocabulary on which to structure a response or question that would delve into the blockage at the centre of a current conversation, and allow the child to release more information about the nature of the problem. This, once more, raised the issue of the inextricable links between possible sources of difficulty in mathematics and language, particularly the precise nature of mathematical terminology and symbols.

In later interviews, I have made valiant attempts to incorporate more of the techniques of a researcher, bearing in mind Piaget's clinical interview (Ginsburg, 1981) and my own reflections and discussions on the subject. Moves forward have really centred around trying to provoke interviewees into revealing more about their mathematics.

To quote from my own research diary here, I am now trying:

- to be more attentive, and pick up on (seemingly) throw-away lines;
- to ask more 'hows' and 'whys';
- not to be embarrassed by silence;
- not to lead the interviewee, even by voice intonation;
- not to talk so much, or interrupt the child;
- to allow the child to express his or her own mathematics, and not impose mine;
- not just to accept answers I 'want' to hear, but consider all responses.

In Altrichter *et al.*, (1993) the phrase 'neutral attentiveness' is used which seems to sum up these elements of my resolution well. In addition, I am also paying more attention to establishing 'proper motivation' (Ginsburg, 1981), during the interview.

In an attempt to probe deeper into the interviewees' responses, and to assist in my struggle to find effective, searching replies, I have tried to compile a list of possibilities. Again, quoting my diary, these include:

- asking 'how did you do that?' (fairly obvious really!);
- trying simpler numbers, or a simpler example;
- trying more difficult examples;
- saying nothing!;
- (if a language problem is suspected) asking a 'non-maths' question using the same vocabulary;
- using counter-examples and counter-suggestions to test 'strength of belief';
- asking 'tell me something (like this) that you do know';
- saying 'ask me a question that you think will help'.

Are the behaviours of teachers and researchers mutually exclusive? I sincerely hope not! Indeed, back in the classroom I have tried to adopt some of the above elementary 'research techniques' during my conversations with children, although, at the moment, I admit, with limited success. When a pupil (or a group of children) articulates a difficulty during a lesson, I attend to his or her needs as best I can. This usually means an intervention which lasts a (very) short period of time, and is not conducted with 100 per cent attendance to the 'subject', since, being a teacher, I need to be alert to other activity in the room.

With what, then, do I leave a child after such an intervention? It may be an 'answer' (to the original query), or it may be another question, in an attempt to stimulate further thought. Whatever the transference, however, has the assistance been successful, and actually moved the pupil's mathematics forward? My suspicions are that, in many cases, it has not, and I have succeeded only in 'papering over the cracks', the real cause of the initial problem being much deeper in the pupil's schema of mathematics. Consequently, any lasting effect of the intervention must be very limited.

Realistically, I obviously cannot hope to reach the real blockages behind many of the problems arising in a busy mathematics lesson, but this piece of research has raised, substantially, my awareness of my own 'processes of intervention' and has encouraged me at least to begin to utilise behaviours highlighted by my work during one-to-one interviews. I do feel confident that I can add parts of a researcher to a teacher, and make my interventions more effective and efficient.

THE TUTOR'S VOICE

One of the most important preliminary tasks for educators, in their roles both as learners and teachers, is to engage in a process of critical reflection upon their outmoded implicit theories of learning, for while these remain tacitly installed in their minds, neither the necessity nor the possibility of a different view of learning can be seriously entertained.

(Claxton, Chapter 4)

Whilst Alan was working on pupils' blockages, and encountering dissonance between the researcher and teacher roles, my focus was on that process of critical reflection. He was bringing to the surface a range of outmoded implicit theories which he then worked on to widen his ideas of what he was doing as a teacher and as a learner. He was trying out new behaviours related to these perceived problems to facilitate the learning of mathematics in his classroom, although, as he says, 'at the moment with limited success'. What was it possible for my perspective to add to this situation?

I want to draw attention to a particular strand of the data which highlights for me how useful it is to have co-workers who are able to look at one's work and share different perspectives on it. To do this I will describe three different but related strands within the data in the form of 'vignettes, snapshots or perhaps a mini-movie, of a professional at work' (Miles, 1990). These strands overlap and are not in any particular sequential order. I will argue that there was resistance to change in Alan's behaviours because of a strong and deeply held implicit theory of which he was not conscious.

Strand 1: Papering over the cracks

In a diary extract (31.3.94) is the first appearance of what was to become a major focus of Alan's attention: the dissonance between the perceived roles of teacher and researcher. In the margin of the journal, as a 'reflection on a reflection,' is the comment: 'Ask, "what do you know?"; say, "ask me a question you think will help?"' These two questions, added after reflection, are of a different order, asking of the pupils an awareness of their own learning and recognition of their autonomy as learners.

Again, in the diary, amid the abundance of strategies which Alan has listed, he ends with the question, posed to himself, which shifts his own learning onto a different plane: does being a 'teacher' inhibit 'research'? Do we as teachers spot an error, 'paper over the crack' and not delve to find the source – treating symptoms as causes?

My role as leader of the group was to support Alan as he wrestled with these ideas but also to allow the focus to remain. What was this tension hiding in terms of implicit beliefs? I suggested to Alan that at some stage I would like to come and interview him, inviting him to talk in some detail about this issue of teacher versus researcher. This interview provoked an articulation of 'papering over the cracks' in the form of a story from Alan's classroom:

> Yesterday, I had that year 8 group of children with special needs. I was talking to Lianne, who had a report card to sign and the whole class had been doing some work on calculator activities designed to check reasonableness of answers: 'is the answer I am putting down on the paper sensible?'. Lianne was having problems identifying the correct model, the correct operation to use on this particular set of questions. She had done the first couple and in fact they were all multiplication questions. So we talked through the first one and, after a long piece of teaching, we came to the conclusion that it was multiplication and the second one was multiplication, and so the rest must all be multiplication. So she was quite happy then pressing buttons on the calculator and doing multiplication sums. But I knew really that I had done nothing, that I hadn't really taught her that that particular set of situations were to be interpreted as multiplication sums. All I helped to do was get those sums right on that particular page. She was quite happy with that.

This idea of 'rightness' is also mentioned in the context of the pupils working on errors:

> Diary entry (9.6.94): Errors – there is a fair amount of theory around which suggests that the analysis of errors can act as an excellent springboard to learning. But our kids do not make errors comfortably. They are concerned about 'getting things right' and seem to interpret mathematics as learning skills to do the questions.

Strand 2: Right behaviours

During our conversation, the sense of 'right' crops up again, this time related to his own behaviour. Talking about it allows Alan to explore the created dissonance and really work at what the issues are:

> The problem there was that I found first of all I was struggling to find the right questions, they might be the searching questions, the questions that would pinpoint it. Secondly, I guess this is where the teacher mode starts operating, I suppose I was conscious of silence. The child was thinking,

nothing was happening, and I felt I needed to do something and inevitably after listening through tapes afterwards, my interventions were very, although I didn't think so at the time, they were very directed – they were starting to prompt the child and push the child in the direction of the answer that I wanted, not really searching out what the child knew at all. So I guess the interventions were answer orientated. I was thinking the answer. I had this model in my head with an answer at the end of it and that was what I subconsciously did. If you had asked me before the interview with the child I'd say, 'no, I don't want to do that, that's precisely what I don't want to do'.

Initially when interviewing the children Alan had reached a crisis moment when he considered that there were times when he just did not know what to say. In following down a path of developing his behaviours as a researcher, the teacher behaviours that were previously automatic had been inhibited and he was suddenly aware of feeling deskilled. During the interview he said:

That researcher thing then of trying to establish through conversations where the child was and what were the real problems – I started more or less at the same time to take that into the classroom and, in my conversations with the children in the class, I was trying also to develop the skill of trying to find out what it was the child was actually asking, not what the particular problem of the moment was. You go over the problem directly and the child is happy for a brief second but in fact you have done nothing, and, what I felt you needed to do, was to go back a few stages and try and find out where this thing was coming from and then you are faced with all sorts of other problems. When you are talking to children on a one to one basis in the classroom you get used to sort of talking with seventy five, eighty per cent concentration. The other twenty per cent is there looking around and hearing problems and things, whereas the researcher mode I think takes much more than that. It takes almost a hundred per cent attention. You've got to get involved and you've got to get inside and if you do that you lose what is happening. I did a count once, I was observing a colleague teaching and we were looking at something very similar and I timed the average length of a contact with a child and it was one minute. I was talking to the children on tape for up to an hour sometimes trying to find out exactly where things were going wrong. So there are lots of conflicts when you are trying to be a teacher and a researcher in the classroom. There is the time, there is the concentration, there is the dynamics of the classroom.

There are also similar tensions when the teacher is present in the one-to-one researcher mode:

I think in a sort of perverse way the not knowing what to say next [when interviewing] has been solved by not saying anything. The correct response might have been no response. Just to sit and wait and be patient. In terms of actually saying things, this statement, 'all right, you don't know, but tell me what you do know', is quite nice. And that is very powerful in the classroom, trying to get straight to a problem. That has been a definite change of behaviour but is certainly a new technique I am using now that I wasn't using four or five weeks ago.

I am conscious of getting to the right thing to be taught, so it's the researcher bit being used to get to the problem and then the teacher bit being used to overcome the problem, which I think is a slightly different emphasis to the one in the classroom. There was a conflict there, it's getting less, there are slight tensions there which need working on and resolving. But you can never divorce the two.

Strand 3: D'accord

This pervasive sense of needing 'rightness' is a powerful organising principle in many mathematics teachers' minds. Was it any wonder that the way Alan saw the world would encourage his pupils to want to get the right answer? From the work that I have done on the teacher's influence on children's image of mathematics (Brown, 1992) it would not be surprising if Alan's implicit belief in 'right answers' and correct paths led his pupils to be uncomfortable with learning from their errors. Here was a conflict between beliefs and actions which would need resolving. Was Alan aware of carrying around with him this sense of needing to get things right? Or was it too deeply embedded to be conscious?

In the following extract from the interview, I work at highlighting the issue of 'rightness' for Alan so that it becomes possible for him to see this for himself:

L: It's interesting, isn't it, because there is a focus on the answer? You as teacher in those individual conversations in a busy classroom are still answer driven. And yet the researcher can bring that into question and say 'what other strategies can I try to do?' and 'let's play around with that'.

A: Well, that's dead right. There's an awful lot of children who see mathematics as a means of getting answers. I am trying to recall several conversations I have had recently where I have tried to get children to think about what they are doing and they have actually said in words to this effect, 'can't you just tell us how to get the answer?'. Perhaps we [as mathematics teachers] have tried to move away from that over the last ten years but we are still dominated, I would suggest, by a quest for answers both in terms of teaching and in learning.

L: But you were saying that, in fact, your own focus was on the answer, so what if I were to say to you that the children will be interested in answers because you are interested?

A: Yes, you took the words out of my mouth. Is it any wonder that the children are looking for answers if that's the picture that the teachers are putting over? It does become one of the things that I have picked up through listening to myself talking to children on an individual basis; how channelled I am, almost subconsciously, in pushing the children along certain routes towards the goal I want. There are lots of situations where that has to be done, but in fact that can become counterproductive and that's something again that's been backed up by this research and doing lots of reading.

L: But it's interesting to me how dualistic you are actually, because this word 'right', you use it a lot.

A: Do you think I use the word Right, to mean Right?

L: It's just the French *d'accord* really?

A: For one horrible year I taught everywhere in this place and I almost decided to buy myself a packhorse from the consortium to get all my stuff around the site, but I taught in a room right at the top in the humanities block next to the special needs person and at the end of one lesson he stuck his head through the door and all he said to me was 'you use Right a lot, don't you?' and then went.

L: But I bet when we get the transcript that there are some uses of Right in this sense of the Right answer, whether you were going to get the Right question, whether you were going to get the Right, now that's not *d'accord*.

I was now convinced that one key implicit theory for Alan centred on this sense of rightness, and had taken the responsibility of sharing this piece of 'grit' with him. Using that awareness to continue work on extending the range of strategies will necessarily take place over a long period of time. As a tutor I was able to help Alan to highlight and work on a piece of grit which he had begun to discover for himself.

TEACHING STRATEGIES AND PURPOSES

So far we have looked at how an implicit theory was identified and brought into question; but now comes the difficult part of the individual teacher trying to change his or her habitual, automated behaviours to which that belief system had given rise. In the literature concerned with learning strategies there is a model which has proved useful in helping me to describe how teachers learn and change. Nisbet and Schucksmith (1986) outline a hierarchy of learning strategies which has three levels. At the most general level there is a *central strategy*, an overall style or approach to learning, which is closely related to attitudinal and motivational factors. Then come *macro-strategies*, which are executive processes linked to cognition and knowledge. These are highly generalisable; improve with age and experience; and can in principle be developed through training, though this may be difficult in practice. Lastly there are *micro-strategies* which are less generalisable, more task specific, and easier to teach or train.

By 'strategy' they mean 'essentially a method for approaching a task, or more generally attaining a goal. Each strategy would call upon a variety of processes in the course of its operation.' Strategies are in principle distinct from 'non-executive processes', or skills, though this distinction, when related to the complex arenas of learning and teaching, is, as they point out, easier to maintain in theory than in practice. (For a full discussion see Nisbet and Schucksmith (1986).)

To apply the above hierarchy of learning strategies to teaching strategies I am linking the central strategy to teachers' images of mathematics and mathematics teaching, giving an overall sense of direction to their work. Such philosophical and attitudinal perspectives (implicit learning theories and theories of self, Claxton, Chapter 4) build up over time and are certainly not easily transferable, but do inform the decision making necessary to apply lower-order strategies. Next, I associate macro-strategies with the teacher's purposes. For a particular purpose (e.g. gaining access to pupils' thinking) the teacher often has a range of strategies which could be used at differing times and in differing circumstances. And finally micro-strategies are identified with specific behaviours. A tutor or mentor might offer such a micro-strategy to another teacher, who would still need to work at the level of purpose to begin to integrate that behaviour into a broader repertoire of strategies in order to achieve that purpose. Teachers will only fully adopt the micro-strategy if it conforms to their developing central strategy.

To give an illustration of this model, consider a teacher who believes that he or she should try to build his or her teaching from what the pupils already know (central strategy). This belief may be stimulated by a theoretical – for example, a constructivist – perspective, or simply by experience, but once it has become an implicit theory it is difficult to change. In planning the teacher may articulate the purpose (macro-strategy) as (for example) 'Knowing what they know'. The teacher then has to assemble a range of strategies, some of which might be considered micro-strategies, but others of which may not yet be articulated at the level of actual behaviours.

A possible micro-strategy might be to invite the students to make posters or write in response to 'Tell me what you know about . . .'. Another might be to ask pupils to explain how they had begun to tackle a problem, and then to invite other pupils to close their eyes and put up their hands if they had started in the same way. The teacher could then elicit a different way of starting to tackle the problem, and again ask the pupils to close their eyes and put up their hands if this was their way of starting. The variety of pupil strategies thus uncovered could then be used as a basis for further exploration (see Brown, 1992). Experience with such micro-strategies may well provide the grit to stimulate a more thoroughgoing reappraisal of the teacher's macro-strategies, the purposes, and could eventually lead on to the development of different central strategies – as it did in the case of Alan. In the description of Alan's learning the dissonance was provided when his behaviour as a researcher brought into question his behaviour as a teacher. He was drawn to question longstanding behaviours and so bring into focus the purposes under which he was operating, and to seek to change the automatic pilot which had been directing his teaching.

CONCLUSION

In both of the examples I have described, implicit theories of learning and teaching were made conscious through a metacognitive shift of attention (Mason and Davis, 1990), and this greater awareness then raised the possibility of alternative behaviours being considered in the decision-making moment in the classroom. These case studies show how the idea of 'learning to learn' can form the basis of a way of thinking about the professional development of the teacher. Trying out the strategies of others can have marked effects on people's beliefs, provided that they notice the outcomes of the change in behaviour. Trying out a particular behaviour which is alien can provide dissonance and a powerful learning experience.

Let me give a final illustration. Student teachers who spent their early days in the classroom talking all the time and not listening to the pupils could be asked to do a lesson almost in silence. It is of course up to the learner teachers whether they take up the challenge, and a defensive strategy, based on a decision not to take the risk, might be appropriate at the time. However, if they do take up the challenge the potential for learning could be enormous:

• learning to use other 'teaching aids' apart from their mouth
• using their eyes and having to take their cues from the children
• discovering how to base their lesson on something other than themselves.

Such experiences of what happens when fundamental changes are made to behaviours can lead to changes in the students' central strategy.

In conclusion, I was much taken years ago with a statement in *The Little Ed Book* (Claxton, 1978): 'In his introduction to *Mother Night*, Kurt Vonnegut says: "We are what we pretend to be, so we must be careful about what we pretend to be". Be careful about what you pretend to be at school.' Perhaps it would also be true to say: 'We are what we choose to be, so be conscious of what you choose to be at school.' If teachers can be aware of their decision-making processes, as they are happening in the moment, they will become more conscious of underlying assumptions which drive their behaviours, and open up the possibilities of getting rid of entrenched attitudes which have acted as brakes to their learning.

REFERENCES

Altrichter, H., Posch, P. and Somekh, B. (1993) *Teachers Investigate Their Work*, London: Routledge.

Bannister, D. and Fransella, F. (1974) *Inquiring Man*, London: Penguin Modern Psychology.

Brown, L. (1992) 'The influence of teachers on children's image of mathematics'. *For the learning of mathematics*, Vol. 12(2), pp. 29–33.

Claxton, G. (1978) *The Little Ed Book*, London: Routledge & Kegan Paul.

Claxton, G. (1984) *Live and learn: an introduction to the psychology of growth and change in everyday life*, London: Harper & Row.

Claxton, G. (1989) *Classroom Learning*, Open University course E208, Exploring Educational Issues, Unit 13. Milton Keynes: Open University.

Festinger, L. (1957) *A Theory of Cognitive Dissonance*, Row, Peterson.

Ginsburg, H. (1981) 'The clinical interview in psychological research on mathematical thinking: aims, rationales, techniques'. *For the learning of mathematics*, Vol. 1 (3), pp. 4–11.

Jahoda, M. and Warren, N., (eds) (1966) *Attitudes*, London: Penguin Modern Psychology.

Jaworski, B. (Chair) (1991) *Develop Your Teaching*, Cheltenham: The Mathematical Association and Stanley Thornes.

Kulm, G. (1980) 'Research on mathematics attitude'. In R. J. Shumway (ed.) *Research in Mathematics Education*, Reston, VA: National Council of Teachers of Mathematics.

Mason, J. and Davis, J. (1990) 'Cognitive and metacognitive shifts of attention and a methodology for their study'. PME conference paper available from J. Mason at the Centre for Mathematics Education, The Open University.

Miles, M. (1990) 'New methods for qualitative data collection and analysis: vignettes and pre-structured cases'. *International Journal of Qualitative Studies in Education*, Vol. 3(1), p. 38.

Nisbet, J. and Schucksmith, J. (1986) *Learning Strategies*, London, Routledge & Kegan Paul.

Chapter 15

Teacher mentors and student teachers
What is transmitted?

Terry Atkinson

With Chapters 15 and 16 we are back once more with initial teacher education, and specifically with the role, and the training, of school-teacher mentors. In the present chapter Terry Atkinson explores the three-way interaction between mentors' and student teachers' beliefs about each other, the nature of the training, and the learning of school students. He particularly focuses on the implicit theories of the mentors, and examines the ways in which these lead mentors to interact with student teachers in very different ways. One of the most important contrasts to emerge is between mentors who see new teachers' potential as relatively fixed, and those who see learning to teach very much as a developmental process. What seems to be fundamental in determining the mentors' attitudes towards student teachers, concludes Atkinson, is their sensitivity towards their own belief systems. Mentors who see their own professional lives in developmental terms are more likely to take a developmental attitude towards their student teachers.

INTRODUCTION

This chapter deals with the learning of student teachers on school-based teacher education programmes in which the prime mode of delivery is via a system of school-based mentoring. Mentors* are schoolteachers who are identified as having a specific responsibility for one or more student teachers. The responsibilities of a mentor commonly include:

- the supervision of teaching practice;
- observation of lessons and the giving of constructive feedback;
- the tutoring of student teachers;
- guidance as to methods, requirements of curricula and syllabuses;

---

* For convenience of use the following pronoun convention has been adopted: a schoolteacher mentor is referred to as she (her, hers); a student teacher as he (him, his).

- advice on procedures;
- the assessment of the teaching competence of student teachers;
- course planning and design, particularly with regard to the school-based element of the programme;
- joint planning with the training institution of the programme as a whole.

Accounts of school-based initial teacher education programmes in England are well documented elsewhere by Atkinson (1994), Judge *et al.* (1994), Townshend (1994) and Benton (1990). Here, we are specifically concerned with the thinking of school-based mentors.

This consideration of mentoring will start from practical contexts – tutorials, joint planning sessions, apprenticeship models and the like – and will lead in to an analysis of the underlying mental processing. A psychological dimension is characteristic of mentoring relationships be they in initial teacher education, induction of newly qualified teachers (Vonk, 1994) or in other professional contexts.

The object of consideration in this chapter is, then, the potential collision between the separate understandings about teaching and learning of two individuals – that of the experienced schoolteacher acting as mentor and that of the student teacher. Both are likely to hold a set of beliefs about teaching and learning covering student teacher development, the role of the teacher, models of teaching, teaching styles and methods, learning styles, curriculum and the needs of school students. These sets of beliefs are the product of the very diverse experiences – professional and other – of the mentor and student teacher. Some of these beliefs, for example those concerned with equality of opportunity, justice, freedom of expression, stem from ideological or moral conviction long pre-dating professional involvement in education. There is often a distance between mentor and student teacher, not in ideological terms but in understanding of how ideology can be and is applicable in the professional context of the role of a schoolteacher. This gap provides but one of many opportunities for a dynamic dialogue between mentor and student teacher which can challenge both to articulate their practice and, more importantly, the underlying thinking which may or may not be at a conscious level. The chapter will attempt to focus on the less conscious elements of the thinking of each of these participants, the implicit beliefs that each brings and which are the theme of this book.

The preconceptions of student teachers and the impact of these on their (college) course learning was noted by Lortie (1975). Wubbels (1992) distinguishes between the explicit and implicit theories held by student teachers. For Hollingsworth (1989) the particular importance of implicit beliefs is that they act as an unconscious yardstick determining whether incoming ideas 'make intuitive sense'. For Elliott and Calderhead (1993), these implicit theories must be brought into the open so that they can be challenged and, in school-based teacher education, that task falls to the mentor.

The purpose of the chapter is, then, to see what light can be shed upon the consideration of implicit beliefs about learning from a review of school-based mentoring. The outcome should provide not only another plank for this particular Kon-tiki but also a review of school-based teacher education from a somewhat different perspective: an attempt to scrutinise the underlying thinking of school-based mentors. What do they think they are doing? How are they helping to develop student teachers' learning? Are mentors aware of the dangers of their own beliefs about learning and teacher development having an undue and possibly harmful impact and how do they set about avoiding this? What light can mentors shed upon the development of student teachers, the diagnosis and challenging of dysfunctional implicit, and on occasions blatantly explicit, beliefs? What view of the reflective practitioner or other model of practice do mentors hold? How do they support and monitor the critical thinking of student teachers, their reflection on practice and, if possible, their reflection in practice?

In his studies of the mentoring of teachers in the first years of their professional practice, Vonk (1994) found the psychological impact upon the mentor to be considerable, leading to extensive professional development for the mentor as well as the new teacher. In fact, Vonk points out that mentors frequently undergo a greater degree of development than the new teachers they work with. In considering the mentoring of student teachers, we might expect to replicate these results. Of particular interest will be the impact of the mentoring activity and the accompanying professional development upon the beliefs of the mentor. In articulating her practice does she encounter any remaining skeletons rattling around in her professional cupboard? Does she bring to her awareness any implicit theories about learning and professional development?

IMPLICIT BELIEFS ABOUT LEARNING

One of the problems for school-based mentors in approaching their work with student teachers is to make sense of the thinking of someone who probably has little or no professional background in education. The mentor has the difficulty of making sense of a complex web of beliefs about teaching and learning that the student teacher is likely to hold; a difficulty compounded by the fact that these beliefs about learning are likely to be implicit, not articulated or formally stated and frequently contradictory. Student teachers bring their share of implicit theories about life as a whole and these are entangled with their beliefs about learning. They bring a series of implicit theories about living in general and these dictate many of their actions in the new professional context of the classroom and the school.

One of the keys to the problem of understanding learners is to discard an undue preoccupation with overly formalised conceptualisations of teaching and learning. The problem with these is that teachers and educationalists have come to invest a lot in them. As Guy Claxton (Chapter 4) has outlined, there is an implicit theory of learning, to which the professional educator is prone, that sees learning as happening in orderly, formal contexts, being associated with effort, work and discipline, and proceeding according to prescribed curricular norms leading to preconceived assessment outcomes. Guy Claxton points out that this is a self-limiting theory since it discards the enormous learning potential of unpredictable, spontaneous, serendipitous, unplanned or purely anarchic learning events. Lewicki *et al.* (1992) and Seger (1994) have shown that there is a unique learning potential inherent in such unstructured activity.

An implicit view of learning as belonging to formal, institutionalised contexts disconnects learning from the rest of life, thereby giving an incomplete portrait of learners. Such learners only learn when wearing neatly pressed school uniforms and sitting in orderly rows. With such an incomplete view of the learner it is difficult to see the connections between, or rather the integrity of, learning in the formal learning context and in the rest of life. An alternative view of learning might reject a separate concept of learning altogether, seeing it merely as a part of the continuum of living. In a sense, all life is learning since life-forms continually adapt to their environments, and in so doing they continually learn. Equally, all formal classroom-based learning is a part of life and those who are termed learners during this formalised school time are in fact living beings. Seeing learners holistically has the advantage of seeing their behaviour in the classroom as being continuous with their behaviour outside of the classroom.

It thus becomes possible to make sense of the implicit beliefs that learners have. These are simply the core beliefs of the individual developed through his or her life experiences. If, throughout my whole life, I am a thoughtful individual who likes to consider all sides of a question, be it what I am going to have for breakfast, who should be selected for my favourite football team or what book I am going to take out of the library, then this is a self-defining characteristic that I am going to have in all situations – it is a lifestyle, not a learning style. Moreover, it is self-defining in that it defines who I am and any challenge to its validity is, in effect, a challenge to my self-image.

There are many formal learning situations in which it is hard to perceive raw learning/living styles because the learners themselves conform to the expectations of learning that they perceive their teacher to have. However, in some situations the acculturation is incomplete, yet to take place, or incapable of taking place. With less sophisticated learners one finds instances of those who simply exhibit their normal living style openly and un-ashamedly. The child in the reception class wants to know where the teacher's volume, rewind and on/off controls are located. The autistic adolescent girl sees no shame in masturbating in class. Analogously, the student teacher draws on his real-life belief systems as he seeks instant recipes for the problems that he encounters in the classroom. Thus, it is important for the school mentor to have a holistic view of the student teacher in order to understand that he brings all of his implicit theories about life into his work as a teacher, to know how to work with the student to adapt and develop these beliefs for positive outcomes.

The ability to see the student teacher holistically may be a key element in constructing the relationship between mentor and student teacher, a relationship which can be seen as the key to the success or otherwise of school-based teacher training. If the mentor is to have the key abilities to support and challenge then she will first need to know and accept the student, to understand that he will have implicit theories and will act according to them. From the understanding and acceptance of the student, a relationship based on mutual trust and respect can be developed. Tomlinson (1995) considers that mentoring always entails counselling and emphasises Carl Rogers' original key concepts: empathy, unconditional positive regard and genuineness. Rogers (1983) himself views these as the key qualities of teachers and their importance for the mentoring role can hardly be challenged since they enable the student teacher to have full confidence in his mentor.

One of the crucial aspects of learning is the learner's decision whether or not to engage (Claxton, Chapter 1). This is equally true of the student teacher and one of the keys to this decision will be the perception he forms of his mentor. Will the student have the unquestioning belief that faith healers require of their patient and is this degree of belief necessary? The faith healer signals that belief in the treatment and the healer are paramount but as Claxton indicates learners are sometimes right to be sceptical. Absolute faith in an unhelpful method is worthless in itself. I will not cure myself of a headache by hitting myself over the head repeatedly with a hammer however faithfully I believe it.

A more pertinent example is the case of a professor who set out to learn German by learning the dictionary off by heart. After the first attempt he was still unable to understand a single word of a lecture on his own field of knowledge. Nevertheless, his faith in the method undiminished, he concluded that his learning had been poor and that he should reapply himself. Despite an attack of temporary blindness which medical opinion attributed to the hours spent in study he completed a second learning by heart but was still unable to comprehend a lecture in German. Finally, his misplaced faith in this way of learning was revealed to him. For the student teacher and the mentor there is a need to take time to engage in the kind of relationship that will eventually bring success. That time is required for the mentor to build up the student's confidence in her skill and for the student to decide to engage fully with the learning opportunity (see Figure 15.1).

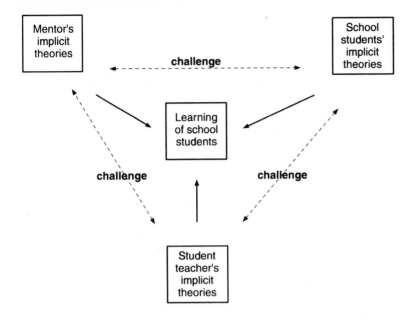

Figure 15.1 Interactions between mentor's, student teacher's and school students' implicit theories

THE MENTOR

Within the mentoring context there is, potentially, a complex web of interactions between the implicit theories of the different participants. The mentor may hold implicit theories about a range of related but separate aspects such as:

- student teachers and their development;
- mentoring;
- learning in general;
- school students and their learning.

These beliefs may impact upon the development and learning of the student but may also be challenged by him and by the interaction between mentor and student.

THE STUDENT TEACHER

The student teacher may hold implicit theories about:

- his own learning;
- his development as a teacher;

- the value and practice of mentoring;
- learning in general;
- school students and their learning.

All of those beliefs will be challenged through the mentoring process and through the student teacher's work in the classroom (see Figure 15.1).

One view of student teacher development might be to see it as a dialectic between the implicit theories of the student teacher about teaching and learning and the practical teaching experiences he undertakes. The mentor's role is to interpret this dialectic, supporting and challenging the student's own reflections as appropriate. However, it is important to remember that mentors have their own implicit theories about professional development. Indeed, a study by Saunders *et al.* (1995) has suggested that these may be derived from the discredited models of teacher education more familiar to many teachers from their own training and from much of their experience in supervising teaching practice.

In order to test the extent to which implicit theories are in play in the context of mentoring an empirical study was carried out.

RESEARCH DESIGN

The methodology chosen consisted of in-depth interviewing with a small number of mentors with varying degrees of experience of mentoring. Once subjects had been chosen, they were interviewed within a loosely structured framework following Burgess's (1984) approach in which the researcher 'had decided the main topics to be covered (but) the actual direction of the conversation was partially determined by the (subjects)'. It was important to allow subjects to talk freely in order to assess their underlying assumptions. I was seeking to avoid directing their answers but experienced the familiar dilemma of being both observer and participant. Inevitably, I had to choose between working with and working on my subjects as discussed by Smyth (1987). I decided to work with them on the basis that this approach engaged them with the subject. I sensed that to ask them to respond to research questions without a dialogue would not have brought the enthusiastic response I was seeking and did, in fact, get.

Each subject was interviewed three times and interviews lasted for about one hour. The first interview was basically the same for each subject and always began with factual questions about the subject, her school and her career to date. For the second and third interviews a structured set of questions for all subjects was prepared but these were then adapted in the light of answers given in the previous interview and scope was given for follow-up questions seeking clarification or further detail.

Much thought was given to how to probe for the implicit theories of the subjects and the main strategy adopted was to use reflective listening so that the subject was encouraged to talk through her own ideas in a relaxed and honest manner. In the course of interviewing this was added to by the successful tactic of asking subjects for their views on the assumptions made by student teachers and by their own colleagues as it became apparent that this seemed to yield some interesting insights on the subjects themselves.

THE PRACTICE OF MENTORING

In constructing the practice of mentoring and differentiating it from university-based teaching, Wilkin (1992) felt that we should proceed by reviewing the desirable content of training – that is, what it is the student needs – and then deciding where the various aspects of that training should be located and by whom they should be taught. In practice, a less well-ordered, more eclectic model seemed to characterise mentors' thinking.

When questioned on how they fulfil the role of mentor, teachers reported various activities including scheduled tutorials as part of a programme, interactions related to actual lessons taught to school students, guided research – often for assessment purposes and informal contacts. Tutorials could function as input sessions from the mentor, as structured discussion or as open discussion and often combined elements of all three. Mentors drew on materials such as university-provided resources, school documentation, the media, educational publications and broadcasts, journal articles and books by educational theorists. They drew heavily on their practical experience as schoolteachers and used the school context, often in imaginative ways, to provide illustration, case studies and research opportunities. They also made use of access to the wide pool of expertise within the school staff group. A common pattern for tutorials would be to link them to some recent practical experience and provide an opportunity for group reflection. Three examples of tutorials which illustrate the range of approaches are given below.

Tutorial 1

The session began with the mentor reviewing the contents of her in-tray in order to convey to students the range of duties fulfilled by a teacher. This raised an interesting discussion and lead in to a greater appreciation not only of the extent of the role but also of the need for good personal organisation and time management. The mentor here assumes that student teachers have a restricted understanding of the role of the teacher. Interestingly, this teacher uses an authentic activity to demonstrate the demands made upon her. This is an instance of a mentor drawing on familiar pedagogy in order to transform it into *androgogy*. The mentor is attempting to make the loop (Woodward, 1991) by provoking a consideration of the role of the teacher and demonstrating the method of making use of authentic materials and tasks.

Tutorial 2

The mentor arranged for student teachers to spend a day tracking the learning experiences of a group of learners and briefed the students to audit the range of teaching and learning styles that were observed during the day. The subsequent tutorial provided the opportunity to discuss various teaching and learning styles as well as the continuity or lack of it within the day-to-day learning experience of school students.

Tutorial 3

The mentor prepared notes of the main points of relevant chapters in a study text (Marland, 1975). This could be characterised as a reversion to a discredited, overly theoretical model of teacher education – another instance of the syndrome referred to earlier which Saunders *et al.* (1995) describe. However, in this case the mentor could be construed as providing a bridge between Marland's theoretical, but highly practical, text and the day-to-day practical experiences which construct student teacher learning during the practicum. This mentor had a clear intention to integrate theory and practice.

Observation of lessons and providing structured feedback is a key task of mentoring and one in which mentors are highly skilled. To take but one example of feedback – a commonly cited problem is that of the student teacher attempting to imitate the teaching style of an established teacher. Mentors used such instances to encourage a reflection on the teaching style, of its suitability and of how the student teacher could best adapt it to his own style. Mentors noted this problem as characteristic of the early phase of student teacher learning and revealed in discussion an awareness of the developmental nature of student teacher learning. Several mentors had evolved sound working practices to support and challenge at each stage of development. Many of these practices encouraged reflection and critical self-awareness. For example, one mentor encouraged student teachers to team-teach so that they would have to plan together and engage in meaningful discussion about teaching and learning.

Mentors considered informal contact with student teachers an important aspect of their work. They valued the chance for regular, spontaneous contact because this built the relationship and gave the opportunity to deal with numerous practical details. These unplanned contacts were often seen as of even more value than formalised tutorial sessions, perhaps because it is through informal contacts that it is easiest to offer support. Mentors were very aware of their pastoral role and drew on their experience of acting in this role with school students and junior colleagues.

School-based investigations were commonly used. For instance, one student had carried out an audit of display in his practice school and concluded that 90 per cent of displays were male dominated – a finding used by the school to underscore a perceived gender problem. Thus, the student teachers were often engaged in meaningful learning activities which trained them to observe critically and act rationally. Their commitment to such activity was enhanced by the fact that the resulting data was used to improve and develop school policy and practice.

IMPLICIT THEORIES OF MENTORS

Interestingly, implicit theories were consistently identified by subjects as of importance. A recurrent theme was that of the quality of the school as a whole. Mentors implied that good initial teacher training was a function of any or all of the following:

- the school ethos;
- the socio-economic breakdown of the catchment area;
- the school's senior management team;
- the academic performance of the school students.

It was assumed that these factors would equate more or less directly to the quality of training; and that the location and context of training would play a significant role. The implication is that students can only learn from good practice: that student doctors should examine and diagnose only healthy patients – not sick ones.

Where mentors lacked confidence about themselves and their schools was in the breadth of experience that they felt they could offer. They referred to the school providing a narrow context from which it was hard to generalise. They felt that they themselves had a limited knowledge of education and of a limited range of educational establishments. One mentor said: 'although I can talk from personal experience, and I can talk about this school, and what we do, I'm certainly no theorist'. Implied here is a belief that school-based training is fundamentally incomplete, for what school can offer a truly representative context? Although all mentors interviewed were strongly in favour of school-based training, they were nonetheless insecure about their own ability to deliver it within the context of their school. This boils down to a belief that they can provide training suited to their own school context but that they are unsure about its transferability or applicability elsewhere – an implicit belief in the non-transferability of learning.

Whilst it was true that the interviewees tended to repeat the same ideas about student teacher learning and school-based training there was a good deal of variation in their awareness of these views. At one end of the continuum stood the mentor who discussed the problems highlighted in the last two paragraphs at a conscious level. For her, it was a question of making the most of the school context, exploiting what it could offer and supplementing its deficiencies through clearly thought-out strategies. At the other end of the continuum, the mentor saw the narrowness of the school context as an intractable problem – for herself, for student teachers and for school students.

THE MENTOR'S VIEW OF THE STUDENT TEACHER

Mentors reported a familiar litany of shortcomings of student teachers on teaching practice. Students had inappropriate views of learners, making invalid assumptions about their backgrounds and their needs. They expected too much of the majority of school students, but their expectations of those with special educational needs were too low. Student teachers tended to misunderstand the origin of misbehaviour; for example, they assumed that it was always the fault of the school student.

Mentors saw the explanation of these shortcomings in such factors as the student teachers' backgrounds. Those who had been pupils at selective grammar schools were presumed to have no idea of average ability level. One mentor perceived a look of disbelief on the faces of the student teachers when they saw the kind of children they were asked to teach and concluded that they had obviously come from backgrounds where they had never come across that sort of behaviour. It was felt by one mentor that some students see their own problems in others, for example they might seek the explanation for a school student's learning difficulties in a problem that they themselves had experienced, generalising from their own personal learning base. Equally, it was felt that students tended to generalise from their own feelings and experience.

There was a general consensus that student personality is very determining expressed in such words as: 'they'll probably go through their whole teaching career being the same sort of person'. Mentors seemed to take this as either positive or negative. There were those who saw the individuality of student teachers as central to their development. They were interested in working with that student to see what kind of teacher he could become. Typically, they had a holistic view of learning and of student teacher learning. Other mentors saw the student teacher's personality and learning capability as fixed and given: 'He is like this and so he will be able to develop into a good teacher or not'. The implicit belief of the mentor about teaching and teacher development was the key variable here and, with this limited sample, the strategy of asking mentors to talk about student teacher assumptions was fairly successful in bringing these to light. One mentor felt that students didn't so much come to teaching with their own assumptions as pick these up from other teachers, especially the 'more down to earth' ones. Of course, student teachers do come with their own assumptions and preconceptions but it is probable that these resonate more readily with the younger and less experienced teachers than with mentors, who tend to be middle or senior managers in the school.

When asked directly about the qualities of student teachers, reference was made to the difficult ones who 'think they know everything already, you can't tell them anything'. Mentors were surprised by students who appeared not to have any empathy for children, perhaps unsurprisingly at this stage in their development, and wondered 'if they don't like kids, what are they doing in the job?' Although mentors thought that empathy was a very important quality in students, they reported that some very sensitive students had problems. For instance, the student with most empathy for one school cohort withdrew because he couldn't cope. Mentors especially valued commitment and students who asked questions, seeing insecurity as a necessary trait at this early stage.

Again, there was a variation between those who were able to see the developmental possibilities of student teachers and those who were not. With no parallel study to see the impact of these two types of mentor on student teacher learning one can only speculate that those who do not see the dynamic possibilities inherent in student teacher learning are more likely to deny it – leading to such unhappy conclusions as the withdrawal of the most sensitive candidates.

CONCLUSION

The best practice in school-based teacher education as revealed in this study was far from atheoretical, though the quality of experience of students was enhanced by the rooting of theoretical issues in practice and the opportunity to reflect upon real experiences. This provided a highly relevant training in practical skills which also helped to develop the capacity for critical self-awareness and reflection. The skilful mentor not only enabled students to perform adequately in the classroom but challenged them to evaluate the lessons they taught as well to participate in and reflect upon the full range of school activity.

School-based teacher education need not represent a regression to an atheoretical model. It can be seen as a progressive model that incorporates, modifies and goes beyond the idealised theoretical model that was rejected in the 1960s but still prevails in some countries. It is a model of partnership between university and school to bring about the reconciliation of theory and practice – giving value and status to reflective theory (Smith, 1992) arising from practice as well as academic theory and practice itself. Thus it can be viewed not as an extreme model in which the practical aspect dominates but as a well-balanced model allowing true integration of theory and practice. It is a model of training which challenges what Zeichner (1992) described as:

> a persistent mind-set . . . that places theory exclusively in universities and practice solely in elementary and secondary schools. In this view held by many, implementation is seen as merely the translation of the theories of

the university into classroom practice. That theories are generated by practices and that practices reflect theoretical commitments, either is not grasped or is deliberately ignored. The relationship between theory and practice is seen as one-way rather than dialogic.

It remains to be seen if a model predicated upon the principles of partnership and reflection upon practice can produce new entrants to the profession who will be enabled to transcend this old prejudice.

This study has shown that implicit theories about learning/living do play an important part in the development, or lack of it, of student teachers through the mentoring process. Such implicit theories may be held equally by mentor and student teacher and are not in themselves either negative or positive. What seemed to be important was *the sensitivity of the mentor towards her own belief system*: how aware she was of her own development as an individual whose implicit theories had become increasingly explicit. This degree of sensitivity was likely to lead to a developmental view of student teachers, and to an acceptance of the personality and assumptions of the student as an opportunity rather than as a limitation. Equally, for those mentors who were less self-aware it was likely that both their own implicit beliefs and those of their students would be problematic. Development would be difficult since students were seen as exhibiting fixed and limiting characteristics leading to assumptions that could not easily be challenged. In this situation, it is a short step to the adoption of the kind of excessively directive style of mentoring which Feiman-Nemser *et al.* (1993) reported as leading to a negative learning experience for the student teacher.

To conclude on a positive note, the willingness of the mentor to see the student teacher holistically, and to work with the student to develop his potential, was expressed by the majority of the mentors interviewed for this study. They were sensitive to the necessary individuality of teachers, to the fact that the best teachers are those who most successfully adapt their own individuality to the needs of the job. They were able to see that it was this ability to adapt and to retain one's own idiosyncrasies that was central rather than the cloning of individual teacher characteristics. For these mentors, assessing student teachers against the DFE's (1992) prescribed list of competencies is of marginal importance since they are able to understand why students act in the way they do, seeing action underpinned by knowledge and understanding (McElvogue and Salters, 1992). They are able to do this because they have a holistic view of the student teacher, of his personality, his implicit theories, his assumptions and his intentions.

In his seminal book on the coaching of tennis, Gallwey (1979) describes the 'bounce–hit' method in which the novice player thinks 'bounce' as the ball bounces in front of the player and then thinks 'hit' as the ball is struck by the racket. The purpose of teaching beginners this simple mantra is to occupy their conscious minds with the most elementary details of the task rather than let confused and inadequate thoughts take hold. This simple approach proved highly effective (apart, of course, from in the teaching of how to volley). The 'bounce–hit' of mentoring might be 'get to know your student teacher'.

REFERENCES

Atkinson, T. (1994) 'National case studies: the United Kingdom'. *European Journal of Teacher Education*, Vol. 17, No. 1/2, pp. 79–82.

Benton, P. (ed.) (1990) *The Oxford Internship Scheme*, London: Calouste Gulbenkian Foundation.

Burgess, R. G. (1984) *In the Field: An Introduction to Field Research*, London: George Allen & Unwin.

DFE (1992) Circular 9/92: Initial Teacher Training (Secondary Phase), London: DFE.

Elliott, B. and Calderhead, J. (1993) 'Mentoring for teacher development: possibilities and caveats'. In D. McIntyre, H. Hagger and M. Wilkin (eds) *Mentoring: Perspectives on School-based Teacher Education*, London: Kogan Page, pp. 166–90.

Feiman-Nemser, S., Parker, M. and Zeichner, K. (1993) 'Are mentor teachers teacher educators?'. In D.McIntyre, H. Hagger and M. Wilkin (eds) *Mentoring: Perspectives on School-based Teacher Education*. London: Kogan Page.

Gallwey, T. (1979) *The Inner Game of Tennis*, Toronto: Bantam Books.

Hollingsworth, S. (1989) 'Prior beliefs and cognitive change in learning to teach'. *American Educational Research Journal*, Vol. 26, pp. 260–89.

Judge, H., Lemosse, M., Paine, L. and Sedlak, M. (1994) *The University and the Teachers: France, the United States, England*, Wallingford: Triangle.

Lewicki, P., Hill, T. and Czyzewska, M. (1992) 'Non-conscious acquisition of information'. *American Psychologist*, Vol. 47, pp. 796–801.

Lortie, D. (1975) *Schoolteacher*, Chicago: University of Chicago Press.

Marland, M. (1975) *Craft of the Classroom*, London: Heinemann.

McElvogue, M. and Salters, M. (1992) 'Models of competence and teacher training'. Paper given at UCET conference, Oxford.

Rogers, C. (1983) *Freedom to Learn for the 80's*, Columbus, OH: Charles E. Merrill.

Saunders, S., Pettinger, K. and Tomlinson, P. (1995) 'Prospective mentors' views of school-based initial teacher education', *British Educational Research Journal*, Vol. 21, p. 2.

Seger, C. A. (1994) 'Implicit learning'. *Psychological Review.* Vol. 115, pp. 163–96.

Smith, R. (1992) 'Theory: an entitlement'. *Cambridge Journal of Education.* Vol. 22, No. 3, pp. 387–98.

Smyth, J. (ed.) (1987) *Educating Teachers: Changing the Nature of Pedagogical Knowledge*, London: Falmer Press.

Tomlinson, P. (1995) *Understanding Mentoring*, Milton Keynes: Open University Press.

Townshend, J. (1994) 'Developments in school-based initial teacher training'. *European Journal of Teacher Education*, Vol. 17, No. 1/2, pp. 49–52.

Vonk, J. (1994) 'Mentoring teachers during induction'. Paper given at ATEE conference, Prague.

Wilkin, M. (1992) 'On the cusp: from supervision to mentoring in initial teacher training'. *Cambridge Journal of Education.* Vol. 22, No. 1, pp. 79–90.

Woodward, T. (1991) *Models and Metaphors in Language Teacher Training: Loop Input and Other Strategies*, Cambridge: Cambridge University Press.

Wubbels, T. (1992) 'Taking account of student teachers' preconceptions'. *Teaching and Teacher Education*, Vol. 8, pp. 47–58.

Zeichner, K. (1992) 'Rethinking the practicum in the Professional Development School Partnership'. *Journal of Teacher Education*. Vol. 43, No. 4, pp. 296–307.

Chapter 16

The supervisory process in teacher education

Learning event or learning bind?

Peter D. John

In this chapter, Peter John complements the previous one by zooming in on one crucial facet of the mentor–student relationship: the post-lesson discussion. Where Terry Atkinson focused on what mentors know about their own implicit theories, Peter John analyses in some detail the ways in which these belief systems manifest in the heat of the conversational moment. He shows how easy it is for tutor/mentor and student to 'get across each other': to pick up messages that may or may not be intentionally communicated, and to adopt a stance that is in the last analysis self-preservative rather than developmental. The tutors/mentors' art, and their responsibility, is to present their enquiries and comments in such a way that the chances of this 'closing down' are minimised; and to be adept at repairing the relationship when it does go wrong. In defensive mode, both are convinced of their own rightness, take their judgements about each other as literal truth, and are quite unable to reflect on their contributions to the situation.

INTRODUCTION

The purpose of this chapter is to examine a number of pertinent issues which surround professional learning in the practicum.* Essentially, it deals with the way in which professional growth can be enhanced or retarded by the quality of the dialogue between tutor and student teacher. The case study harnesses the concept of theories-of-action (Argyris and Schon, 1974, 1977) to investigate the contextual features upon which the success or otherwise of a supervised practicum depends; the sorts of theories-of-action the participants bring to their patterns of interaction; and the ways in which these theories manifest themselves in supervisory conferences.

---

* The practicum is here defined as a series of supervised professional experiences in which student teachers learn the art and craft of teaching.

THE PROCESS OF SUPERVISION

The supervision of student teachers by classroom teachers and tutors from the training institution is a central feature of all courses of initial training, and yet despite its universality the practicum remains an enigma. Research suggests that part of its mystery stems from the fact that supervising tutors have little or no effect on the professional development of their students and that their practice is often inconsistent with their espoused theories. Furthermore, tutors appear to be ineffectual in countering the powerful effect of school socialisation. Nonetheless, the school-based experience remains one of the most potent interventions in courses making the supervisory process potentially one of the most singularly important learning events in the student teacher's professional development cycle.

The main focus of interaction between the participants is the diadic post-lesson supervisory conference. However, the emergence of 'pedagogical thinking' (Feiman-Nemser and Buchmann, 1985) during the practicum appears to be inhibited by the quality of the relationship between supervisor and student. In order to increase levels of learning during this process, various approaches and strategies have been suggested. Foremost among these is clinical supervision (Goldhammer and Gordon, 1969) and its offshoot partnership or diagnostic supervision. These techniques stress the isomorphic relationship between tutor and student as the essential precursor to learning. More traditional approaches, on the other hand, tend to involve the encouragement of concept leakage whereby the application of knowledge and practices offered in higher education is seen as paramount. The differences are summed up by Smyth (1984) when he comments that the former is predicated on a desire to work with teachers while the latter is an attempt to work on them.

Despite its apparent simplicity the supervisory relationship is still fraught with difficulties. This is not altogether surprising given the fact that the participants in the process are coming to the situation with their own particular concerns, preoccupations and experiences. These competing perspectives often give rise to a series of tensions and ambiguities which can interfere with the learning event. Teachers, for instance, have reported that students bring a welcome if artificial novelty to classes and departments while simultaneously introducing an unwelcome temporary disruption. Also teachers and mentors sometimes collude with the student in managing the visits of the tutor who is seen as having to balance the twin roles of enabler and assessor. Furthermore, professional learning is seen, on the one hand, as requiring enough freedom to experiment and make mistakes while at the same time being restricted by curricular and departmental structures. Finally, students often feel they deserve support, sympathy and guidance but also want the autonomy and respect of a fully fledged professional practitioner (Winter, 1980; Terrel et al., 1975).

Other studies which have examined the effects of particular supervisory practices on the self-concept of student teachers have found that some strategies induced greater tension and anxiety than others. For instance, tutors who were over-prescriptive and evaluative tended to focus too much on the specific details of lessons thus inducing a negative self-concept in their students. This was often exacerbated by conflicts about educational and pedagogical ideals between the participants. Strategies associated with an improvement in self-concept, on the other hand, were those based on mutual goal setting combined with diagnostic feedback where tutors were sensitive to the locational factors and variables that can influence practice (Berg *et al.*, 1986).

These tensions and ambiguities are thrown into sharp relief when the discrepancy between the tutors' espoused theories and their actual practice becomes apparent. Sergiovanni (1985) hypothesised the notion of 'mindscapes' to explain this discrepant behaviour. These he claims are 'implicit mental frames through which supervisory reality and the participants' place in this reality are envisioned'. He suggests that the crux of the problem is that the dominant mindscapes for supervision do not reflect the reality of supervisory practice.

THEORIES-OF-ACTION: AN ANALYTICAL FRAMEWORK

Argyris and Schon (1974, 1978) propose that human beings, in their interactions with one another, design their behaviour and hold theories for doing so. These theories-of-action include the values, strategies and underlying assumptions that inform deliberate behaviour. These theories are distinguished at two levels: espoused theories that are used to justify and explain behaviour; and theories-in-use – implicit theories – which are embedded in patterns of spontaneous behaviour and interaction. Like many other kinds of knowledge, these theories are usually tacit and sometimes beyond description in the formal sense, and are only redeemable when individuals reflect on the actuality of practice.

Argyris and Schon (1974, 1978) then went on to construct a general model of theories-in-use to describe interpersonal behaviour in situations that are complex and sometimes stressful. Model I is a theory of unilateral control over others. Action is designed to maintain four underlying values: achieving purposes as defined by the actor; winning; suppressing negative feelings; and being rational. The primary strategies are those of unilateral advocacy, controlling enquiry and protection of the self and others. The consequences of these actions include defensive interpersonal and group relationships, limited or inhibited learning and decreased effectiveness. The result is self-sealing, 'single-loop' learning and very little public testing of personal theories.

Model II, on the other hand, aims at creating a behavioural world in which people can exchange valid information about complex and sensitive issues, subject private dilemmas to shared enquiry and make public tests of negative attributions. In essence, it is a theory of joint control and enquiry. Its underlying assumptions are based on valid information, informed choice and internal commitment. Thus reasoning can be made explicit and confrontable, thereby increasing the capacity for what Argyris and Schon (1974, 1978) call 'double-loop' learning which means choosing from competing norms, goals and values.

THE CASE STUDY

Case studies have a long pedigree in qualitative research, particularly where the aim has been to develop a reflective language which has theoretical, analytic and descriptive concepts embedded in it. In addition case studies have always been attractive because they allow researchers to present many of their findings in the language of those being studied (MacDonald and Walker, 1977). Given that this study is an attempt to understand the espoused theories and theories-in-use of the participants in a supervisory relationship, a single case study of the supervisory sessions over an entire school-based practice period seemed appropriate. The enterprise involved a university tutor and student agreeing to tape-record their post-lesson conferences over a three-month, spring-term, school experience placement.

The data collection method was chosen because it was relatively non-intrusive. The recordings lasted from three-quarters of an hour to one and a half hours. Prior to the placement both the tutor and the student were interviewed at length about their beliefs regarding professional learning and their expectations of the supervision. After each conference the researcher and the tutor had a brief discussion about the exchanges; these are reported in the findings at the end of each section.

The tutor in the study was male and in his middle fifties. He had worked in teacher education for nearly twenty years and had supervised hundreds of student teachers. The student was a male in his early twenties and had recently left university with an upper second class honours degree in geography. The school chosen for the placement was a suburban comprehensive on the edge of Bristol.

The analysis was based on the principles of ethnographic semantics (Spradley, 1979) and focused on the following key features (Gardiner, 1993):

- the language used by the supervisor and student;
- the conceptions each appeared to have of the teaching and learning process;
- the expectations each brought to the learning event;
- the extent of hierarchy and directiveness in the relationship;
- the changes and patterns of interaction that emerged during the placement.

The analytical presentation which follows relates to the sorts of conversations that took place in the four meetings between the tutor and the student. The commentary that accompanies it not only relates to the most significant themes but is also an attempt to convey the general style of the proceedings. The results of the laborious analysis may give perhaps an unfortunate impression of a stilted and contrived manipulation, but in reality the conversation flowed naturally and spontaneously for the most part. During the conversations the participants relied heavily on intuitive judgement and it is in retrospect difficult to be explicit about what precisely prompted one to speak or to define his specific intentions. This does not mean, however, that the discussions were random and undetermined.

It is hardly necessary to add that in presenting the descriptions I have not been able to do justice to the richness and complexity of the verbal interactions, let alone to the non-verbal ones. In the interests of brevity and clarity the 'ums' and 'ers' etc. have been omitted from the illustrations chosen. It was also impossible to convey any sense of the changes in tempo or of the quality of silences; some were tense, some contemplative. It was even more difficult to describe the pervading mood of the participants and their emotional fluctuations, let alone the idiosyncratic variations in manner and style of speech.

SETTING THE SCENE

The supervisor's comments tended to cluster around three main themes: the importance of the school setting in which the student would be operating; general opinions about the character and ability of the student in relation to teaching; his expectations for the practice and a prognosis of its likely outcomes.

The geography department was seen as solid and reliable if a little staid. The humanities faculty had been used by the geography PGCE for three years and the associate tutor (AT) was experienced in dealing with student teachers. He was seen as a solid professional who had worked his way up through the ranks. The tutor felt he tended to operate with students the same way he ran his department, 'tightly structured along the lines outlined by the National Curriculum rather than being based on a particular philosophy of geography education'. At the operational level the AT was expected to give the student 'solid support' and 'help him to develop some basic classroom skills'.

The student teacher was seen as a typical male geography student. He had an upper second class degree from a major university and was interested in rugby and outdoor pursuits. After his first school experience his tutor commented that he was 'already competent in the classroom and good at relating to pupils and staff'. These interpersonal skills were regarded by the tutor as his strong point and in the classroom he felt he was 'relaxed and well planned with the majority of his lessons being clearly presented'. The tutor felt the student would get through the practice comfortably but thought he was not 'terribly creative or innovative', and in this respect he was 'typical of most of the new teachers who pass through my hands annually'. Overall he was described as 'a solid trooper who many schools would be glad to have in their departments'.

The tutor's personal theories about the process of learning to teach and the role of supervision in that process were also explored. He claimed to work within the clinical supervision framework but qualified his remarks with the view that he and other tutors were forced to adjust their approach and strategy according to the needs of the student they were supervising. He also said he preferred the diagnostic model but felt it was not always 'possible to use it given the time, travel and timetable demands being made'. Overall, he felt his style had developed with experience and was now a 'mishmash of the personal and the theoretical'. This self-confessed eclecticism was underpinned by a firm belief in enquiry-based forms of learning and the need for new teachers to experiment with such approaches during their school experiences. He commented:

> Despite being a bit mushy, I still like to see students take risks in the classroom. Seeing dull, routine lessons, tightly focused and information driven, leads me to concentrate on techniques at the expense of the wider more important things to do with teaching and learning. The basic skills are important – classroom management, blackboard work, voice and communication – but my main aim is to get them to be more innovative and try out varied teaching styles. I suppose it's tied to my belief that children learn more effectively and efficiently when they are engaged in active modes rather than processing information that is either being shown or told. Sitting and soaking up teacher talk must be less efficient and is certainly a less enjoyable way of learning.

The tutor's conceptions of professional learning were also complex. Lack of space means that only a brief outline can be given. In essence, he saw learning to teach as being applicatory and saw the practicum as an arena where the students could apply what they had read, witnessed, thought about and practised in method sessions. His views on teaching and learning, on the other hand, stemmed from a conception of geography and geography teaching which was based on a humanistic and enquiry-orientated perspective. The tutor recognised the problems inherent in this approach and realised that not all schools and teachers adhered to this line of thought. He was also aware of individual differences in his students and the nature of their concerns.

Initially he saw his role as part advisory – giving advice about teaching methods and approaches; part ambassadorial – making sure that schools were satisfied; and part evaluative – ensuring his students were reaching an acceptable standard using his peripatetic knowledge (John, 1995) to compare and moderate their performance.

The student teacher in his interview said he was looking forward to positive feedback, advice on lesson structure and ideas for teaching from the tutor. The bottom line though was still assessment and although he didn't think he would fail, he recognised the importance of the tutor in confirming his progress.

One of his main concerns was control and classroom management. His first objective was therefore 'to get the control right and to feel confident in front of the class'. He didn't expect major problems because the school was not a difficult one but he felt he had to be 'on his guard' and was keen to develop and practise the basics throughout the term. He felt he was already well versed in the process of planning and organising his lessons but needed to be more confident with certain groups. In the following extract he outlines his beliefs about professional learning.

> Well learning to teach, it's a bit like baking a cake, you have to have the basic ingredients first before you can really start on the cooking. The trouble is there are no simple answers to some problems, especially bad behaviour. All the advice and theory you're given about good classroom control, well it doesn't always work because kids don't always behave as they should or as the book tells you. Take Kyriacou, for instance, I tried following the rules he set out – sometimes they worked sometimes not. Teaching is like that – it's experience that really counts. That's why the spring term is so important, it can help you learn by your mistakes and you have teachers on tap to give you advice that fits.

The associate tutor (AT) was seen as central to his learning and great store was laid on the advice he would get from him. His knowledge of the classes and the school was seen as invaluable and he hoped to be able to learn from his style and approach in the classroom. Finally, the student said he enjoyed the school experience elements of the course most because they taught you about teaching.

From the outset then, the student recognised the uncertainty of classrooms and the problematic relationship between theory and practice. However, rather than adopting a reflective stance towards these issues he seemed to have already decided how his learning will best proceed. This will be an amalgam of recipe knowledge gained from the tutor and other practitioners in the field and craft knowledge gained from first-hand experience in the classroom.

VISIT 1

The early exchanges between the student and the tutor were mainly pastoral and organisational. They discussed the nature of the placement, the make-up of the groups that had already been encountered, the timetable and other personal–professional problems that had arisen during the first fortnight. The student was content with his placement and commented positively on the department and the nature of the support being given by the AT and other colleagues.

The tutor then focused on the lesson to be observed which was an issues-based approach to the building of an imaginary bypass around a town. The student showed the tutor the worksheet and explained how he had been advised and how he intended to use it. During the observation the tutor sat at the back of the class and took notes on the lesson.

The debrief opened in a relaxed and friendly manner. Personal relations were cordial and after the exchange of a few pleasantries the tutor asked his first major question. The conversation centred on the choice of method and the reactions of the pupils.

T: They seemed lively – are they always like that?

S: Well it's been raining and they were wet and soggy and sweaty – it's always difficult to get them settled then – perhaps I didn't make a good job of it?

T: So what would you have done differently?

S: I probably would have settled them a little more first but I didn't want to get into a shouting match with them; we've been told to avoid that at all costs – confrontations – so I gave out the sheets as they came in to get them started as quickly as possible. We've been told that by the teachers here – 'get their heads down' – it's a way of establishing basic control.

T: Yes I see, the problem was that it stayed that way because you had a problem getting them back together again as a group and every time you tried you had to shout at them.

S: I know it's a problem that – I wanted to have a more interactive question and answer lesson but I had to settle with just helping them individually. I thought the instructions on the sheet were clear and I felt I kept them going even though I had to wander around quite a lot as well as foregoing my inputs.

T: You planned to have more of an input didn't you?

S: Yes but in the end I had to settle for the bits I knew they had covered.

T: You could have started with something more punchy – some pictures or a video clip for instance, something that might get their attention. You don't need to have a long intro. but it does help to have one – it sets the tone for the lesson.

S: That would be great but the department have very few resources of that type. Most lessons are worksheet based. I know it could have been livelier but they did get through quite a lot after they got going and they were reasonably quiet when they were working – it was just hard to get them back together when they were all at different points in the worksheet.

The extract shows the power of the student's own concerns and dilemmas to influence his actions (Fuller, 1969). He clearly wanted to have an interactive lesson but found himself unable to get order and quiet from the front. He therefore departed from his plan, distributed the sheets and serviced the pupils individually. This led to numerous attempts to re-establish himself later, all of which failed. The tutor recognised this and suggested alternatives. The student, although seeing some value in his ideas, soon began to bemoan the lack of resources in the department and the lack of time to prepare such materials. He was in effect operating an early set of coping strategies based on internalised adjustment and strategic compliance (Lacey, 1977; Woods, 1979).

The debrief continued with the tutor exploring the positive elements of the lesson and comments being exchanged about the student's energetic input and the generally good classroom management. These supportive remarks were interspersed with some occasional comments about the personal idiosyncrasies of the student's style, in particular his tendency to 'shh, shh' the class continually. The tutor ended by saying quite firmly, 'I'd stop that if I were you; you sound like Ivor the Engine.'

Midway through the debrief the tutor returned to the issues flagged at the start and asked when the student intended to introduce his own resources and ideas into lessons. The student replied by claiming he had very little time to do that given his teaching load and that he preferred to use the departmental resources because 'they fit into the scheme of work which is built around the National Curriculum. They are very keen for me to follow the syllabus and get through the material because we only have a set time on each topic.'

The tutor continued this line of enquiry attempting to encourage the student to introduce his own materials into lessons in an effort to develop creative teaching which he thought might lessen his control anxieties. 'Having your own lessons', he claimed, 'may make you more confident about trying new things instead of relying on the worksheet syndrome.' This issue was then discussed in more depth:

T: You see worksheets are fine as far as they go – but are they learning? Often they are just filling in the answers blindly or copying them from each other; all they want to do is finish the sheet. It's all rather mechanical – do you see what I mean?

S: Yes of course but I give personal support where I can and I know I can't see all of them. But that leads to the 'shh' problem because the moment my back's turned they start to have their own conversations and that leads to off-task talk.

T: I noticed quite a bit of that although it wasn't too noisy.

S: The problem is getting them working can be a good control tactic but you're right it does have drawbacks. I really need to be able to control them before I can begin to think of creating my own lessons and experimenting.

   T: Perhaps an interesting lesson may help improve your control and they may be more motivated to work?

   S: I'd like to think so but it's a risk and the department wants me to get through the set work. It's important for me to get into a routine with them first, I feel.

The student's own personal agenda is again evident in his anxiety over control and discipline. This he felt was preventing him from using more open-ended strategies, a factor which was exacerbated by the limitations the department was placing on him. Both reasons were used extensively throughout the transcripts as inhibiting factors.

At the end of the session the tutor gave the student some written comments which included a breakdown of the good and bad points of the lesson. The tutor reiterated the need to be more adventurous as well as preparing his own material. The problem of control was seen as less troublesome than the student supposed and the tutor was generally satisfied with his classroom management.

In a discussion with the researcher following the debrief the tutor felt the lesson had gone reasonably well and that the student had many of the basic competencies already in place. But the urge to 'get their heads down' combined with the perceived need to get through the material had made a 'promising lesson rather dull'. In conjunction with this, the tutor felt the student was not very 'critical of his work' and that he was already 'resting on his laurels' and becoming 'comfortable with a limited approach to his teaching'.

VISIT 2

The second debrief followed a similar pattern to the first. The tutor opened the discussion with a comment about the physical nature of the classroom and the need to keep an eye on the temperature. He then took up the point made at the end of the first session, namely the need for a more creative personal input. He began by trying to tease out the student's view of the lesson and asked him to empathise with a typical pupil:

   T: If you were a pupil evaluating that lesson what would you say?

   S: I'm not sure, I suppose I would have learned something although it was a bit repetitive–the video at the start was very short and I may have confused them slightly with my explanations – but I think overall they enjoyed the lesson, they worked hard and there were no major discipline problems.

From this rather relaxed opening the tutor made a more explicit link to the lesson plan which he had seen prior to the lesson.

   T: You had in your lesson plan that you wanted them to understand the location and origins of volcanoes? Did you achieve that do you think?

S: Yes by and large – but this is only a background lesson, the more detailed stuff will follow.

T: I'm not sure what they learned – they may have some notes and answers in their books but does that equal learning?

S: Maybe, maybe not, I'll let you know when I mark them and when they've done their end of topic test. But it is important for them to have things down in their books; they like it and the parents demand it. The school is very keen and we have to fall in line.

At this rather tense point the tutor changed his tack by concentrating on the positive things he had observed in the lesson. He felt the student had good control and his relationships with the pupils were respectful and friendly. But after a few minutes the tutor returned to the theme of the need for him to try preparing more creative and innovative lessons. The student immediately diverted attention away from the question and claimed, once again, that he was hamstrung by the needs and demands of the syllabus and the department. The tutor continued more forcefully:

T: My main message, and I'll say it again, the one I'd really like to convey, is that I feel you have the control but the lessons are still very routine. Try to introduce some more variation into the task; try experimenting a little more with the content, try a more open-ended strategy.

S: I have done that sort of thing in history, the department encouraged me – I've also done a Channel Tunnel role-play and I've begun introducing my own materials [he shows the tutor a sheet from a previous lesson] but I can't do a lot because of time and the syllabus– the department likes you to use their materials.

The tutor accepted the reply and carefully shifted the agenda onto a more neutral footing. The discussion now revolved around the techniques deployed by the student in the lesson in explaining and handling the content. He was clearly concerned about the lack of specificity and accuracy in the students' explanation of Pacific volcanoes and the concept of viscosity. The tutor also described the student's blackboard diagrams as 'scrambled eggs' and pointed out the need for him to improve them. The student was receptive to this which was probably indicative of his need for confirmation and technical advice. The discussion ended with the tutor saying 'if you are going to be didactic then the kids need to be told about the topic in detail, in particular subduction theory and the melting of the continental margins'.

At this point the tutor again returned to his earlier theme and said quite forcefully that the lessons being delivered were 'akin to producing an itinerary without the pleasures of travel'. He continued by suggesting some alternatives. The student outwardly recognised the need but again emphasised the lack of equipment and resources and ended his answer by explaining in detail his use of overhead projection (OHP) overlays in history.

By now the student was becoming increasingly frustrated at the continued exhortation to change. This manifested itself in a discussion of his use of the blackboard.

S: Using the blackboard is still useful though, don't you think?

T: Of course it is but we are approaching the year 2000 and we are still using the same 19th Century implements to teach – it seems absurd!

S: Well I'm not convinced by that – the board is still vital and useful. I agree I should improve the quality of my presentation and diagrams but if I have no other equipment what can I do? What would you do?

T: Ah well, I would perhaps use some of the approaches we've discussed in method sessions, something like the Euro-Tunnel role-play or using place perhaps and basic geology to explore volcanic eruptions.

S: Very interesting and I'm sure I would use them too if I had a different classroom; it's the terrapins and the noise levels in them. Those sorts of lessons are inevitably noisy and I don't want to disturb other teachers. They might think I can't keep control. At the moment I seem to be doing all right in their eyes, all the teachers who have observed me have been very positive and I don't want things to slip; I don't want to go down in their estimation just because you feel I should do a role-play!

From this exchange one gets the feeling that the student felt trapped in a bind of wanting to please his immediate colleagues while at the same time feeling the need to justify his position to the tutor. The demands of the school clearly played an important role in his choice of lesson and were used as mitigating circumstances in his defence. Both individuals were clearly becoming locked into a mutually incongruent set of understandings (Schon, 1987).

The session ended soon after with the tutor summing up the pros and cons of the lesson and arranging a date for the next visit.

In the discussion following the lesson the tutor recognised the limitations placed on the student by the school and the department but felt that his reluctance to change said as much about his own inadequacies as it did about the department imposing restrictions. He also felt the student was 'missing the point' and was 'like a drain that needed to be unblocked'. 'The problem is', he claimed, 'it can be messy and I simply don't have the time to clear it up'. He also prophesied that the excuses would continue and that at times like this he felt like a 'vicar trying to give people an experience beyond their own immediate concrete concerns'.

VISIT 3

After the initial informalities the tutor returned to the question set and discussed at the last meeting. The student's reply reads more like a position statement:

S: I do feel more confident since your last visit and I feel I can use and try different things instead of just using the text book or the department's worksheets. I've used the Information Technology room quite a bit since your last visit and more of the Audio Visual equipment. Knowing people helps, I'm more familiar with certain key people now, like the librarian and the technicians and I know my groups a lot better. So I'm more comfortable now in the school as a whole; I know a lot more people and their interests. Also I'm more confident with classes and so I feel I can experiment a little more and take a few risks. Can you see the display up there? That's part of a project with my year 7s–it's a process I'm trying to develop.

This litany is clearly aimed at diffusing any further attacks and illustrates a change in tone from earlier conferences. The student in these early exchanges is more forceful and less reactive.

The debrief then moved into a discussion about the general points of the lesson which was a group work task on volcanoes. The tutor began with a question about the noise level; the student still felt uncomfortable but claimed he deliberately booked a classroom as far away from the main department so 'the class could make a lot of noise without disturbing others'. He then asked the tutor for his views on the noise 'was it unacceptable?' The tutor tentatively replied with a question about the classroom management tactics that might be used to gain quiet in role-plays. The conversation then moved to an exploration of the make-up of the group and the choice of grouping criteria.

The tutor in these exchanges appeared to be less concerned about persuading and in consequence the debrief centred on the pedagogy of the role-play and the substantive issues surrounding it. The questions asked moved from being specific and technical early on, to the more general and interrogative later. The tone, however, was still confrontational:

T: Do you feel all the energy you committed to getting the video cassette recorder set was worth it considering the short clip?

S: Well a video is always difficult to evaluate in terms of its impact. I know I got lost a few times trying to track down the right snippet but them seeing Mount St Helens blowing off is so powerful and I wanted them to see a real picture of a volcano erupting. This was to help reinforce the images built up from previous lessons and to get them to think about the impact such an eruption might have on a locality. It would have been simpler on my part to have said, well it's not worth showing, just five minutes and they can do without it, but the impact – well, it can't be compared to pictures and sheets.

T: OK I take your point; but do you think all the time you spent setting it up – perhaps ten times the length of the clip – was worth it?

S: Yes I do! Otherwise I wouldn't have done it!

Later on in the discussion the questions became more evaluative requiring the student to justify his choice of strategy.

T: Are such lessons valuable as teaching strategies? Or do you feel that more formal methods are better on the whole?

S: You can give formal lectures or expositions – they're good for getting the message across to the majority of kids but there has to be a place for developing geographical skills especially for a broad and balanced education. Key skills are important so breaking classes down into smaller groups and giving them responsibility is the only way to develop them. But I don't think you should use role-plays just for the sake of it. You know, do a role-play today because I haven't done one for a fortnight – that sort of thing. You should choose when to use them and shape them according to the topics – use them opportunistically.

T: The problem is that many will say that lessons like that one I've just observed are too open ended and a bit indeterminate. It's like being in a bog – you are moving but you're not sure in which direction and how fast.

S: Obviously you have to give them the main points and sort out the knowledge first – the worksheets and the exposition can get that done reasonably efficiently.

T: But where do lessons like that lead?

S: Basically it fits on top of the other lessons on volcanoes. It was a chance for them to have their say before they start glaciation. Barry, the head of department, suggested I do it even though it's not strictly on the syllabus because he felt it would be a good one for you to see.

Throughout these exchanges the student wanted the tutor's approval and tried to get it by offering him reasoned justifications interspersed with interpretive leaps of his own. The tutor listened carefully but continued with his own train of thought. At no point does the student ever fully succeed in diverting the tutor away from his main line of questioning. And yet at the same time the tutor never fully explained the reasons why he was insisting on following this particular line. He never revealed the thoughts and feelings that underpinned his beliefs. In a sense the student's relationship with the tutor was akin to the pupils' relationship with him. He felt stuck with a person who was there supposedly to help him, often wanting more than he was getting and then getting angry for wanting it.

A further problem arose when the student pointed out his own dissatisfaction with the lesson. The noise level perturbed him and he was still fearful of the looseness of the outcomes and the effect the noise may have on his next set of lessons. It also became clear from the concluding section of the above extract that he had, to a certain extent, colluded with the AT in staging the lesson for the benefit of the tutor. The tutor recognised this and in the post-conference interview described the lesson as 'a bit of a sham'. His suspicion was based on the student's inability to justify his use of this particular teaching strategy and was instead driven by the need to 'satisfy me he's doing the right thing and to make me think he's in line with good practice'.

VISIT 4

The final session was much more low key. The lesson was a straightforward one on latitude and longitude with the student teacher returning to the routines established earlier in the term. The tutor began the debrief with some congratulatory comments regarding the practice and the improvements he had noticed in the student's teaching. These clustered around management and basic control. His blackboard work and basic explanations had also improved. However, the need to develop more flexible teaching patterns and the use of more enquiry-orientated methodologies were not mentioned. Instead the questions were focused on substantive issues brought up in the lesson.

The tutor first of all took issue with the student's definition of latitude and longitude. He then asked him for any alternative ways of explaining the concepts.

T: The questions surrounding latitude and longitude were straightforward but your explanations were purely verbal – can you think of any other ways of explaining the concepts?

S: Well last week I saw a teacher in the maths department use superimposed OHPs – it was great. I would have used those but this room – well it's not suited to an OHP, it's too light and there are no blackouts. If I'd had been in the maths room I would have used layered OHPs so the kids could actually see the lines.

T: Yes that sounds good but couldn't you have used the blackboard instead?

S: I'm trying to develop their listening skills at the moment and often if I use the blackboard they all start copying things down and I think it's important for them to listen -the department are very keen on that.

T: But don't you think latitude and longitude need visual representation?

S: I suppose so but it was just impossible given the conditions.

The conversation was all too familiar with the student teacher again blaming his lack of variation on organisational difficulties. The tutor felt that this was typical of the practice and was related either to his inability to think creatively or to the fact that he had settled for an easy life. Later in the debrief the student again mentioned the Head of Department's concern that the pupils have a record of definitions in their book; hence the stress on explanation. The tutor again offered some alternatives and explained how a simple cylindrical projection could have been used by getting them to unwrap a drawn diagram.

Near the end of the conference the tutor offered another possibility by outlining a travel task which would help the pupils calculate the distance between lines of latitude and longitude. The student listened intently and commented positively on its usefulness. Again, however, the problem of time and the need to cover the syllabus was omnipresent in his reply, 'It's only on the syllabus for one lesson. I agree it deserves more time and weight but I have to follow the scheme. I can't go off and do my own thing as much as I might like to do.'

The frustration felt by the tutor at not being able to penetrate the outer shield put up by the student led him to comment after the conference that:

> I may have been preaching from the wrong pulpit for all these years. Maybe I'm not harsh enough with them but you have to work with them and support them as well as being critical. It's a fine line. Maybe I should lay the law down and say what I want to see but that would probably lead to an even greater conspiracy and even more collusion between the AT and students.

His concern was not solely with this particular student but that he was all too typical of the majority.

LEARNING EVENT OR LEARNING BIND?

If we consider the dialogue of the tutor and student from the general conceptual issues raised by Argyris and Schon's (1978) theories-of-action, then we can describe the process as one in which both succeeded in constructing a world in which a potential learning event turned into a learning bind. Throughout the exchanges the student sought to defend himself against what he perceived as the tutor's attacks while at the same time trying to secure approval. Thus we can describe his theory-of-action as being based around self-defence and the need to gain appreciation for his accomplishments – as he defined them. In this sense, he did not seek out the tutor's reasons and goals for the practicum or for the conference. Instead, as the dialogue progressed, he began to see himself as being involved in a win or lose game in which he tried to succeed by adopting strategies of excuse, unilateral control and self-defence (Schon, 1987). He thus brushed aside questions he did not really want to answer, clung tenaciously to his position and gave answers that invited approval. Despite the negative feelings that emerged, the student rarely accused the tutor of hostility and tried at all times to maintain a reasoned position supported by justificatory arguments. When eventually he was driven into a corner he did go on the offensive.

Such interactions are not uncommon in the annals of student teaching (Feiman-Nemser and Buchmann, 1985; Zeichner et al. 1988). From the evidence presented in this chapter it seemed that the student was unable to become more actively involved in one domain (his learning) while simultaneously developing in another (his teaching). His conception of learning therefore rarely shifted from seeing the professional development process as external – something that happened to him.

This narrow conception of his own learning was reflected in his belief that successful teaching could be attained by imitating the practices of his immediate colleagues. In this sense his tutor's expertise was seen as being derived from his position within the course rather than stemming from any real practical basis. As a result the associate tutor and other co-operating teachers exerted a greater influence on his learning and subsequent theories-of-action, not simply because he was anxious to fit in with their needs but also because they conveniently mirrored his world views about teaching and learning. In this sense, the learner's approach to the process of learning to teach was to a large extent dependent on his own perceptions of the task confronting him and on his perception of the circumstances in which the tasks were set. The situational context not only confirmed his theories-of-action but also helped him define and refine his understandings of his own professional development.

At the outset then, the student saw his professional growth as being based firmly on reproductive and passive conceptions of learning. His thinking therefore reflected Claxton's (Chapter 1) view that he tacitly believed his acceptability as a colleague and co-professional depended on being seen as competent in their eyes. Hence the fear of making mistakes or being found wanting in the areas of classroom and pupil management. This led him to err on the side of caution, thereby maintaining his self-worth and self-concept.

This urge to be accepted rapidly became the 'trigger' in the conferences for a series of avoidance and defensive strategies which manifested themselves in his general inability to engage in any meaningful sense with the tutor. This was achieved by sidestepping problems and by presenting over-massaged excuses about the demands of the department and the constraints of the National Curriculum. His use of the automatic intercept (Schon, 1987) was therefore sparked by negative feelings of anger, resentment, fear and impatience. When meaningful and significant dialogue did take place it appeared after the student had 'done what the tutor asked' but even then the amount of positive interaction was minimal.

Similarly, many of the ideas presented by the tutor fell on stony ground because they were perceived as unworkable within the confines of the situation in which the student found himself. This manifested itself as a 'maintenance strategy' based on a keen cost–benefit analysis linked to the relative merits of success and failure (Claxton, Chapter 1).

The tutor also employed a similar theory-of-action. He too had an objective for the conferences – to get the student to think about his practice and to adopt and experiment with more enquiry-based approaches to teaching and learning. Many of the interactions were therefore aimed at getting the student to try to see the inadequacy of his lessons, not in a critical way but in a manner that might provoke change. However, as he made no attempt to understand what the student may have wanted from the discussions and visits, he therefore saw himself as being in a similar win–lose situation (Schon, 1987). He tried to control the dialogue, shifting from one target to another and from one opportunity to another; he asked the questions and yet appeared to know the answers; he tried to use arguments to convince the student and at some points drove him into corners. But he still withheld the intellectual basis of his own interventions and failed to reveal openly the basis of his own frustrations. He made statements about it but never got near explaining it in a way that would encourage mutual exploration.

In terms of style, the tutor tended to move frequently between two well-grounded positions: idea interpretation and behaviour prescription (Zahorik, 1988). In terms of the former, he presented his beliefs to the student in a recognisable form. These were for the most part based on his own personal theories of teaching and learning which manifested themselves in an idealised version of how schools and classrooms should be. In relation to the latter most of his prescriptions were based around telling the student to eschew certain instructional and managerial strategies and to use others. Rust (1988) further reinforces this notion of the tutor working individually from his own implicit images of good teaching. For the tutor in the case study this centred on a view of the teacher as a facilitator and the classroom as enquiry orientated. These images were then presented to the student teacher after he was satisfied that he had reached basic levels of competency. The strategies used then fluctuated between the directive and the facilitative.

Throughout the conferences the tutor had a real problem in persuading the student teacher to adopt a more self-critical approach as well as encouraging him to use more open-ended pedagogical strategies. The tutor recognised the power of the school to influence and thereby 'wash out' the effects of method courses with its powerful socialising impact. Thus co-operating teachers, the mentor, the subject department, the ecology of classrooms and the culture of school were all seen as culpable in buttressing the student teacher's theories-of-action.

In terms of the tutor then, the data supports Schon's view that although 'one may be comfortable in viewing supervision as a logical process of problem solving, a more accurate view may be to see it as a process of managing messes' (p. 14). The theories-of-action that emerge from this study conform to the first of Argyris and Schon's (1978) models. This is a model of unilateral control where strategies of mystery and mastery combined with the withholding of feelings create the appearance of surface rationality. They comment:

When the parties to a pattern of interaction sustain Model I theories in use, they tend to create a certain kind of behavioural world, that is, a certain kind of communicative context which they perceive as reality. This is a win-lose world in which defensiveness and unilateral self-protection are the norms. Characteristically, however, within this world each perceives the other, and not himself, as defensive and as unilaterally bent on winning. It is a model in which each tends to see himself as caught in a dilemma which he keeps to himself; negative attributions about the other are not publicly tested but are simply taken at face value.

(p. 68)

Both student and tutor in the case study were as unlikely to reflect on their own implicit theories of teaching and learning as they were on their own lack of communication. Far from suspending his views about the tutor, the student persisted in fending off his attacks with excuses while at the same time seeking approval and confirmation. It never occurred to him to explore with the tutor the underlying reasons for his beliefs. Likewise, the tutor could not fully explore the student's understandings of his statements and questions as long as he continued to convince him of the need to change. Thus a learning opportunity turned into a learning bind.

At the end the student had become, to some extent, a 'counterlearner' refusing to suspend his own theories-of-action or to enter into a dialogue with the tutor about them. In the third visit he conspired to give the tutor what he thought he desired – an enquiry-based lesson. The problem was that by simply doing it, the student grafted the method onto an alien set of beliefs. His frustration was clearly evident and the contrived nature of the task contributed to the tutor's evaluative line of questioning. Thus the supervisor could only conceive of the lesson as a limited illustration of a much more complex idea. As a result the student developed 'a closed-system vocabulary' (Schon, 1987) whereby he could state the tutor's principles while performing them in a manner incongruent with their underlying meaning.

CONCLUSION: TOWARDS A REFLECTIVE PRACTICUM

In Chapter 1 Claxton comments that:

unless we understand equally the dynamics of engagement, which enables learners to commit themselves and their learning resources whole-heartedly to the process of learning, and of disinhibition, which enables learners to avoid or overcome tendencies to defend or withdraw unnecessarily, then our attempts at facilitation are always liable to founder.

Improving the quality of supervision then is not only central to the process of disinhibition but also vital to the continued professionalisation of teaching (Hoyle and John, 1995). Schon (1987) suggests that learning blocks can be overcome if both coach and learner search actively for a 'convergence of meaning through a dialogue of reciprocal reflection-in-action' (p. 137). Essentially, this would mean both supervisor and supervisee extending their ladder of reflection by adding an extra rung to it (Schon, 1987).

Responsibility for breaking the learning bind, however, must still predominantly lie with the supervisor. So let us for the sake of conjecture explore how the tutor in the case study might have gone about things differently. He could have expressed his own frustrations in a way that might have invited discussion rather than forcing them into his evaluative dialogue. He could have, for instance, expressed his anxieties in a way that encouraged exploration by empathising with the student and by engaging him in a discussion about the institutional and personal barriers that appeared to influence his learning. This may have led the student to express his feelings more directly as well as helping them both to examine perceived problems in a mutually meaningful way.

The issue of greater personal input and experimentation might then have been approached more personally rather than being seen as an essential demand. Here the AT might have been invited into the discussions and some of the issues explored collectively. This may have led to the setting up of a situation where the student was encouraged to experiment in a protected way and may have even led to team teaching and joint planning of lessons.

Each of these interventions and strategies involves empathising as well as revealing. They require the participants to show their dilemmas and actively explore each other's meaning. Above all they require the tutor to ask himself what the student reveals in the way of knowledge, ignorance or difficulties and then to encourage discussion by first being as descriptive as possible about what has been observed and then to particularise the descriptions by playing the events of the lesson back to the student thus creating a reflective dialogue. The student should simultaneously reconstruct and test what he sees and hears working back and forth from the events and the descriptions to rediscover the thinking in his actions. In this way the tutor's behaviour acts like 'two vectors' each contributing to the student's learning cycle with two kinds of practice entering the practicum: the actual teaching abilities he is trying to learn and the reflective process by which he comes to learn them (Schon, 1987).

Essential to this relationship is the establishment of a learning contract where what each participant will give and what each will receive is set out very early on. So when a student and tutor or mentor do become caught in a learning bind their ability to escape from it may depend on the tutor/mentor's ability to reflect on and encourage reflection on the learning dialogue itself. The pathologising of the learner by the tutor/mentor, seen typically in such dismissive comments as 'they aren't creative', 'they lack basic talent', 'unable to grasp what is required', may also be unhelpful and say less about the student's inadequacy and more about the tutor/mentor's failure to 'negotiate the ladder of reflection'. But as Schon (1987) points out, the ability to encourage reflection both in and on a 'dialogue that may have gone awry requires a theory-in-use that minimises unilateral protection and places a higher value on inquiry than on winning'.

REFERENCES

Argyris, C. and Schon, D. A. (1974) *Theory in Practice: Increasing Personal Effectiveness*, San Francisco: Jossey-Bass.

Argyris, C. and Schon, D. A. (1978) *Organizational Learning*, Reading, MA: Addison-Wesley.

Berg, M., Harders, P., Malian, I. and Nagel, A. (1986) 'Partners in supervision: a clinical supervision programme'. Paper delivered at the annual meeting of the Association for Teacher Educators, Atlanta.

Feiman-Nemser, S. and Buchmann, M. (1985) 'Pitfalls of experience in teacher preparation'. *Teachers' College Record*, Vol. 87 (1), pp. 53–65.

Fuller, F. F. (1969) 'The concerns of beginning teachers'. *American Educational Research Journal*, Vol. 6, pp. 207–26.

Gardiner, W. E. (1993) *An Anatomy of Supervision: Developing Professional Competence for Social Work Students*, Milton Keynes: Open University Press.

Goldhammer, C. D. and Gordon, S. P. (1969) *Clinical Supervision*, New York: Holt, Rinehart and Winston.

Hoyle, E. and John, P. D. (1995) *Professional Knowledge and Professional Practice*, London: Cassell.

John, P. D. (1995, in press) 'The subject method seminar and the role of the teacher educator'. In V. J. Furlong and R. Smith (eds) *The Role of Higher Education in the Initial Training of Teachers*, London: Routledge.

Lacey, C. (1977) *The Socialization of Teachers*, London: Methuen.

MacDonald, G. and Walker, T. (1977) 'Case study on the philosophy of educational research'. In D. Hamilton (ed.) *Beyond the Numbers Game*, Basingstoke: Macmillan.

Nettle, T. (1988) 'A teaching and learning approach to supervision within a teacher education program'. *Journal of Teacher Education*, Vol. 14 (2), pp. 125–33.

Rust, F. O. (1988) 'How supervisors think about teaching'. *Journal of Teacher Education*, Vol. 39 (2), pp. 56–63.

Sergiovanni, T. J. (1985) 'Landscapes, mindscapes and reflective practice in supervision'. *Journal of Curriculum and Supervision*, Vol. 1 (1), pp. 5–17.

Schon, D. (1987) *Educating the Reflective Practitioner*, San Francisco: Jossey-Bass.

Smyth, J. (1984) 'Teachers as collaborative learners in clinical supervision: a state of the art review'. *Journal of Education for Teaching*, Vol. 10 (1), pp. 24–39.

Spradley, J. (1979) *The Ethnographic Interview*, New York: Holt, Rinehart and Winston.

Terrell, C., Tragaskis, O. and Boydell, D. (1985) *Teaching Practice Supervisors in Primary Schools: an Ethnomethodological Perspective* (Research Report), Cheltenham, UK: College of St Paul and St Mary.

Winter, R. (1980) *Perspective Documents on Teaching Practice*, Chelmsford, UK: Institute of Higher Education.

Woods, P. (1979) *The Divided School*, London: Routledge.

Zahorik, J. A. (1988) 'The observing conferencing role of university supervisors'. *Journal of Teacher Education*, Vol. 39 (2), pp. 9–16.

Zeichner, K. M., Tabachnik, B. R. and Densmore, K. (1988) 'Individual, institutional and cultural influences on the development of teachers' craft knowledge'. In J. Calderhead (ed.) *Exploring Teachers' Thinking*, London: Cassell.

Chapter 17

Put it together and what have you got?

Guy Claxton

In this final chapter, Guy Claxton offers a personal overview of the contributions to the book, and draws out some of their common themes. He concludes that the framework of integrated learning theory has indeed been useful in highlighting certain important but neglected questions for adult professional learning in education, particularly those to do with the idiosyncratic affective, motivational and 'personal philosophical' attitudes and experiences of learners. The book has clearly demonstrated the presence of implicit theories of learning in the minds of teachers and learners, and their power to direct, facilitate or inhibit learning in a variety of ways and contexts. Guy also returns to questions of the broader context of education, and argues for the potential of APL to promote a much-needed 'learning to learn' agenda throughout the education system.

This book set out to explore the utility, in understanding and facilitating adult professional learning (APL) in education, of two linked themes. The first concerned the partly explicit, partly tacit belief systems about learning that inform the APL context, coming both from the learners and students, and from those who design and deliver the learning event. Those in the role of learner, we surmised, may bring into an APL encounter implicit and/or unexamined theories and assumptions that 'set' them to perceive the event in certain ways, to engage full- or half-heartedly, to experience some occurrences as potential threats and others as challenges or opportunities, and to select a particular subset of their learning abilities with which to meet the anticipated demands of learning. Those in the role of teacher, trainer or facilitator will likewise have incorporated into their thinking and their practice certain assumptions – those that are ambient in the educational culture in which they move, as well as more personal distillates of their own past teaching and learning experiences – and these are likely partly to mesh and partly to clash with the implicit theories of their clientele.

Thus the way they meet over learning will on the surface be concerned with the transmission of certain content, or the training of certain skills, or the reflective consideration of certain issues; but will also, often at a less conscious level, be concerned with negotiating the differing views of learning and learners that the two parties, teachers and learners, bring with them. (Not neglecting, of course, the fact that the learners – and the teachers, too, if there are a number of them – are very unlikely to be a homogeneous group, and will demonstrate through their expectations and reactions a diversity of implicit theories.)

The second, more practical, theme, which develops naturally out of the first, concerns the blocks or barriers which adult professional learners experience, and the ways in which providers can anticipate, minimise or neutralise these through their design and delivery of their courses. Much attention has been paid in the literature to the ways in which APL can be facilitated, but rather less to the possibility that what is needed is not so much facilitation or 'acceleration' as *disinhibition* – making sure the brakes are off – and *engagement* – ensuring that power from the learning motor is getting to the wheels. I argued in Chapter 1, you recall, that a range of 'defensive strategies' formed as vital a part of one's repertoire of ways for dealing with the unknown as did a good 'tool-kit' of learning strategies. But if one's implicit theories lead one to construe a learning event as more of a threat than it (in some sense) objectively is, then defensiveness and disengagement are likely to be deployed prematurely, to the detriment of one's ability to pursue learning goals that are actually of professional, and possibly also of personal, value.

Taken as a whole, the contributions to the book have clearly demonstrated that these themes do provide a revealing set of spectacles through which to look at APL, and that the more focused discussions and investigations which they have stimulated have resulted in theoretically interesting and practically useful outcomes. Again taken as a whole, the strategy of the book, to explore these themes across a wide diversity of APL contexts in education, with the hope of revealing some generic considerations, has been vindicated. We have looked at the assumptions of novitiate teachers as they embark on an initial teacher education course; at the ways in which their tutors and mentors construe learning; at experienced teachers changing their working habits as a result of national reforms; at educational managers as they take on new responsibilities, experience training support, or undertake a higher degree; at overseas educators coming to grips with new approaches to learning, and at UK student teachers as they also experience education in a different culture; and at lecturers and trainers in higher education as they too grapple with innovations and new demands.

There are indeed a number of issues that recur across chapters and contexts, and it is to an exploration of these that the bulk of this final chapter is dedicated. Perhaps the most consistent message to emerge is that learning in the workplace, preferably in the company and with the collaboration of peers, seems to be preferred, and to be more effective, than off-the-job training or guidance. There are exceptions to this, such as those studying for a research degree whose agendas are different, but in the main the value of peer support, peer tutoring and collaborative learning stands out clearly. Jan Winter's (Chapter 15) review of her in-service course showed that what serving teachers seemed to appreciate most, out of a course that offered a well-designed mixture of ingredients, was the opportunity to work alongside a colleague *from another school*, who could, in the words of one of Jan's informants, 'help you notice what you are doing'. Agnes McMahon's peer mentoring scheme for headteachers also seemed to be appreciated for the opportunity to meet with a slightly more experienced colleague, who could act as a 'critical friend'. We might suppose that teachers, having had to go through the process of being judged during their training, and being agents of an education system that remains wedded (as Patricia Broadfoot reminded us forcibly in Chapter 3) to external evaluation, are sensitive to situations in which they feel themselves on the receiving end of any such judgement, and this anxiety may rear its head even in the presence of a supportive advisor, if a difference in perceived job status or title triggers that vulnerability.

It seems as if there has been a sea-change in the UK over the past ten or even five years, in which teachers' culture now accepts and values collaboration and peer learning much more than formerly; and that the UK is in the vanguard of this trend certainly as far as Europe and, on present evidence, some Asian and African countries are concerned. Elisabeth Lazarus's Swedish teacher educators (Chapter 6), Marilyn Osborn's French primary school teachers (Chapter 5), and Terry Atkinson's Spanish student teachers (Chapter 9), all gave evidence in different ways of systems where collaborative learning and collective autonomy were less familiar and, in the case of the French teachers, took some getting used to when a shift in policy made such opportunities more common.

Where the implicit theories of learning of the educational culture had been, to speak very broadly, scholastic and individualistic, now, at least in the UK, received wisdom goes some way towards accepting the value of teachers' experience as a common resource, and accepts also that teaching is an irreducibly personal business: individual teachers have to be allowed leeway in which to develop and negotiate an idiosyncratic solution to the core question of how to 'be themselves' while they are being teachers. For those who do not find a satisfactory solution, there is only the choice to cling to personal styles and values that are unequal to the complex professional task; to adopt a teacher persona that does violence to their personal integrity; or to leave the profession. We are not yet at the point where the intricate interweaving of professional competence and personality is fully understood, or fully respected, but we are some way towards it.

Interestingly, it is precisely in this area that we find illustrations of the second general theme to emerge: that of the potential for misunderstanding, confusion or even open conflict when the implicit theories of tutor, mentor or course organiser are at odds with those of the students or consumers. Perhaps the clearest examples of these come from Peter John's two chapters (7 and 16) and Terry Atkinson (Chapter 15). Peter's first study shows that some student teachers tend to have implicit theories of teaching and learning that are an uneasy amalgam of the personal and impersonal. On the one hand, they accept that teaching is a 'personal' business, though their analysis of what this means tends to be somewhat stereotyped: 'warmth, enthusiasm, commitment, humour and patience [are seen] as being at the epicentre of exemplary teaching'; while on the other they have an equally simplistic 'transmission' view of learning, and a crude faith in the necessity, if not the virtue, of 'control'. The business of learning to teach, within this framework, is largely construed as grafting a set of technical competencies – organisation, preparation, communication, group management, and so on – onto a basically static character or style, some aspects of which need to be capitalised on as resources, while others of which may need to be suppressed.

Tutors and schoolteachers can have a rather different philosophy of learning, when it comes to student teachers. Terry Atkinson finds that, though some teachers also see 'personality' as the major determinant of a student's style and success, they tend to see this as a 'given', rather than as something which provides the raw material to be selectively shaped by learning. Such teachers may make premature judgements about the 'suitability' of a student for teaching which can act as a powerful barrier to communication, and therefore to the student's learning. It will, he argues, be by mentors (in the first instance) developing a more relativistic view of teaching and learning, in which the existence of valid differences in implicit theories are recognised, that such misunderstandings will be minimised. As Terry concludes, it is those teachers who are most alive to the possibility that *their* views of learning and teaching are capable of being problematised, who will be most able to offer the reflective space to students to develop a critical awareness of *their* implicit views.

There is a suggestion that the mentor–student relationship is potentially at least much more symmetrical than it is sometimes construed. While it is clear that the mentor has responsibility for prompting the development of skill and self-awareness in students, the reverse potential – that for the students, by their freshness of perception and the 'naivety' of their questions, to stimulate the development of articulation and reflection in the mentor – has been undervalued. The core issue here is the familiar one of socialisation. While teachers are gaining experience and expertise, they are also only experiencing a very small sample of educational cultures, and it is very understandable that, as they are tacitly imbibing the mores and values of those institutions, they are also coming unwittingly to take these for granted, and to assume that they have greater validity and universality than they do. The pressure placed on experienced teachers in the role of mentor is to deconstruct both their own practice and the values and assumptions that they have taken on board from the milieux in which they have been training and working.

Peter John's second contribution analyses in some detail the ways in which communication breaks down when these implicit differences of view are not acknowledged. He draws on Argyris and Schon's important distinction between 'espoused theories' – what one consciously believes and articulates – and 'theories-in-use', which are largely implicit and embodied in the way people act, rather than in what they say. It is these latter belief systems that are the source of conflict when either or both parties in a practice-related conversation fail to appreciate the personal premises on which judgement and performance are based. Without this basis of self-awareness, the conversation can easily become polarised, hostile or defensive, and learning is blocked. The lesson is clear: if lines of communication and learning are to be kept open, and goodwill maintained, both tutor/mentor and student must be willing to reflect on and take responsibility for their theories-in-use. There are implications here for mentor and tutor training, for it is they who must not only espouse but model this open and reflective attitude.

And this leads us on to a third theme: that of the anxieties created by the conflict between the necessity to learn and the implicit view of the (seasoned) professional as one who knows; whose mind is clear, grasp is firm and practice confident and competent. Those who hold such a view of themselves are bound to have trouble when they are, through choice or necessity, forced back into the 'twilight zone' of learning, where actions are experimental, issues are confused, and unconscious assumptions are being brought to light. Several of the chapters explore this theme. Laurinda Brown, in Chapter 14, through her work with Alan Dobson, develops a model of in-service tutoring which involves the dual aspects of support and stimulation. It is uncomfortable to allow your experience of yourself as a teacher to resonate discordantly with the educational principles, and the personal self-image, which you espouse. Laurinda's view, that such fruitful dissonance is best stimulated by getting someone to act in a new way, and *then* sympathetically to encourage the awareness of this experience to rub abrasively against what had been 'taken for granted', is a powerful alternative to the more usual assumption that one first has to re-theorise one's practice, and then translate this new understanding into action.

But the emphasis on the tension between role and reaction, and the need for gentle and empathic support if this frequently threatening and destabilising process is to be allowed to happen, is as important as the need to stimulate dissonance in the first place. And the difficulty of allowing oneself to become a learner seems, not surprisingly, to be directly proportional to the status that one has achieved in the profession. In Chapter 12, for example, Agnes McMahon shows how headteachers feel that they have to keep their insecurities and their learning invisible from colleagues and staff. It is almost a dereliction of duty, a shameful inability to fulfil the trust placed in you by the school, to be seen to be other than perfect right from Day One. Thus the peer mentoring scheme turned out indeed to be a skilful way of getting round this considerable barrier to learning. To be able to talk to someone who is neither a judging superior, nor a member of one's own staff, is about the only context in which one can feel safe enough to admit doubts and inadequacies, and to dare to be tentative and exploratory.

This is an example of designing the learning experience so that barriers are minimised. But if the underlying assumptions on which the barriers are based remain unarticulated and unchallenged, then the dynamics of that particular blockage or anxiety is unaffected. If your image of the competent headteacher is someone who never makes a mistake and never has to say 'I don't know', then to be able to sidestep the risk of exposure as incompetent, by being able to reveal yourself, as it were, only within the confidentiality of a Headteachers Anonymous encounter, gives you relief but not insight. The implicit theory of self-as-professional will continue to demand the bombast, evasiveness or whatever in contexts – like staff meetings – where honesty threatens loss of face. (It is interesting how such implicit theories create their own reality. While it is true that some members of staff do collude with the headteacher in expecting omniscience, I have often heard of headteachers who have been astonished when they have finally been exposed as fallible, and fearing the worst, have been met with the response: 'Thank God you're human!')'

If we are to take seriously the challenge to schools to become 'learning societies', in which the emphasis is on helping all young people to become good learners, rather than to get as great a proportion as possible through their GCSEs, then the onus on headteachers to take the risk of leading by example, and of daring to be seen to be a learner in their job, just as much as they are expecting their teachers, and their students, to be learners in theirs, becomes all the greater. Now it is no longer adequate to slip away for a private chat with your mentor once a month; the implicit assumption that being a professional means being perfect has itself to be uprooted and examined. And this requires a different type of educational experience, one more like those which are discussed in Chapters 13 and 14. Headteachers who want to promote a learning culture in their schools may need to consider 'outing' themselves as learners – just as heads of department acting as mentors may need to see that their contribution is to allow themselves to be discomfited and confused by the questions of their mentees.

Right down the line, the development of an educational philosophy that puts learning at the centre demands the overturning of the pervasive implicit theory that links self-esteem with competence. When teachers are genuinely able to value travelling hopefully, gamely, ingeniously and creatively over arriving – learning over achievement – in themselves, then we might guess that they will be better able to model these qualities for their pupils and students, and 'learning to learn' will take on a more powerful meaning than a few lessons of 'study skills' or a flirtation with Matthew Lipman or Edward de Bono.

In this context, Valerie Hall's exploration of the concept of 'resilience' in senior professional learners is very illuminating. The ability to bounce back from learning difficulties or disappointments seems, in her sample, to be closely related to the wish, and the ability, to be self-directed as learners. This association offers another important method for liberating the learner. Instead of finding a way round the barriers, or trying to reduce them by gaining insight into the personal belief systems that generate them, we can try to tip the motivational scales by increasing the incentive and the self-belief to push through the barriers when they occur. We can try to maximise the 'benefits' as well as minimise the 'costs'. As Valerie notes, here again peer support is a vital ingredient in the process of recovery and reaffirmation; but so too is an attitude which encourages the development of students' resilience on the part of the providing institution and its agents. Seeing learners as self-directed consumers, rather than as the lucky recipients of whatever educational wisdom is currently being dispensed, helps to create an atmosphere of greater responsiveness and equality of esteem. Lecturers and professors are not exempt from the reciprocal demand to share themselves as learners, and to see participants on programmes such as the EdD as authors of their own learning, as well as being apprenticed to the research community (Lave and Wenger, 1991; Salmon, 1992).

Two useful ways of promoting reflection on implicit theories of learning, and the learning blocks to which they may give rise, are through immersion in a different culture, and through guided reflection on past experience. The role of a cultural shift is explored in several of the chapters. Paul Weeden and John Hayter's (Chapter 8) reflections on the experience of taking a group of PGCE students for a two-week trip to The Gambia show how, for both tutors and students, the 'culture shock' may act either to promote reflection or to elicit a more self-protective stance. Paul's refreshingly open account of the conflict between his feeling of being at sea, and his perceived need to stay 'on top' of things as a tutor, provides another example of the status/role problem I have just discussed. But their emphasis on the *timing* of reflection, its need to take account of the emotional phases that learners go through as they come to terms with an unfamiliar culture embodying values and principles that are potentially at odds with their own, is also thought provoking. Reflection seems to require a 'warm' attitude towards one's own concepts and experience: too 'hot' and the situation may become too threatening, leading to denial or defensiveness; too 'cool' and there is insufficient 'grit in the oyster', to borrow Laurinda Brown's phrase (and to mix my metaphors), to make the work of reflection seem necessary. Again what emerges is that the importance of reflective enquiry into the pre-suppositions of experience is balanced by its subtle, slippery and delicate nature.

Terry Atkinson's Chapter 9, which looked at the slightly more extended experience of modern languages students teaching in a range of European countries, echoes this concern with the possible negative effects of pushing learners into reflection prematurely. They need, he points out, to hang on to their implicit theories long enough for them to have some structure for interpretation, as a seedling may need a stake to support its growth before it is capable of standing on its own. 'The critical time for deeper reflection', he suggests, 'may be when their growth takes them beyond the useful life-span of these preliminary understandings'. The implications for APL facilitators may be that it is their job to wait patiently for the opportune moment at which to offer a judicious nudge, rather than to set out with a pre-established agenda and time-scale. This requires a very different set of attitudes and skills from the more formal, and familiar, approach of the 'calculated curriculum'. Sensitivity to occasion, empathy, and intuition, will be of greater value in such a learning context than meticulous planning. Here lies a considerable challenge for APL in education which we are only just beginning to articulate, let alone to which to develop an appropriate response – though we might hazard the conjecture that here again the ability of tutors to model the desired mode, rather than simply to espouse it or exhort it, will be central.

John Hayter's solo contribution, Chapter 10, also identifies the time course of adaptation to a new learning culture as being important, this time in the context of overseas educators coming to grips with the unfamiliar demands of higher-degree work in the UK. His juxtaposition of the principles informing the course with the dissonant implicit theories of the students highlights the possibility of making a discussion of this dissonance an explicit part of the educational programme. Much more work needs to be done before we shall be able to identify with any confidence the conditions under which, and the learners for whom, the approach of deconstructing their current educational milieu explicitly is appropriate and effective. There is the risk, as we have seen, of sending people even deeper into shock by such tactics.

We could, of course, include several of the other chapters under the rubric of 'culture'. Valerie Hall's Chapter 11 looks at the adaptation of professional learners to the doctoral 'research' culture. Marilyn Osborn and Elisabeth Lazarus (Chapters 5 and 6), as we have seen, explicitly look at cultural differences in teachers' attitudes to change. And more generally we can look at initial teacher education very much as a process of new teachers' adjustment to, and assimilation by, the culture of a particular school. For many secondary PGCE students, for example, a preliminary experience in a primary school, or the first few weeks in a secondary, can involve just as great a culture shock as a visit to a foreign country. And we could argue that the same considerations of timing and sensibility should apply there too.

Two of the chapters explore a complementary way of investigating implicit theories and the effect they have on current learning, by unearthing their roots in personal history. Peter John's use of 'life histories', in Chapter 7, to investigate the origins of student teachers' implicit theories of teaching and learning in their own educational experience is particularly instructive. Their views of what makes for good teaching, and a good teacher, are heavily influenced by their own experience as school pupils, and they therefore tend to arrive with a pupil-centred view, and one which often tacitly assumes that all pupils are as they were. As these views are both intuitive and strongly held, they can result in a resolutely atheoretical view of education, and a concomitant resistance to reflection and conceptual analysis. (One might argue that some senior politicians have likewise failed to outgrow this attitude.) And this in turn fuels the common pragmatism of student teachers who demand recipes and maxims, and treat anything else as 'waffle'. Peter, like Laurinda Brown, Jan Winter and others, notes that the requisite shift in attitude needs to be stimulated by a felt dissatisfaction with current models, and cannot successfully be imposed; and that the *process* of transmitting and integrating new and old views must be carefully managed and supported. He offers some powerful suggestions as to how this can be operationalised.

Elisabeth Lazarus (Chapter 6) also used life histories, though more within an 'action research' framework designed to illuminate her own practice as a relatively newly recruited teacher trainer. Her interviews nicely complement Peter John's in focusing more on the students' expectations of their teacher training itself – she catches her informants right at the beginning of their course of study – than on their views of themselves as nascent teachers. She reminds us of the diversity of students' preferred modes of learning, and how the lack of an explicit rationale from the training institution can lead to misunderstandings and disaffection. The theme of co-operative working and learning emerges yet again.

Chapter 15, by Terry Atkinson, provides a foil to these studies of students' implicit theories by revealing something of the history of tutors' and mentors' theories of teaching and learning. Just as students carry forward tacit images of teaching from their own school experience, so do mentors, especially when new to the role, automatically fall into attitudes and practices derived from their own experience of teacher training. And just as mentors need to loosen and broaden students' preconceptions, so may mentor trainers need to work gently on freeing new mentors from the sway of outmoded approaches to teacher education.

Many of the contributions bear on the vexed question of transfer. Mike Wallace's Chapter 2 sets the scene by arguing strongly for the ineffectiveness of APL which relies on activities offering some sort of logical analogue to workplace performance, but which fails either to ensure that the clothes in which this analogical skeleton is dressed match those of the workplace, or to offer any continuing coaching or support which helps the disembedded competence to reimplant itself within the complex world of everyday professional practice. This is not good news for APL providers, for such courses are often easy to mount, are tidy and easy to budget, and can provide a stimulating experience. But the implicit assumption that learning in one context ought, somehow, to translate automatically into competence in a different and more naturalistic context seems not to be borne out by experience. Several of the chapters substantiate this. A brief immersion in a different culture, such as that of Weeden and Hayter's students in Chapter 8, may provoke some learners to reflect on their home situation, but its pay-off in terms of practical competence remains to be demonstrated. Likewise further research is needed (as they say) to establish the extent to which the studies of experienced overseas educators translate back into the very different conditions of their home culture (Hayter, Chapter 10). A vital part of any effective APL must be to ensure that what is learnt comes to manifest spontaneously in the workplace; and this requires the rejection of any lingering hopes that such transfer should happen automatically, or is dependent on some simplistic psychological notion such as 'ability' or 'motivation'.

Learning is impeded or facilitated, for adult professionals just as much as for children, in a variety of subtle and personal ways, and to liberate the learner, at any phase of education, is to seek to understand and appreciate these personal, delicate subtleties at an ever deeper and more intuitive level. Adults, it appears, do not grow out of the apprehensions and frailties that are the inevitable associates of learning. We may learn to conceal them and manage them better than an 8-year-old, but, for many of us, loss of control or loss of face is still experienced as a significant hazard of the learning adventure. One need only to recall the improved performance of anxious adults when they were told that a learning task was 'very difficult', and so were able to relieve themselves of some of the fear of failure reflecting badly on themselves as individuals (which I referred to in Chapter 1), to see what a dramatic effect even the casual way in which a learning task is presented – 'challenge'?; 'opportunity'? – can have. Patricia Broadfoot in Chapter 3 reminds us, in this context, of the power that anticipated forms of *assessment* have to drive learning, and how it will continue to do so until we can replace the implicit theory on which current attitudes towards assessment – in professional as well as classroom contexts – continue to be founded.

Clearly there is much more work to be done in articulating an approach to APL that is sophisticated enough to do justice to the complexity and diversity of adult professional learners. Some of the studies presented in this book are small illustrations, which need investigating on a larger scale if their conclusions are to bear much weight. And there are many issues on which we have hardly touched. Only Agnes McMahon in Chapter 12, for example, has anything to say about gender differences in APL, and while we have laid the foundations for an integrated learning theory, it needs developing so that it can naturally incorporate the differences of learning style, belief and habit between different groups. Recent work on 'women's ways of knowing', such as that of Belenky *et al.* (1986) for example, and the match or mismatch between these and the styles of learning and tacit epistemologies embodied by formal institutions of education, will have much of value to teach us. Meanwhile we hope that this book has made a contribution not only towards the facilitation of adult professional learning, but also towards the creation of a genuine culture of 'learning to learn' at all levels of the education system.

REFERENCES

Belenky, M. F., Clinchy, B. M., Goldberger, N. R. and Tarule, J. M. (1986) *Women's Ways of Knowing: The Development of Self, Voice and Mind*, New York: Basic Books.
Lave, J. and Wenger, E. (1991) *Situated Learning: Legitimate Peripheral Participation*, Cambridge: Cambridge University Press.
Salmon, P. (1992) *Achieving a PhD: Ten Students' Experience*, Stoke-on-Trent: Trentham Books.

Name index

Subject index